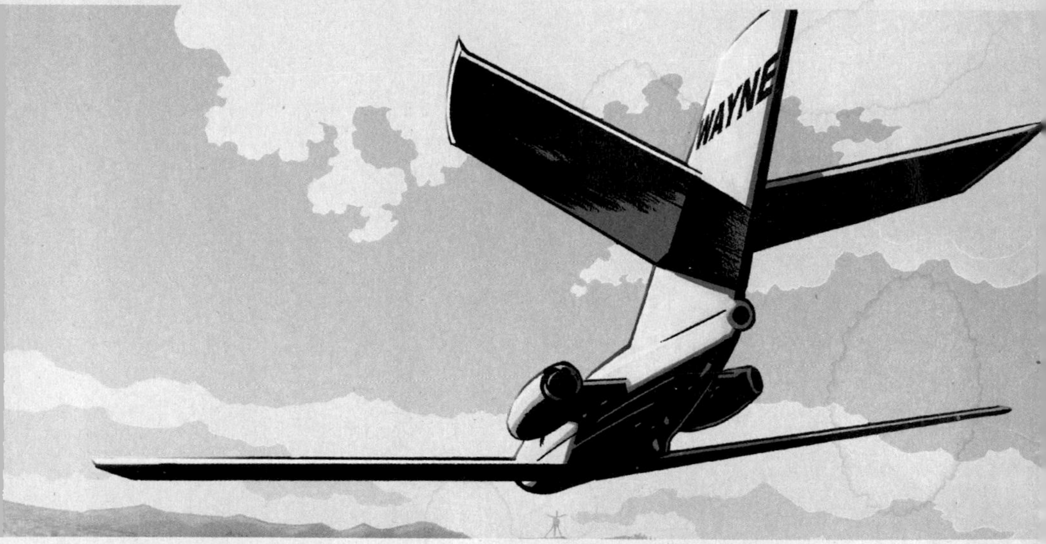
WAYNE

BATMAN INTERNATIONAL

BATMAN INTERNATIONAL

SCOTTISH CONNECTION
ALAN GRANT Writer
FRANK QUITELY Artist
MATT HOLLINGSWORTH and **BRAD MATTHEW** Colorists
BILL OAKLEY Letterer

BATMAN IN BARCELONA: DRAGON'S KNIGHT
MARK WAID Writer
DIEGO OLMOS Artist
MARTA MARTINEZ Colorist
STEVE WANDS Letterer
Special thanks to David Macho and Paloma Joga

TAO
ALAN GRANT Writer
ARTHUR RANSON Artist
DIGITAL CHAMELEON Colorist
WILLIE SCHUBERT Letterer

Batman created by Bob Kane

DAN DIDIO SVP-Executive Editor
DENNIS O'NEIL MIKE MARTS ARCHIE GOODWIN Editors-original series
JORDAN GORFINKEL BILL KAPLAN Associate Editors-original series
JANELLE SIEGEL Assistant Editor-original series
GEORG BREWER VP-Design & DC Direct Creative
BOB HARRAS Group Editor-Collected Editions
ROBBIN BROSTERMAN Design Director-Books

Cover by Jim Lee

BATMAN: INTERNATIONAL

DC COMICS
PAUL LEVITZ President & Publisher
RICHARD BRUNING SVP-Creative Director
PATRICK CALDON EVP-Finance & Operations
AMY GENKINS SVP-Business & Legal Affairs
JIM LEE Editorial Director-WildStorm
GREGORY NOVECK SVP-Creative Affairs
STEVE ROTTERDAM SVP-Sales & Marketing
CHERYL RUBIN SVP-Brand Management

Published by DC Comics. Cover, text and compilation Copyright © 2010 DC Comics. All Rights Reserved.
Originally published in single magazine form in BATMAN: SCOTTISH CONNECTION, BATMAN: LEGENDS OF
THE DARK KNIGHT 52, 53, BATMAN IN BARCELONA: DRAGON'S KNIGHT 1. Copyright © 1993, 1998, 2009
DC Comics. All Rights Reserved. All characters, their distinctive likenesses and related elements featured in this
publication are trademarks of DC Comics. The stories, characters and incidents featured in this publication are
entirely fictional. DC Comics does not read or accept unsolicited submissions of ideas, stories or artwork.
DC Comics, 1700 Broadway, New York, NY 10019
A Warner Bros. Entertainment Company
Printed by World Color Press, Inc., St-Romuald, QC, Canada 02/03/10. First Printing
ISBN: 978-1-4012-2649-7

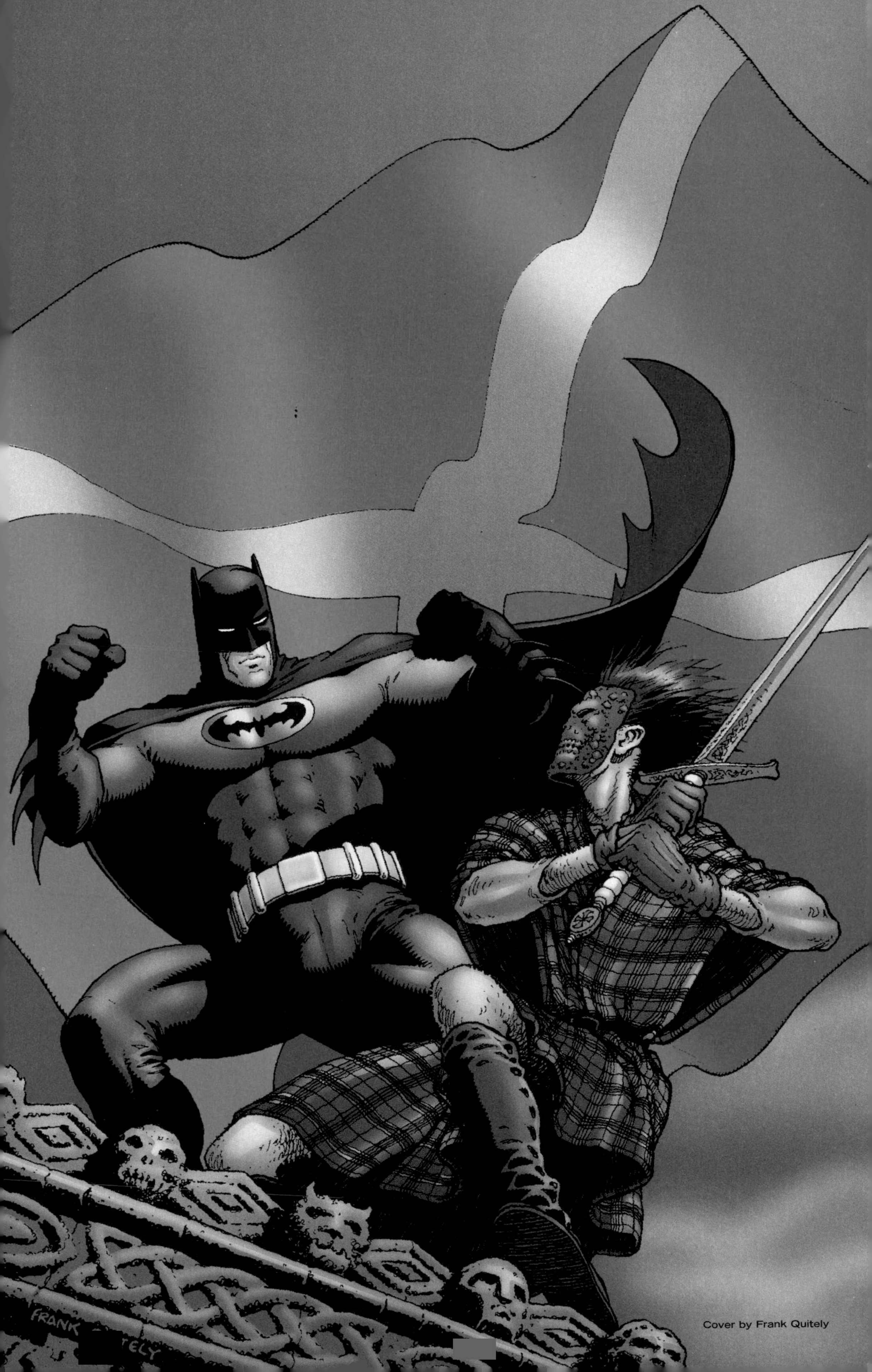

Cover by Frank Quitely

SCOTTISH CONNECTION

CHAPTER ONE: ISLE OF MISTS
DEARLY BELOVED...
...WE ARE GATHERED HERE TODAY TO REINTER THE MORTAL REMAINS OF SIR GAWEYNE de WEYNE, KNIGHT OF THE SCOTTISH COURT, WHO LOST HIS LIFE ON A CRUSADE TO FREE THE HOLY LAND.

ACCORDING TO HIS WISHES, WHEN HE FELL IN BATTLE, SIR GAWEYNE'S *HEART* WAS *EMBALMED* AND RETURNED TO SCOTLAND.

FOR 600 YEARS, IT HAS REPOSED IN DUNVEGAN CASTLE, AWAITING THE *REDISCOVERY* OF HIS *GRAVE*.

TODAY, I RETURN IT TO THE TOMBSTONE WHICH BEARS HIS NAME.

MAY THE LORD HAVE MERCY ON HIS SOUL.

AMEN.

IN WITNESS OF THIS EVENT, I WOULD ASK THOSE PRESENT TO SIGN THE *BOOK OF REGISTERS*.

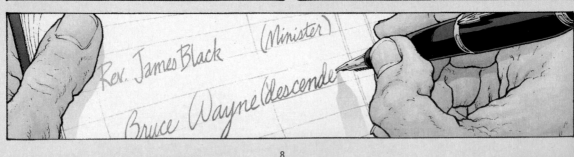

Rev. James Black (Minister)

Bruce Wayne (descende

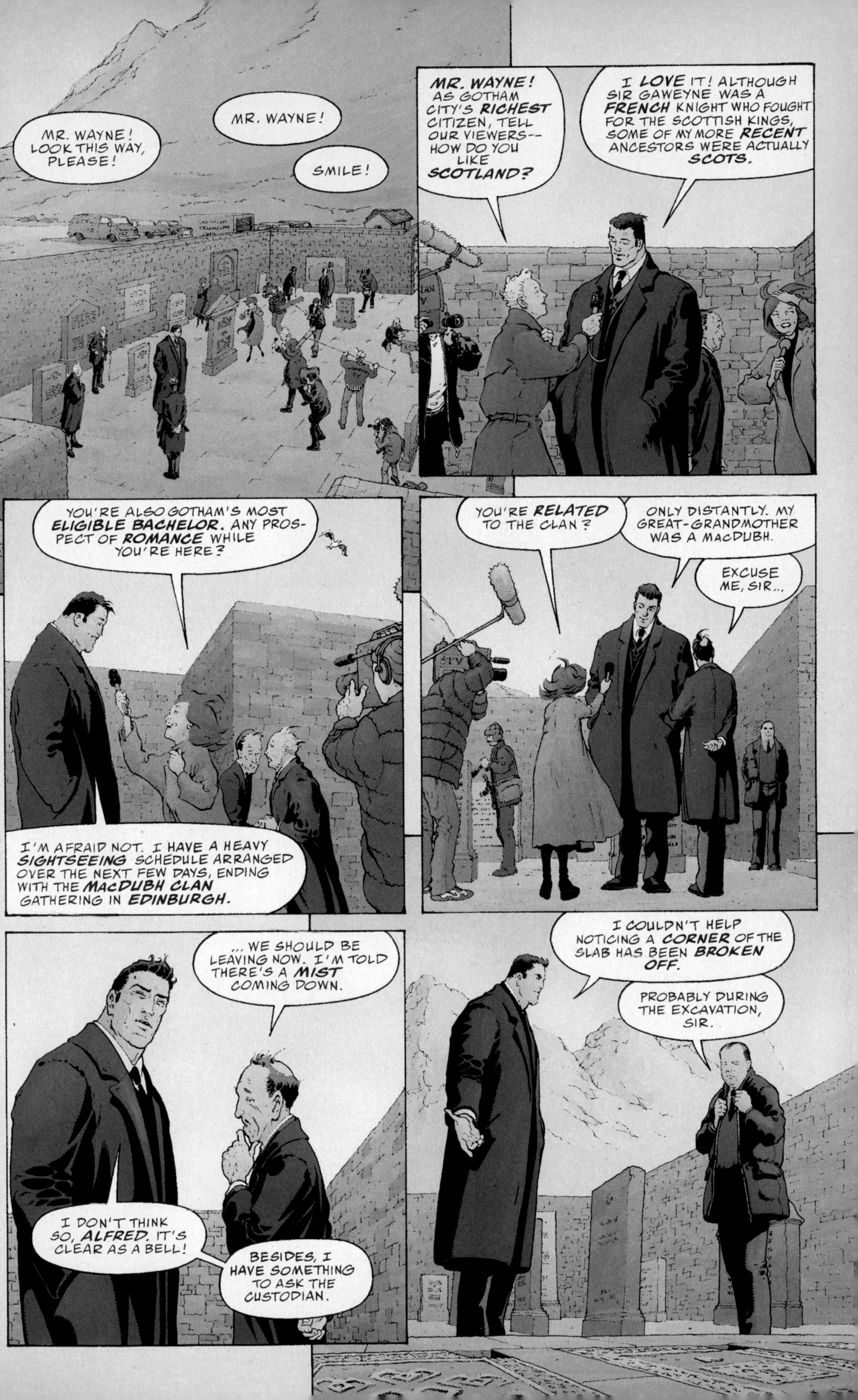

MR. WAYNE! LOOK THIS WAY, PLEASE!
MR. WAYNE!
SMILE!
MR. WAYNE! AS GOTHAM CITY'S RICHEST CITIZEN, TELL OUR VIEWERS-- HOW DO YOU LIKE SCOTLAND?
I LOVE IT! ALTHOUGH SIR GAWEYNE WAS A FRENCH KNIGHT WHO FOUGHT FOR THE SCOTTISH KINGS, SOME OF MY MORE RECENT ANCESTORS WERE ACTUALLY SCOTS.
YOU'RE ALSO GOTHAM'S MOST ELIGIBLE BACHELOR. ANY PROSPECT OF ROMANCE WHILE YOU'RE HERE?
I'M AFRAID NOT. I HAVE A HEAVY SIGHTSEEING SCHEDULE ARRANGED OVER THE NEXT FEW DAYS, ENDING WITH THE MacDUBH CLAN GATHERING IN EDINBURGH.
YOU'RE RELATED TO THE CLAN?
ONLY DISTANTLY. MY GREAT-GRANDMOTHER WAS A MacDUBH.
EXCUSE ME, SIR...
... WE SHOULD BE LEAVING NOW. I'M TOLD THERE'S A MIST COMING DOWN.
I DON'T THINK SO, ALFRED. IT'S CLEAR AS A BELL!
BESIDES, I HAVE SOMETHING TO ASK THE CUSTODIAN.
I COULDN'T HELP NOTICING A CORNER OF THE SLAB HAS BEEN BROKEN OFF.
PROBABLY DURING THE EXCAVATION, SIR.

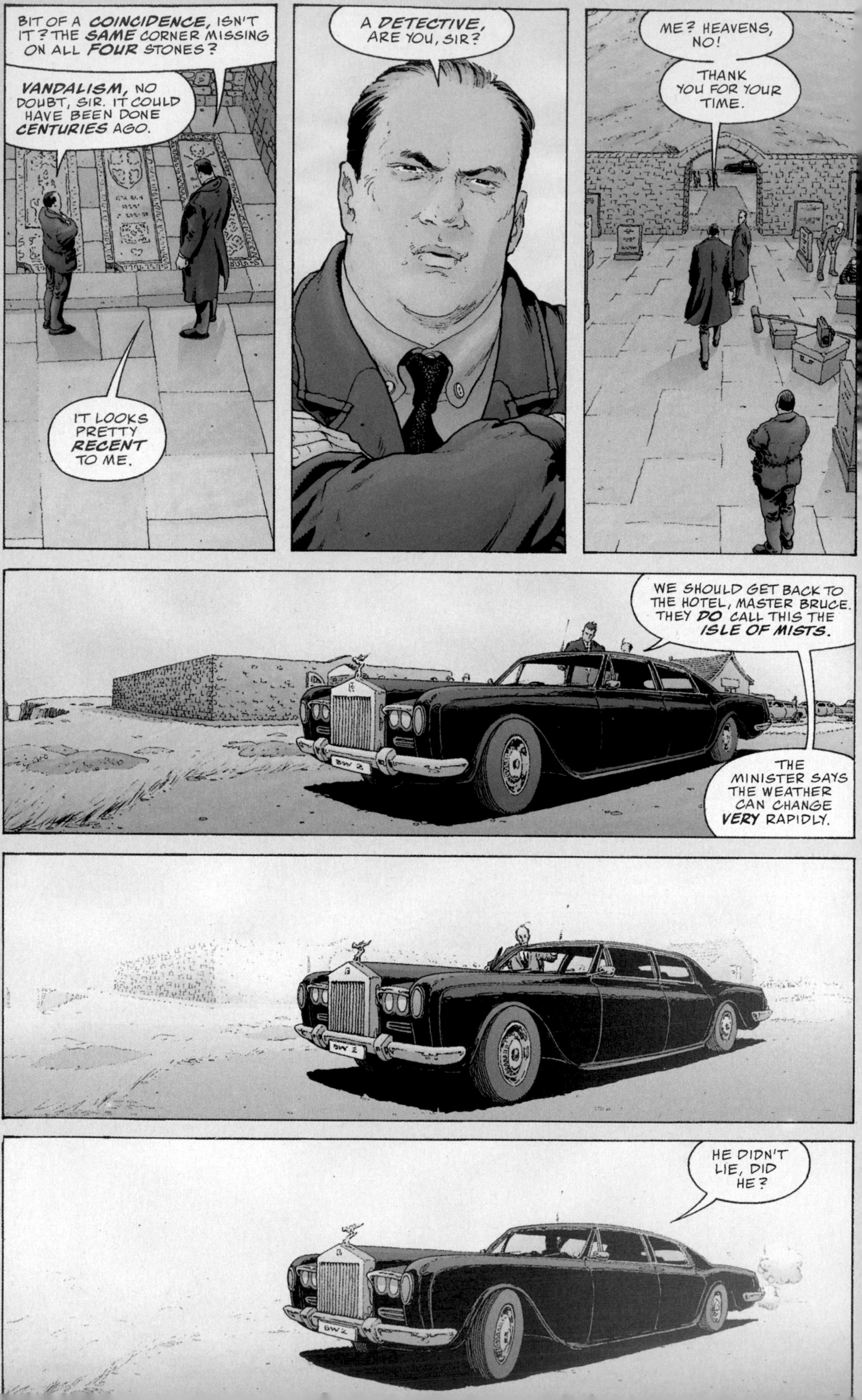
BIT OF A COINCIDENCE, ISN'T IT? THE SAME CORNER MISSING ON ALL FOUR STONES?
VANDALISM, NO DOUBT, SIR. IT COULD HAVE BEEN DONE CENTURIES AGO.
IT LOOKS PRETTY RECENT TO ME.
A DETECTIVE, ARE YOU, SIR?
ME? HEAVENS, NO!
THANK YOU FOR YOUR TIME.
WE SHOULD GET BACK TO THE HOTEL, MASTER BRUCE. THEY DO CALL THIS THE ISLE OF MISTS.
THE MINISTER SAYS THE WEATHER CAN CHANGE VERY RAPIDLY.
HE DIDN'T LIE, DID HE?

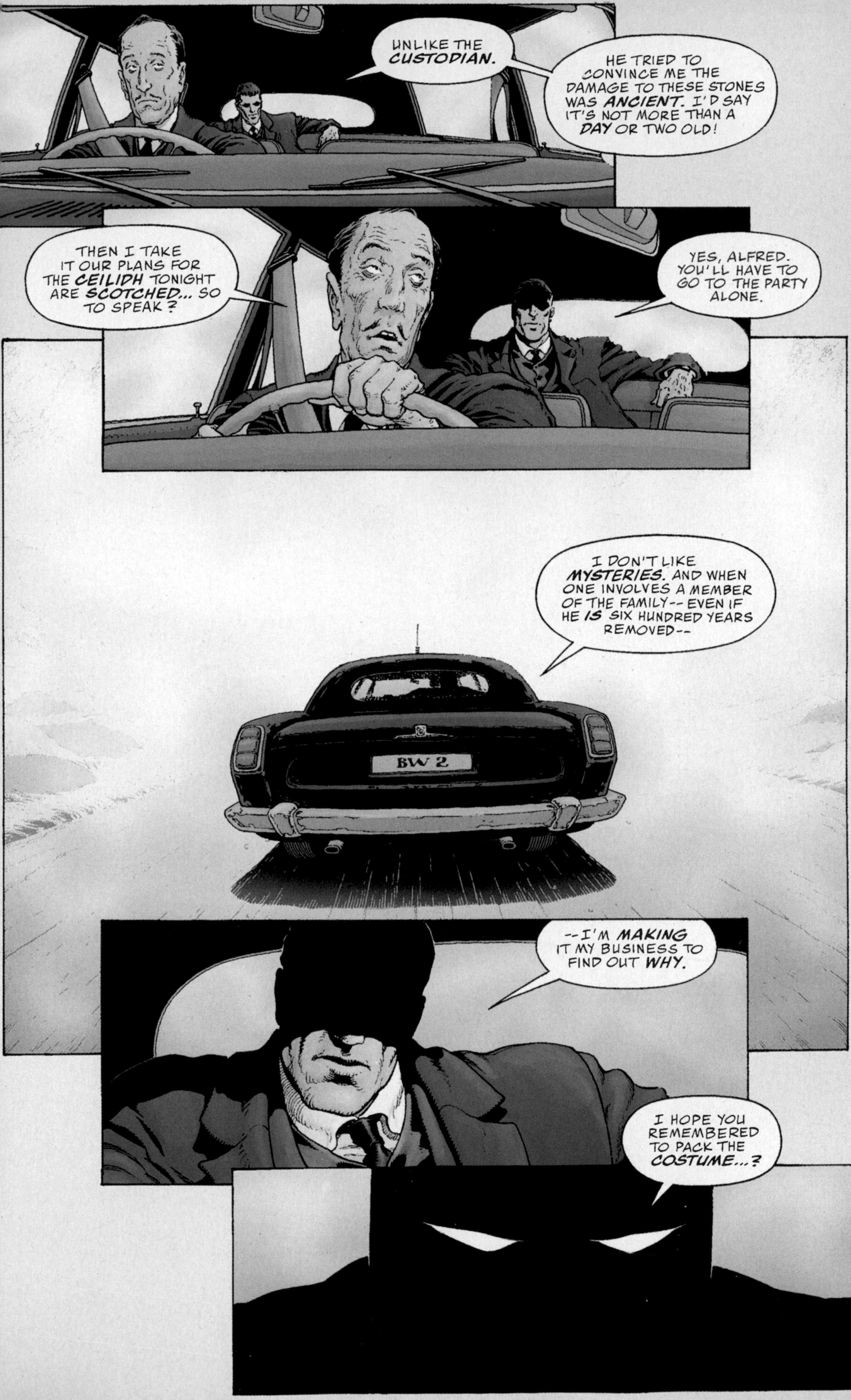
UNLIKE THE CUSTODIAN.
HE TRIED TO CONVINCE ME THE DAMAGE TO THESE STONES WAS ANCIENT. I'D SAY IT'S NOT MORE THAN A DAY OR TWO OLD!
THEN I TAKE IT OUR PLANS FOR THE CEILIDH TONIGHT ARE SCOTCHED... SO TO SPEAK?
YES, ALFRED. YOU'LL HAVE TO GO TO THE PARTY ALONE.
I DON'T LIKE MYSTERIES. AND WHEN ONE INVOLVES A MEMBER OF THE FAMILY-- EVEN IF HE IS SIX HUNDRED YEARS REMOVED--
BW 2
--I'M MAKING IT MY BUSINESS TO FIND OUT WHY.
I HOPE YOU REMEMBERED TO PACK THE COSTUME...?

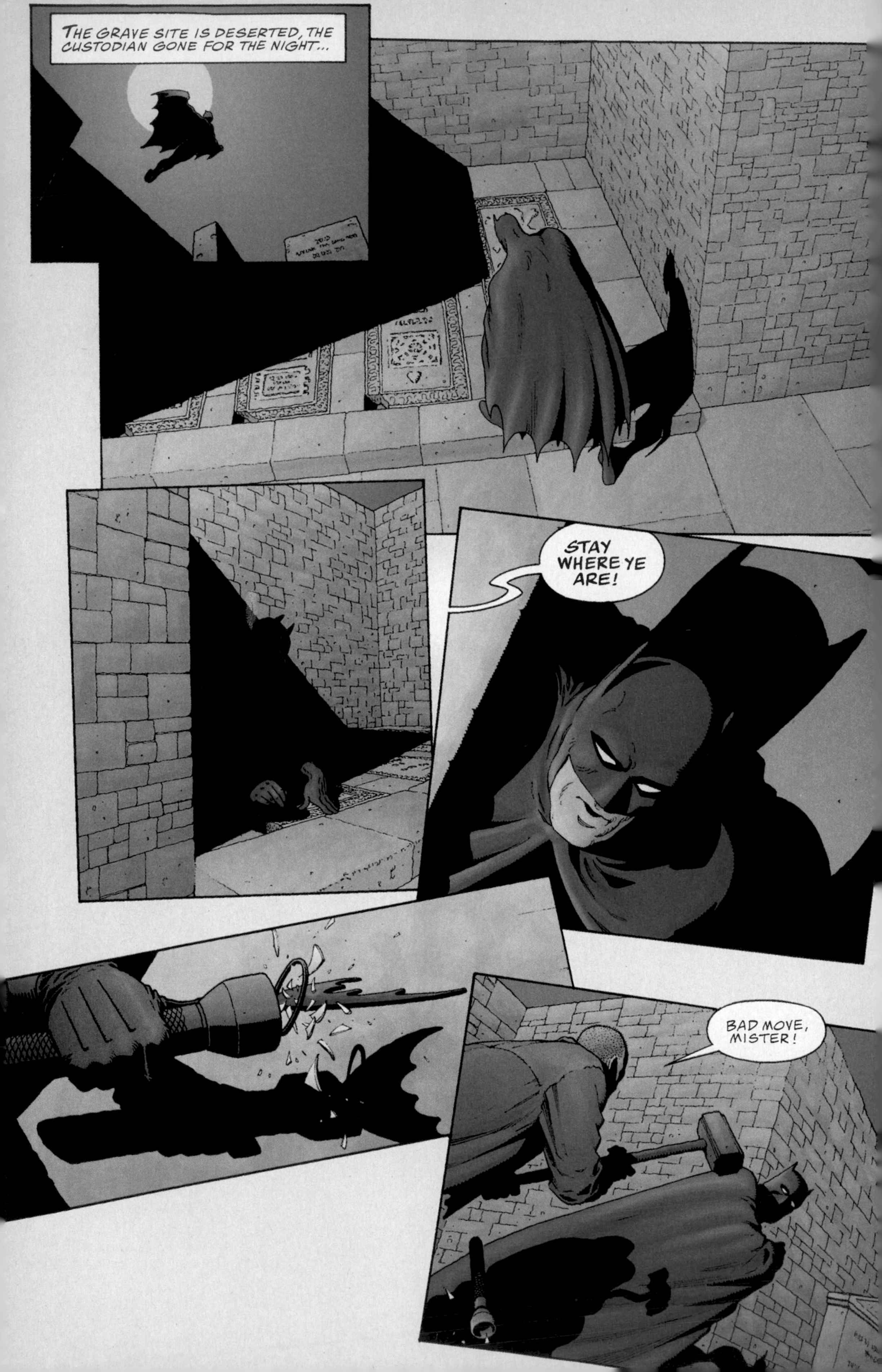
THE GRAVE SITE IS DESERTED, THE CUSTODIAN GONE FOR THE NIGHT...
STAY WHERE YE ARE!
BAD MOVE, MISTER!

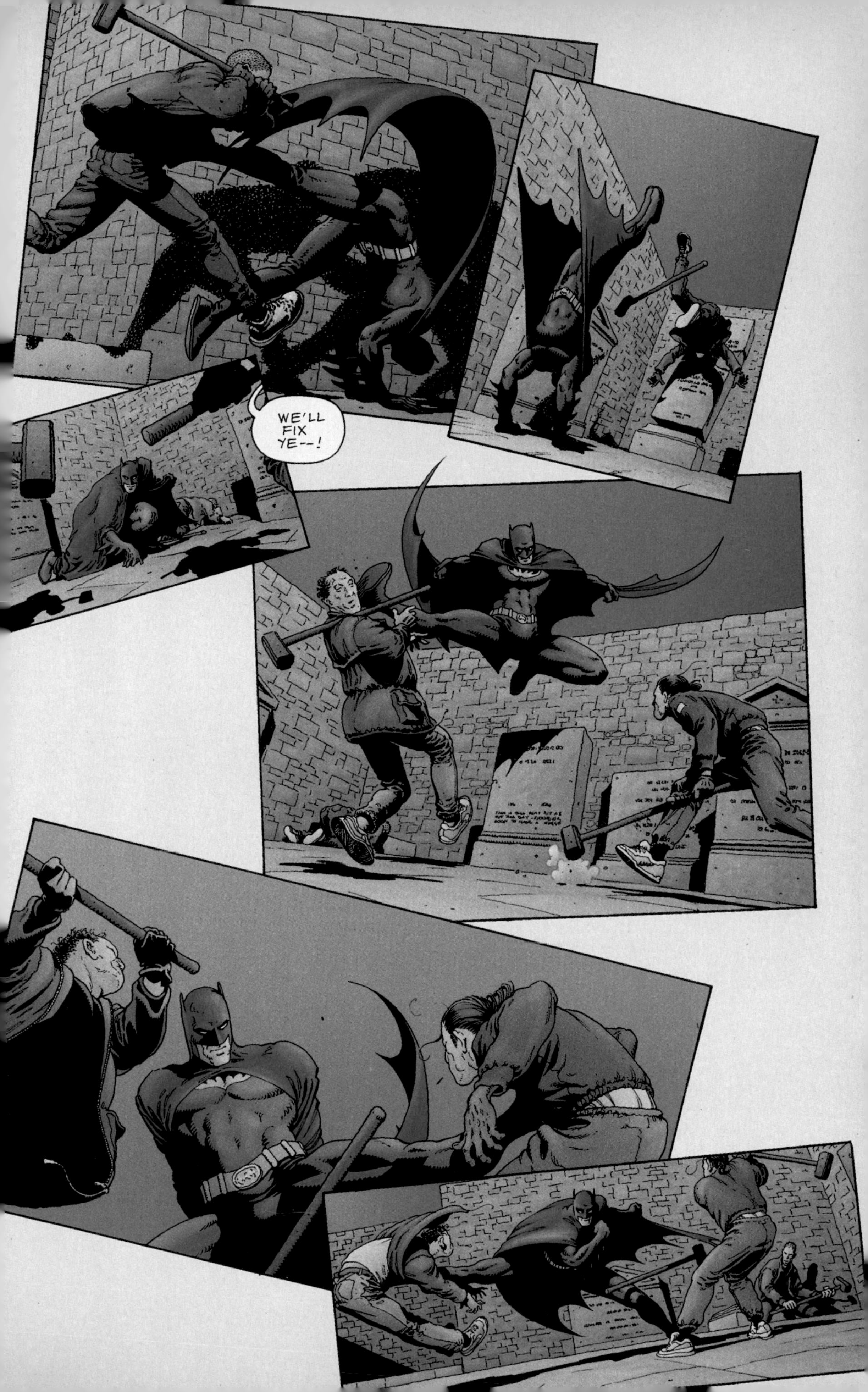
WE'LL FIX YE--!

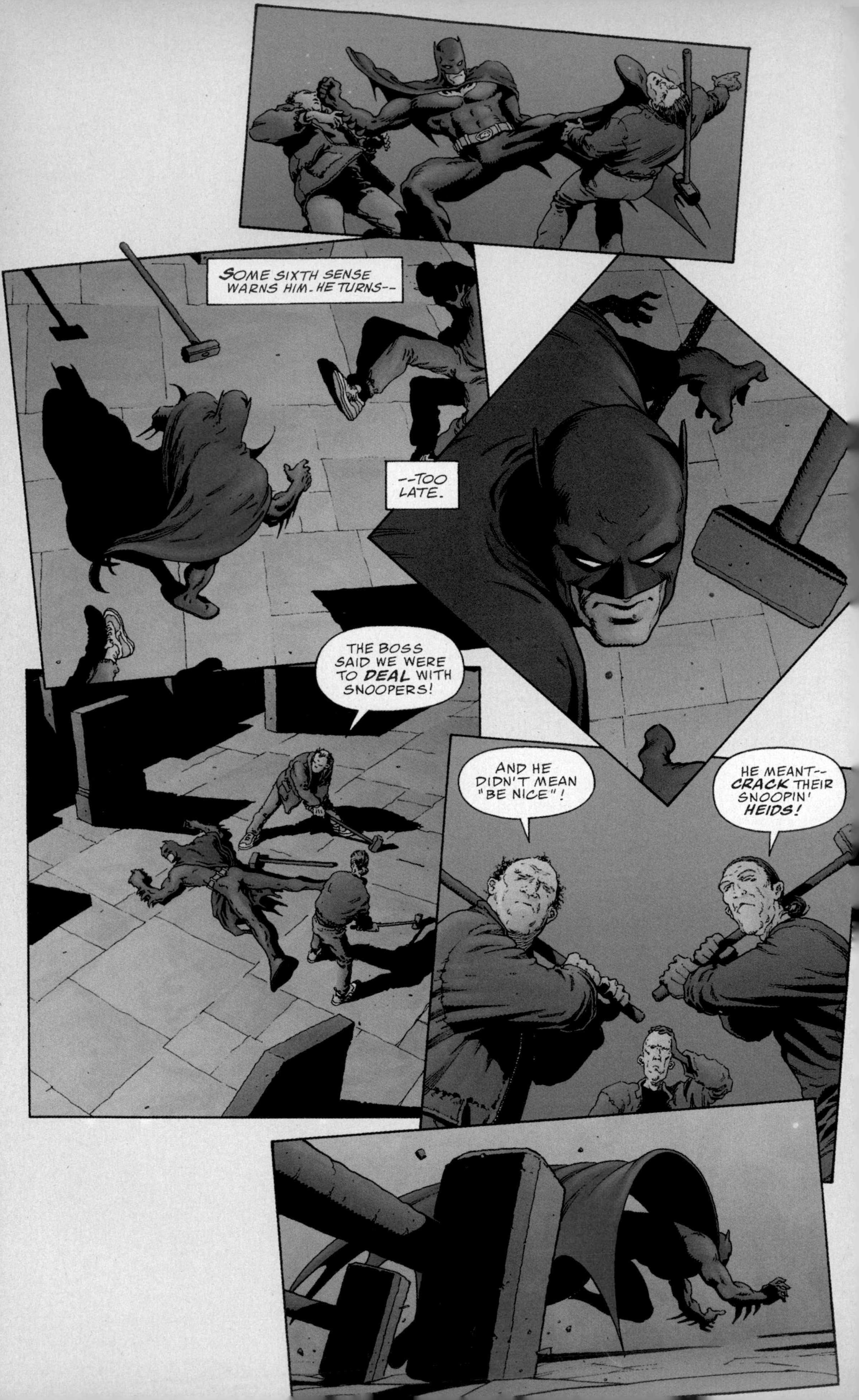
SOME SIXTH SENSE WARNS HIM. HE TURNS--
--TOO LATE.
THE BOSS SAID WE WERE TO DEAL WITH SNOOPERS!
AND HE DIDN'T MEAN "BE NICE"!
HE MEANT-- CRACK THEIR SNOOPIN' HEIDS!

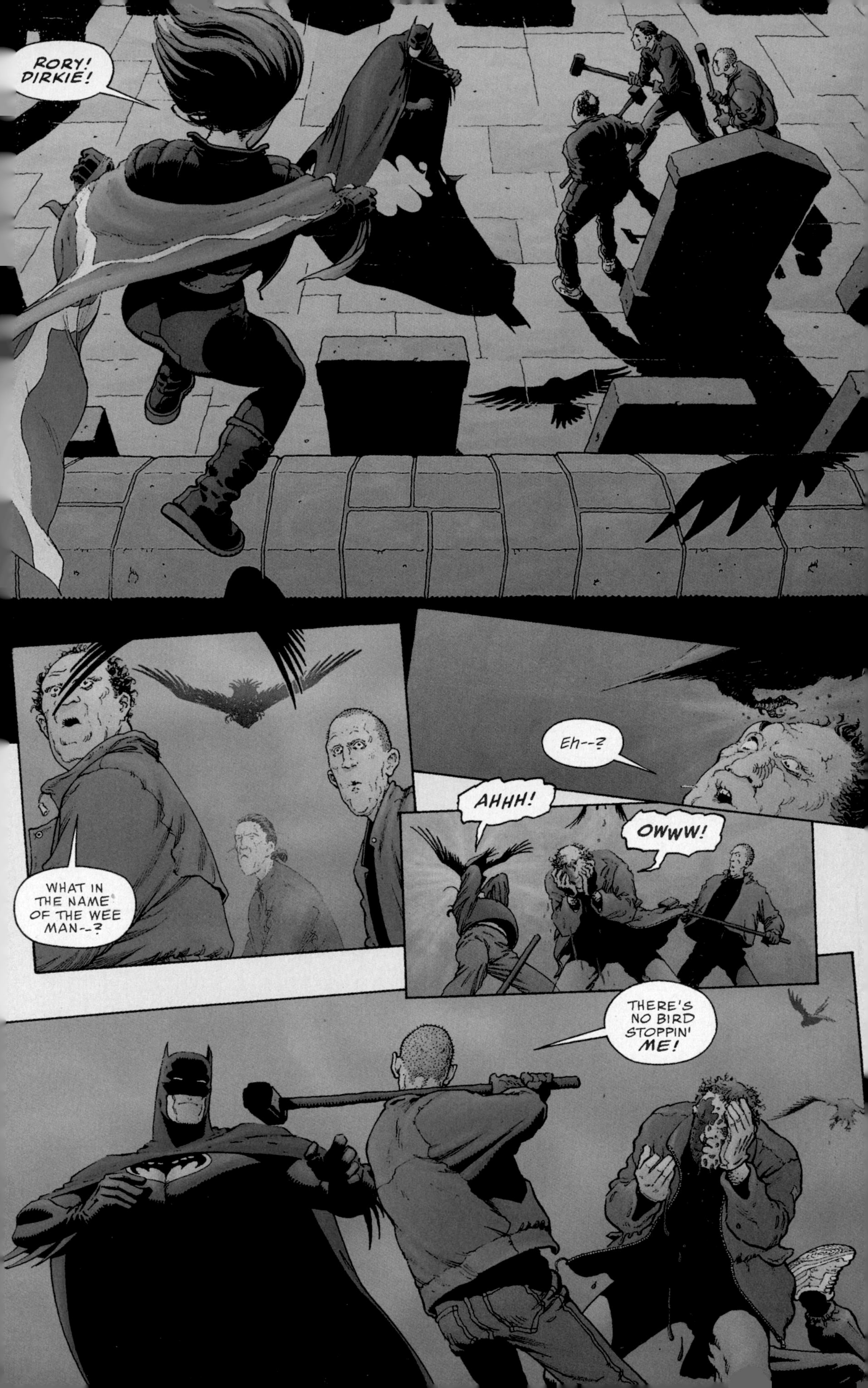
RORY! DIRKIE!
WHAT IN THE NAME OF THE WEE MAN--?
Eh--?
AHHH!
OWWW!
THERE'S NO BIRD STOPPIN' ME!

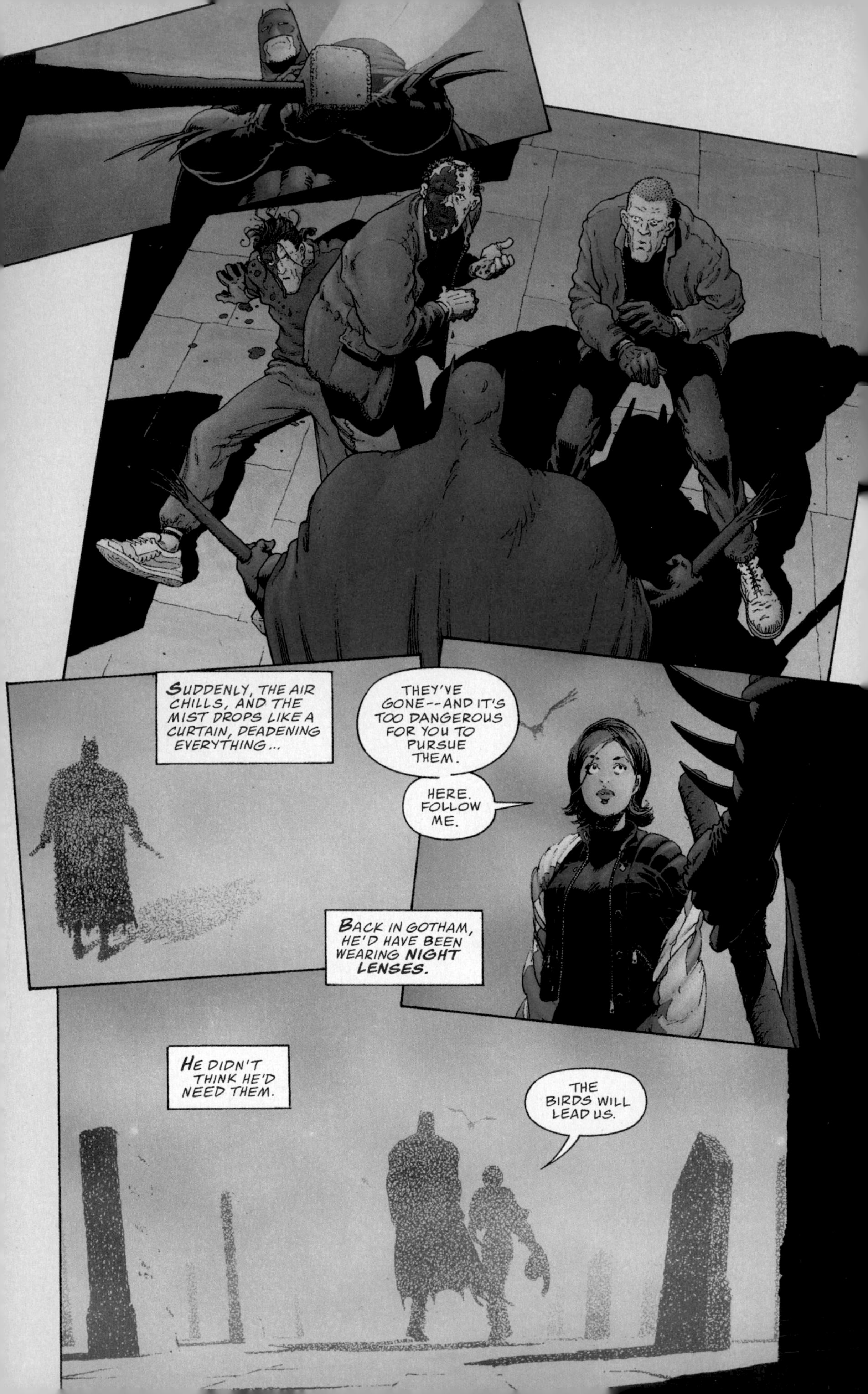
SUDDENLY, THE AIR CHILLS, AND THE MIST DROPS LIKE A CURTAIN, DEADENING EVERYTHING...
THEY'VE GONE--AND IT'S TOO DANGEROUS FOR YOU TO PURSUE THEM.
HERE. FOLLOW ME.
BACK IN GOTHAM, HE'D HAVE BEEN WEARING NIGHT LENSES.
HE DIDN'T THINK HE'D NEED THEM.
THE BIRDS WILL LEAD US.

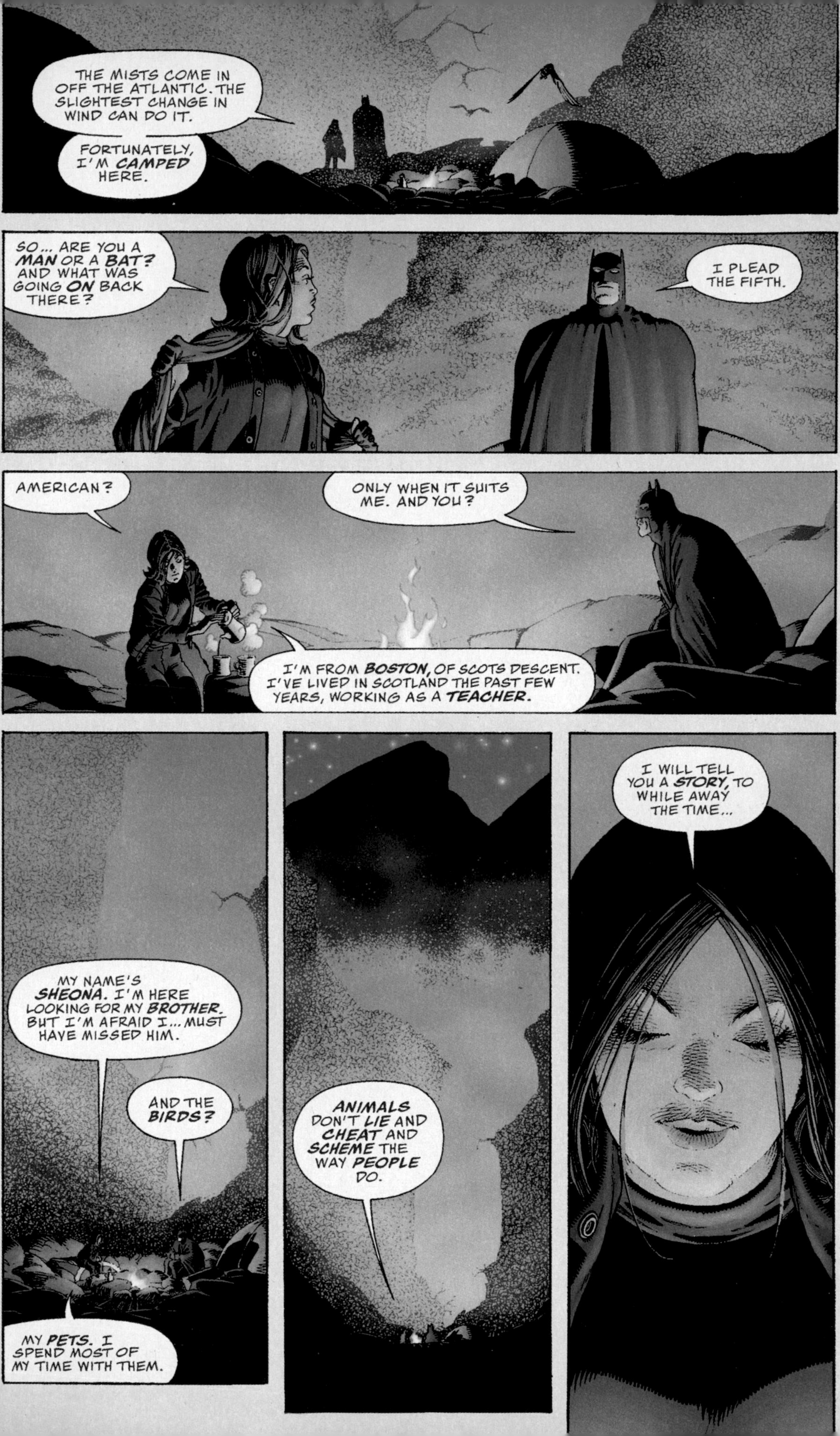
THE MISTS COME IN OFF THE ATLANTIC. THE SLIGHTEST CHANGE IN WIND CAN DO IT.
FORTUNATELY, I'M CAMPED HERE.
SO... ARE YOU A MAN OR A BAT? AND WHAT WAS GOING ON BACK THERE?
I PLEAD THE FIFTH.
AMERICAN?
ONLY WHEN IT SUITS ME. AND YOU?
I'M FROM BOSTON, OF SCOTS DESCENT. I'VE LIVED IN SCOTLAND THE PAST FEW YEARS, WORKING AS A TEACHER.
MY NAME'S SHEONA. I'M HERE LOOKING FOR MY BROTHER. BUT I'M AFRAID I... MUST HAVE MISSED HIM.
AND THE BIRDS?
MY PETS. I SPEND MOST OF MY TIME WITH THEM.
ANIMALS DON'T LIE AND CHEAT AND SCHEME THE WAY PEOPLE DO.
I WILL TELL YOU A STORY, TO WHILE AWAY THE TIME...

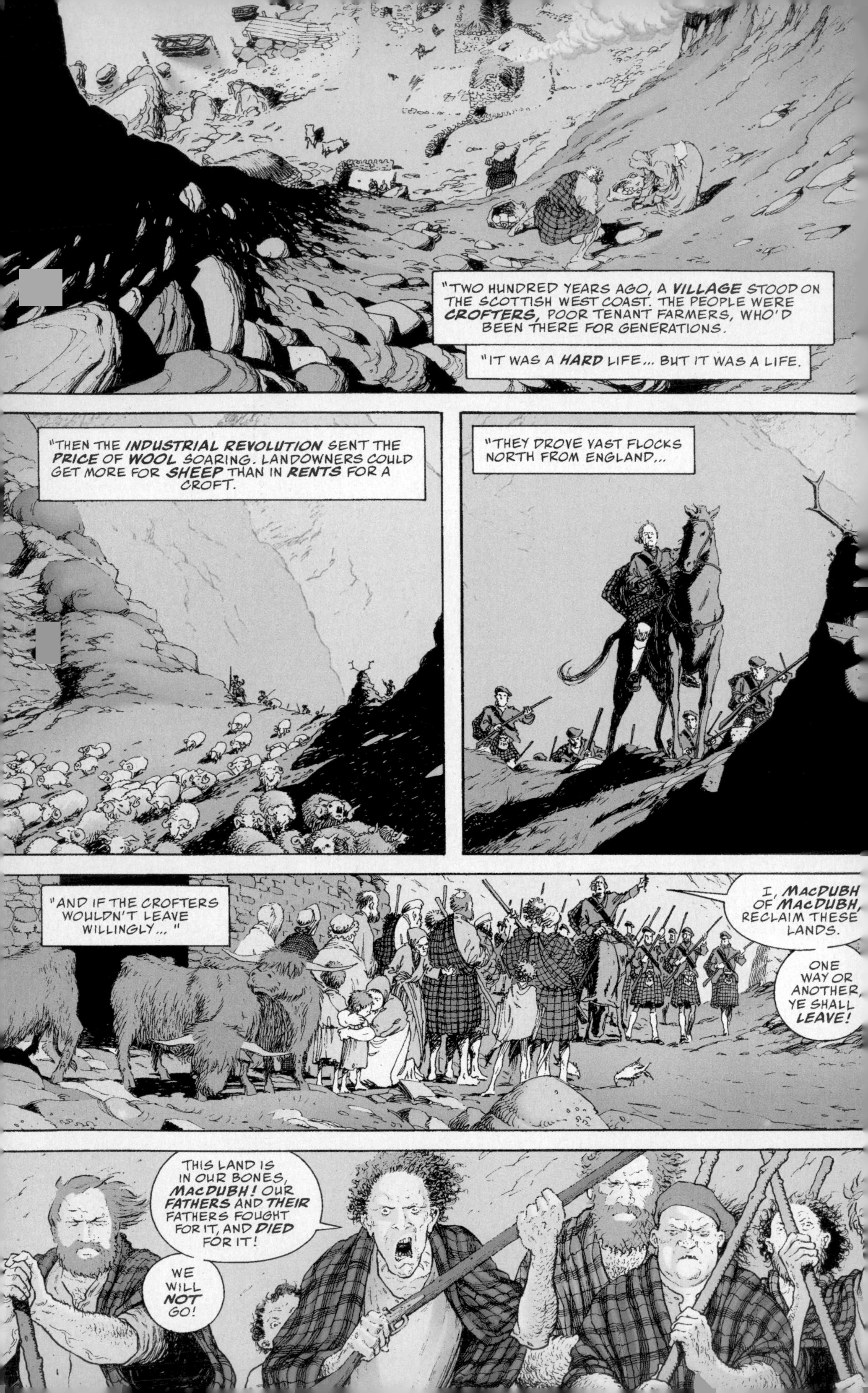
"TWO HUNDRED YEARS AGO, A VILLAGE STOOD ON THE SCOTTISH WEST COAST. THE PEOPLE WERE CROFTERS, POOR TENANT FARMERS, WHO'D BEEN THERE FOR GENERATIONS.
"IT WAS A HARD LIFE... BUT IT WAS A LIFE.
"THEN THE INDUSTRIAL REVOLUTION SENT THE PRICE OF WOOL SOARING. LANDOWNERS COULD GET MORE FOR SHEEP THAN IN RENTS FOR A CROFT.
"THEY DROVE VAST FLOCKS NORTH FROM ENGLAND...
"AND IF THE CROFTERS WOULDN'T LEAVE WILLINGLY..."
I, MACDUBH OF MACDUBH, RECLAIM THESE LANDS.
ONE WAY OR ANOTHER, YE SHALL LEAVE!
THIS LAND IS IN OUR BONES, MACDUBH! OUR FATHERS AND THEIR FATHERS FOUGHT FOR IT, AND DIED FOR IT!
WE WILL NOT GO!

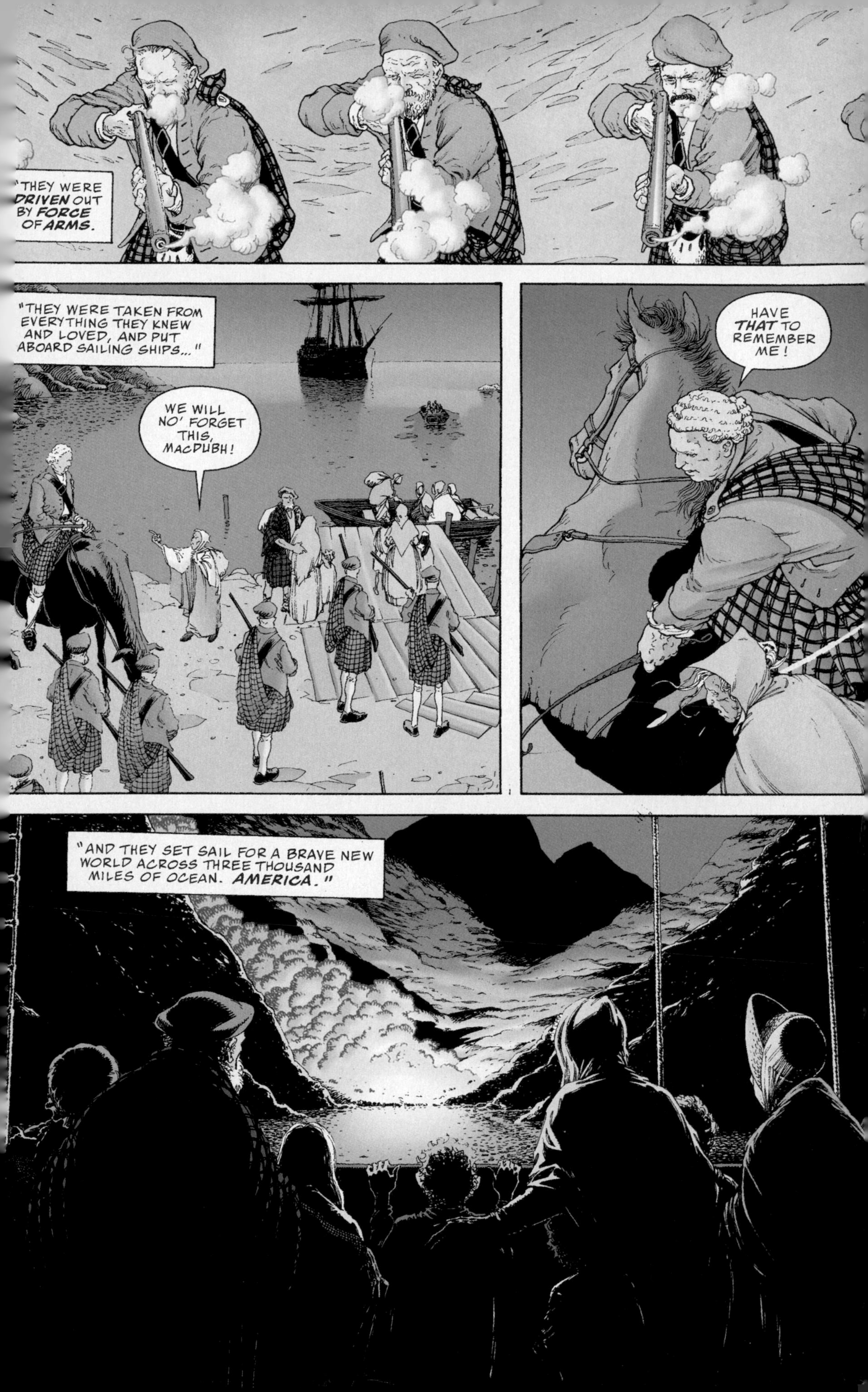
"THEY WERE DRIVEN OUT BY FORCE OF ARMS.
"THEY WERE TAKEN FROM EVERYTHING THEY KNEW AND LOVED, AND PUT ABOARD SAILING SHIPS..."
WE WILL NO' FORGET THIS, MACDUBH!
HAVE THAT TO REMEMBER ME!
"AND THEY SET SAIL FOR A BRAVE NEW WORLD ACROSS THREE THOUSAND MILES OF OCEAN. AMERICA."

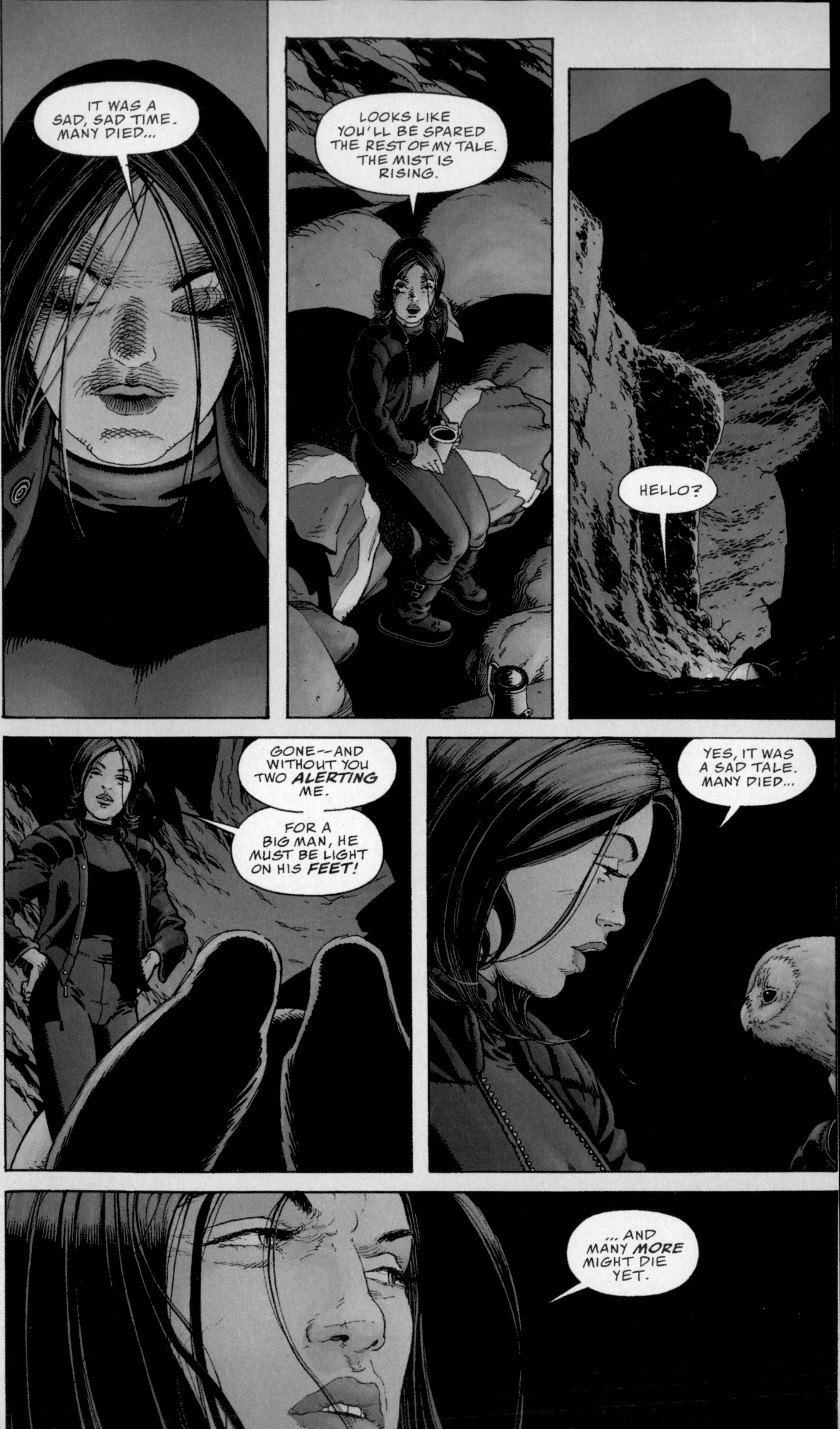
IT WAS A SAD, SAD TIME. MANY DIED...
LOOKS LIKE YOU'LL BE SPARED THE REST OF MY TALE. THE MIST IS RISING.
HELLO?
GONE--AND WITHOUT YOU TWO ALERTING ME.
FOR A BIG MAN, HE MUST BE LIGHT ON HIS FEET!
YES, IT WAS A SAD TALE. MANY DIED...
...AND MANY MORE MIGHT DIE YET.

CHAPTER TWO: THE TEMPLAR MYSTERY

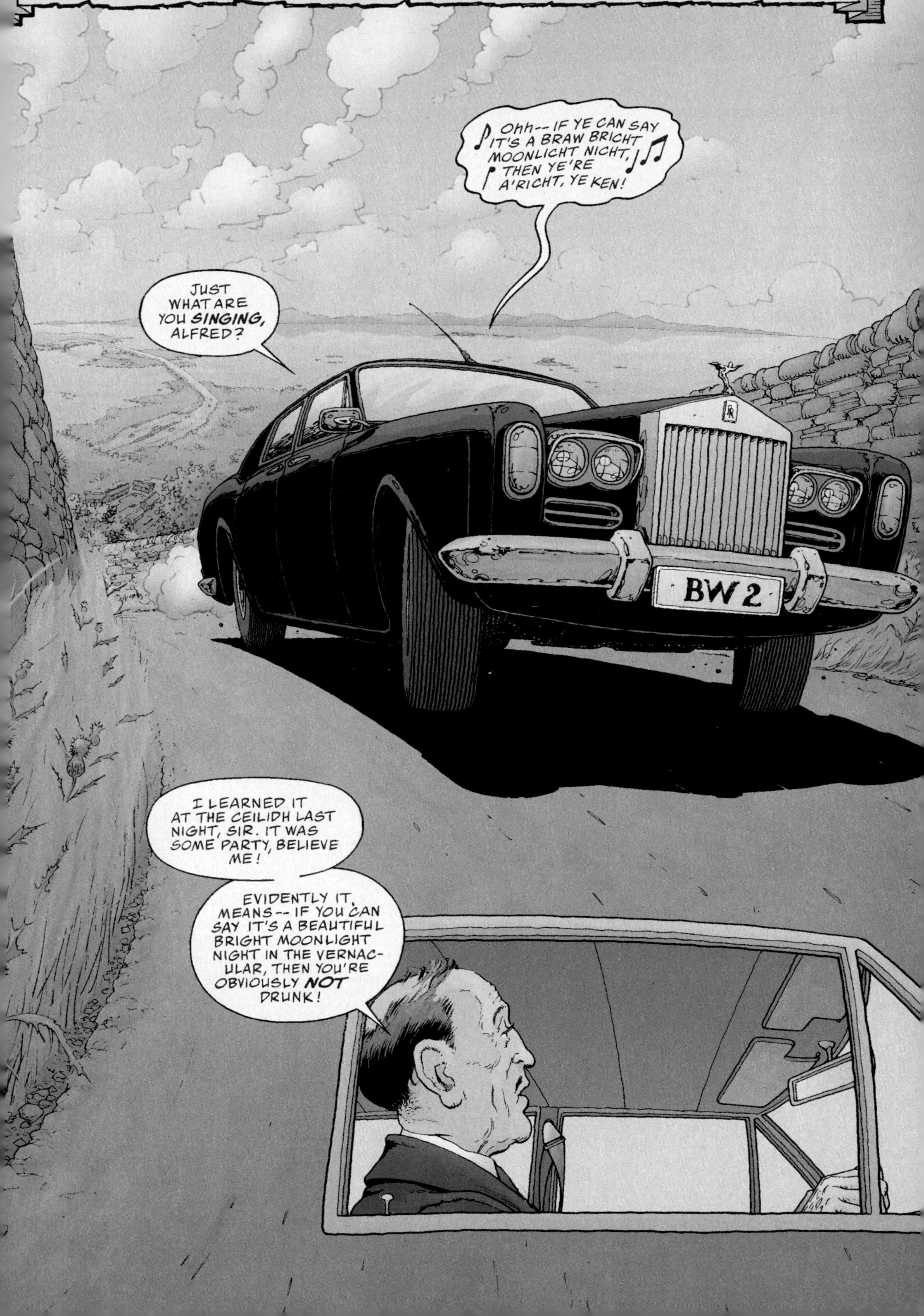
JUST WHAT ARE YOU SINGING, ALFRED?
OHH-- IF YE CAN SAY IT'S A BRAW BRICHT MOONLICHT NICHT, THEN YE'RE A'RICHT, YE KEN!
BW 2
I LEARNED IT AT THE CEILIDH LAST NIGHT, SIR. IT WAS SOME PARTY, BELIEVE ME!
EVIDENTLY IT MEANS-- IF YOU CAN SAY IT'S A BEAUTIFUL BRIGHT MOONLIGHT NIGHT IN THE VERNACULAR, THEN YOU'RE OBVIOUSLY NOT DRUNK!

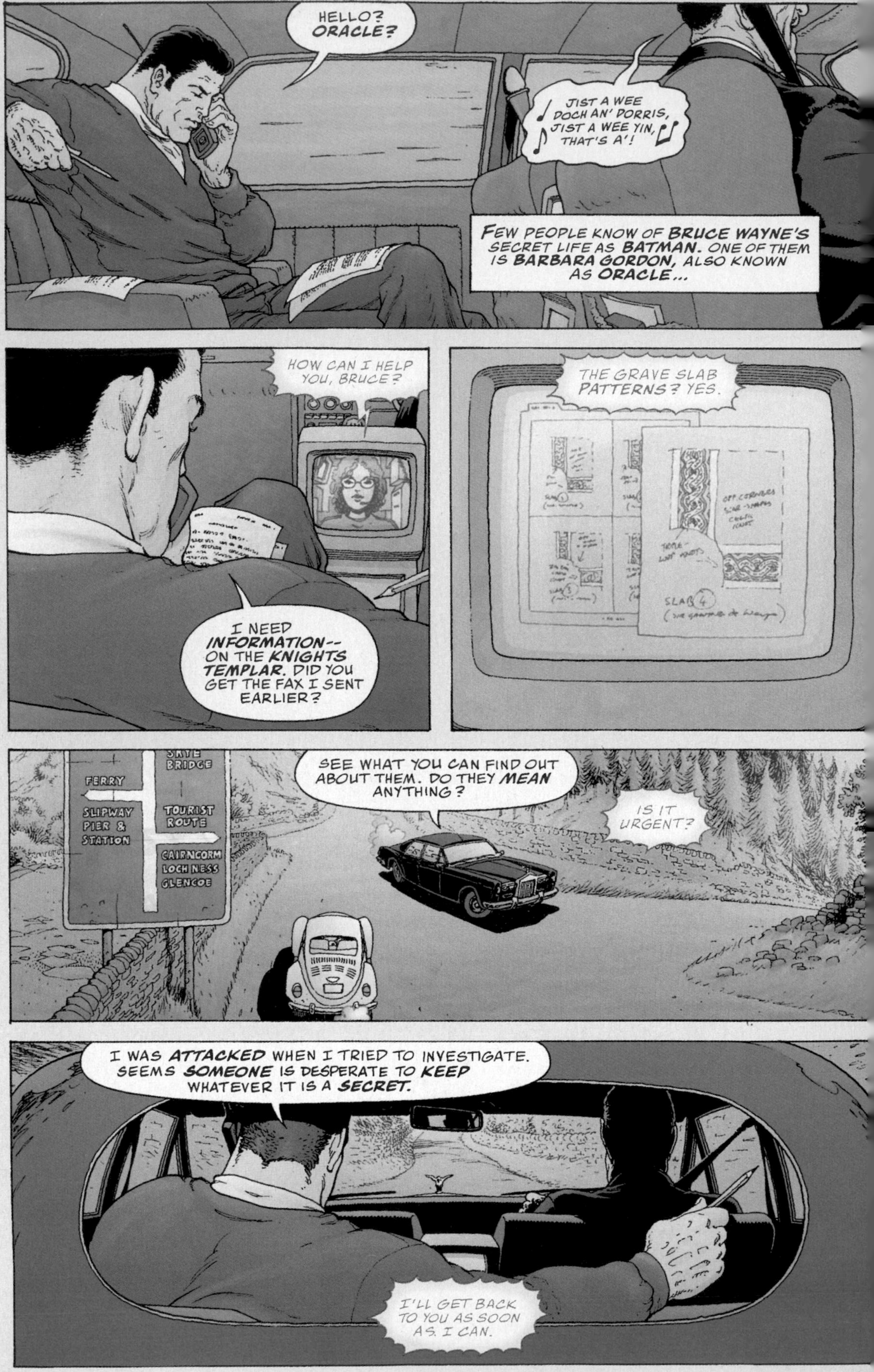
HELLO? ORACLE?
JIST A WEE DOCH AN' DORRIS, JIST A WEE YIN, THAT'S A'!
FEW PEOPLE KNOW OF BRUCE WAYNE'S SECRET LIFE AS BATMAN. ONE OF THEM IS BARBARA GORDON, ALSO KNOWN AS ORACLE...
HOW CAN I HELP YOU, BRUCE?
I NEED INFORMATION-- ON THE KNIGHTS TEMPLAR. DID YOU GET THE FAX I SENT EARLIER?
THE GRAVE SLAB PATTERNS? YES.
SLAB 4
FERRY
SKYE BRIDGE
SLIPWAY PIER & STATION
TOURIST ROUTE
CAIRNGORM LOCH NESS GLENCOE
SEE WHAT YOU CAN FIND OUT ABOUT THEM. DO THEY MEAN ANYTHING?
IS IT URGENT?
I WAS ATTACKED WHEN I TRIED TO INVESTIGATE. SEEMS SOMEONE IS DESPERATE TO KEEP WHATEVER IT IS A SECRET.
I'LL GET BACK TO YOU AS SOON AS I CAN.

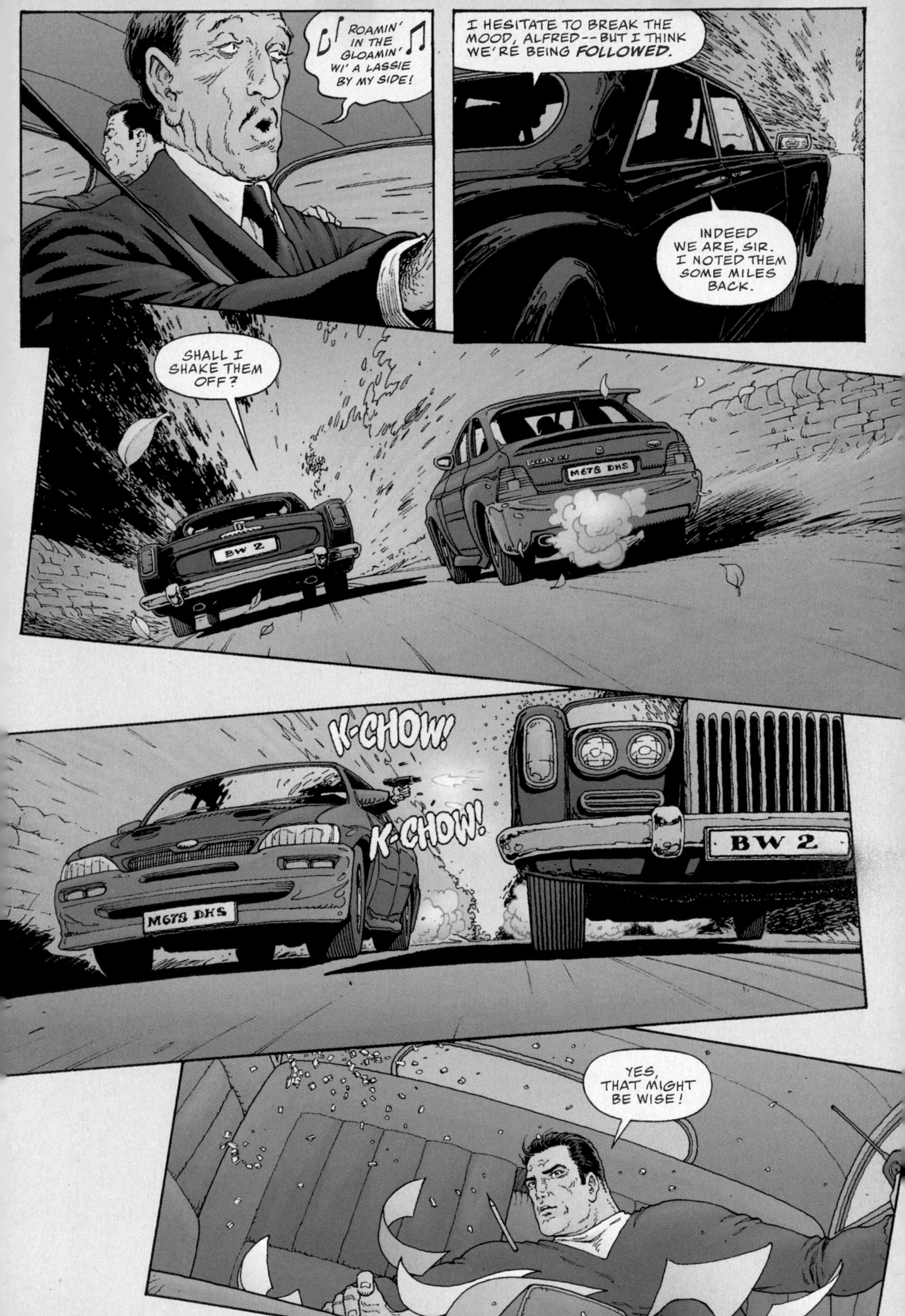
ROAMIN' IN THE GLOAMIN' WI' A LASSIE BY MY SIDE!
I HESITATE TO BREAK THE MOOD, ALFRED--BUT I THINK WE'RE BEING FOLLOWED.
INDEED WE ARE, SIR. I NOTED THEM SOME MILES BACK.
SHALL I SHAKE THEM OFF?
M678 DHS
BW 2
K-CHOW!
K-CHOW!
BW 2
M678 DHS
YES, THAT MIGHT BE WISE!

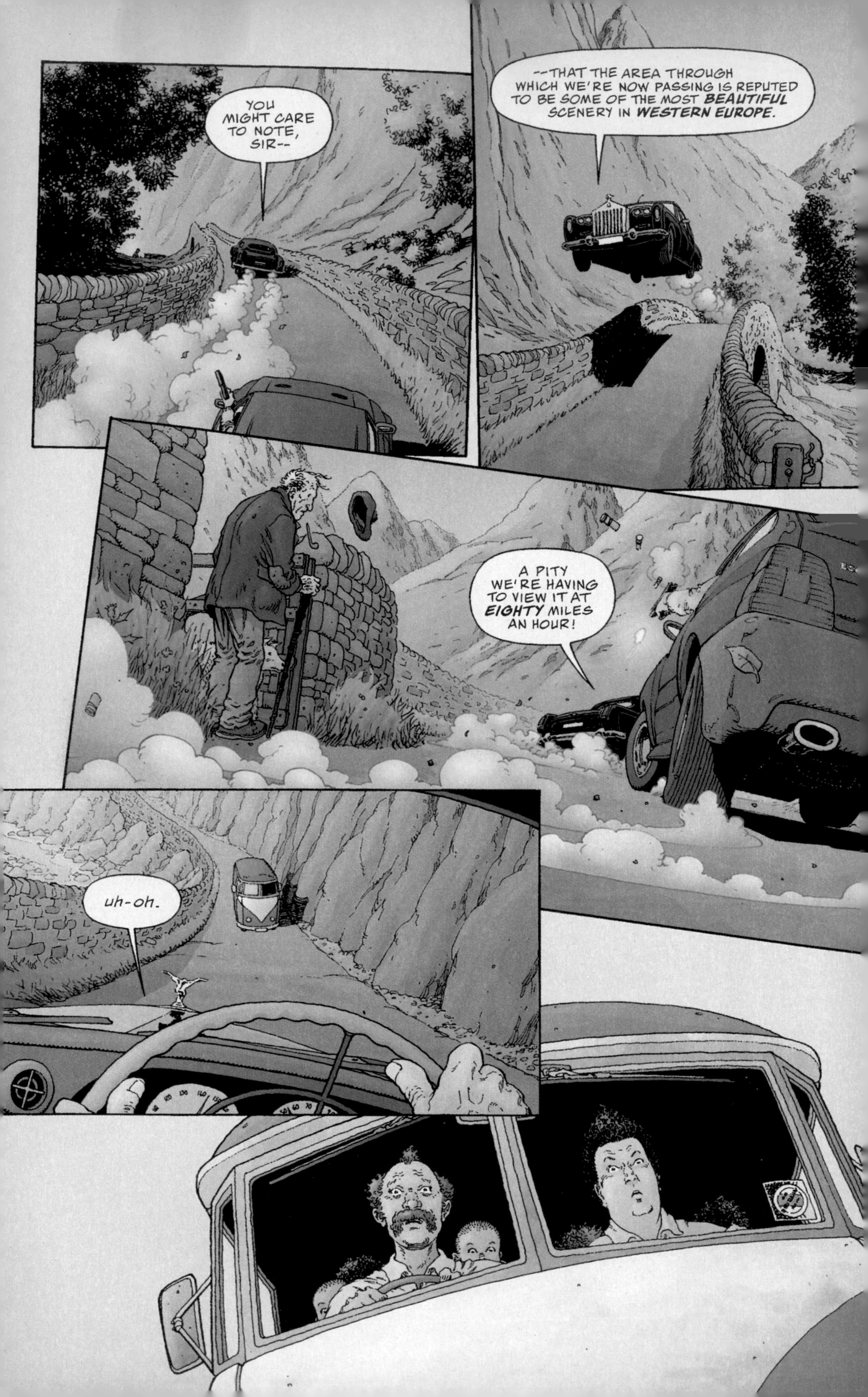
YOU MIGHT CARE TO NOTE, SIR--
--THAT THE AREA THROUGH WHICH WE'RE NOW PASSING IS REPUTED TO BE SOME OF THE MOST **BEAUTIFUL** SCENERY IN **WESTERN EUROPE**.
A PITY WE'RE HAVING TO VIEW IT AT **EIGHTY** MILES AN HOUR!
uh-oh.

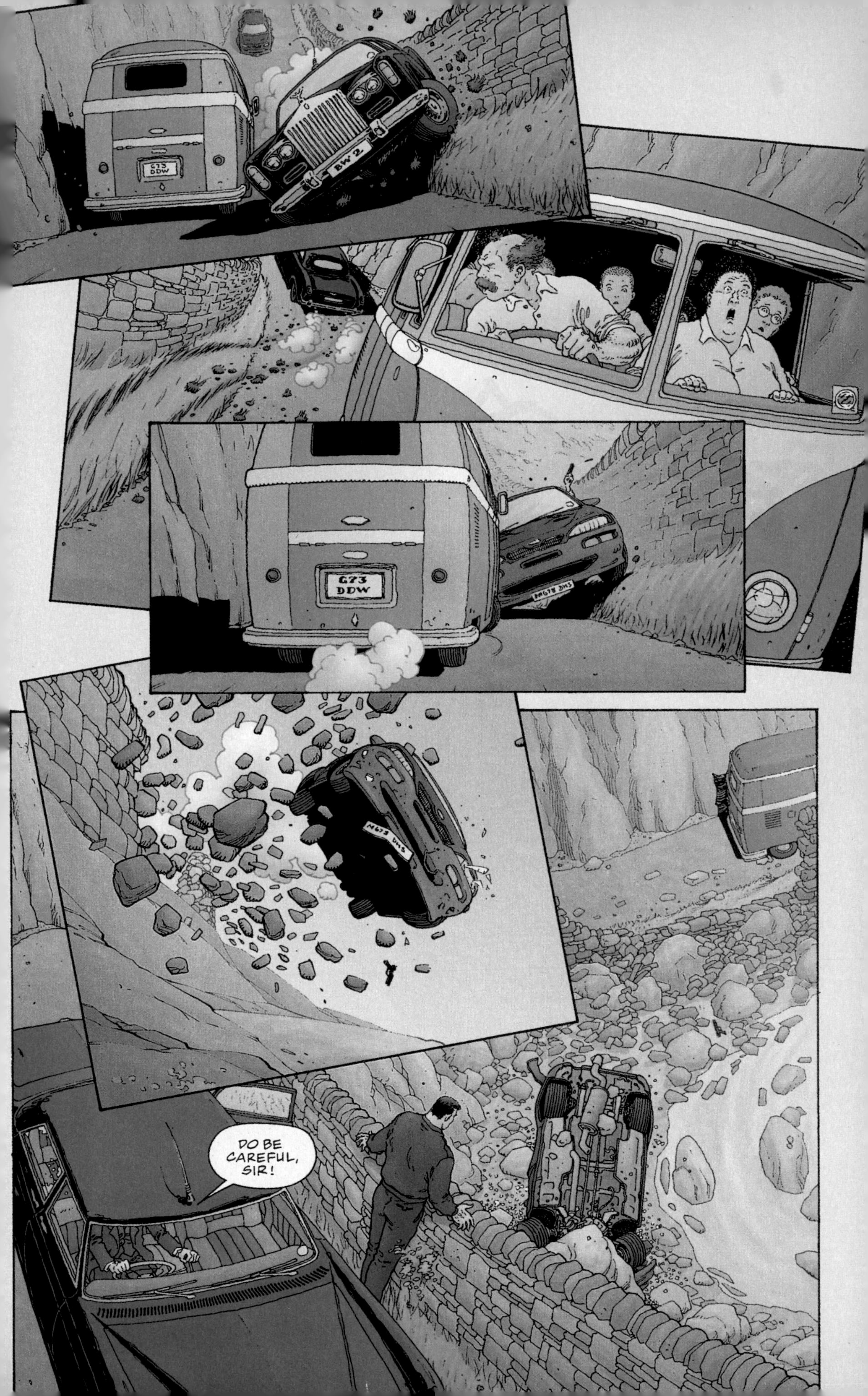
DO BE CAREFUL, SIR!

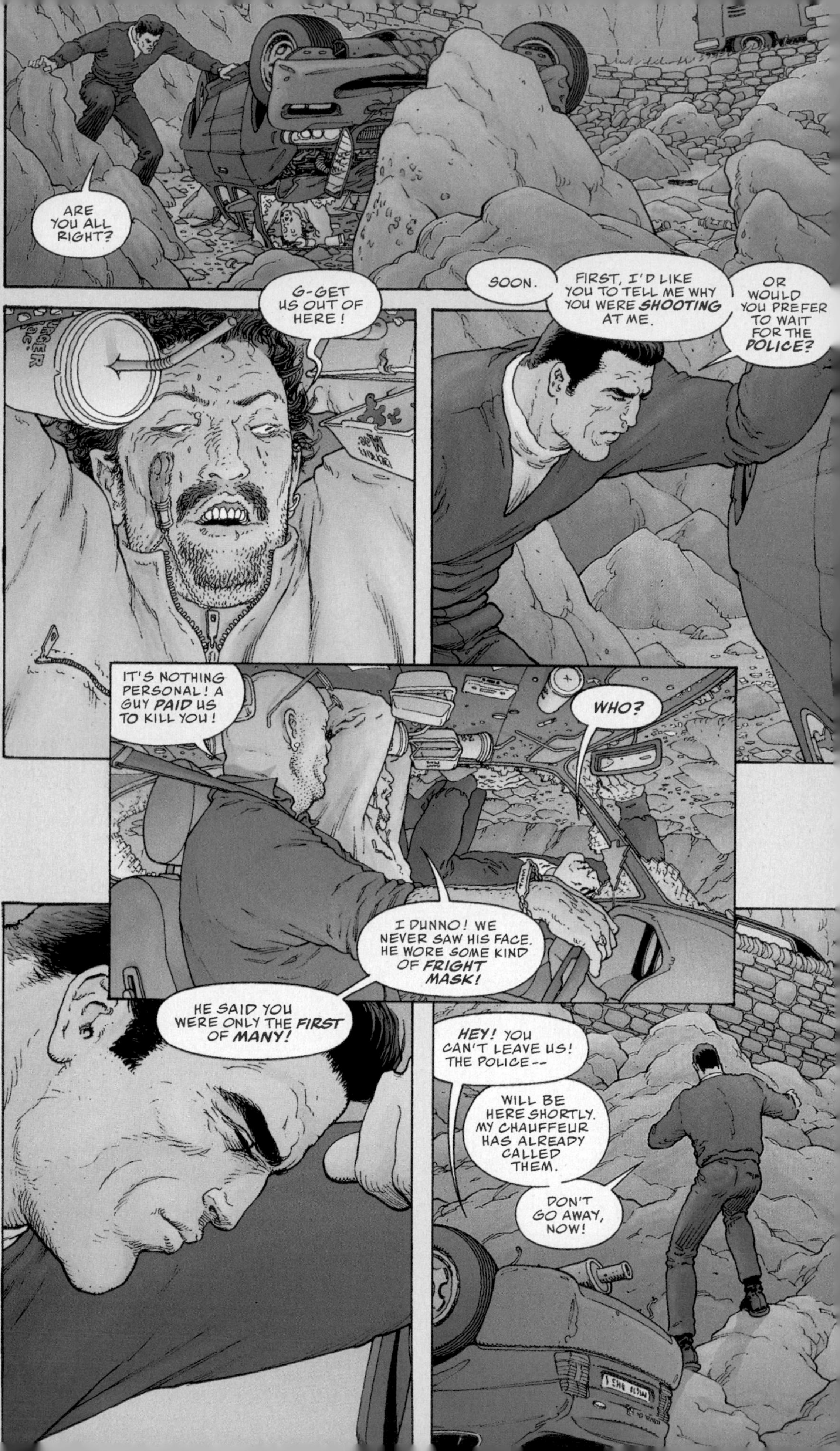

ARE YOU ALL RIGHT?
G-GET US OUT OF HERE!
SOON.
FIRST, I'D LIKE YOU TO TELL ME WHY YOU WERE SHOOTING AT ME.
OR WOULD YOU PREFER TO WAIT FOR THE POLICE?
IT'S NOTHING PERSONAL! A GUY PAID US TO KILL YOU!
WHO?
I DUNNO! WE NEVER SAW HIS FACE. HE WORE SOME KIND OF FRIGHT MASK!
HE SAID YOU WERE ONLY THE FIRST OF MANY!
HEY! YOU CAN'T LEAVE US! THE POLICE--
WILL BE HERE SHORTLY. MY CHAUFFEUR HAS ALREADY CALLED THEM.
DON'T GO AWAY, NOW!

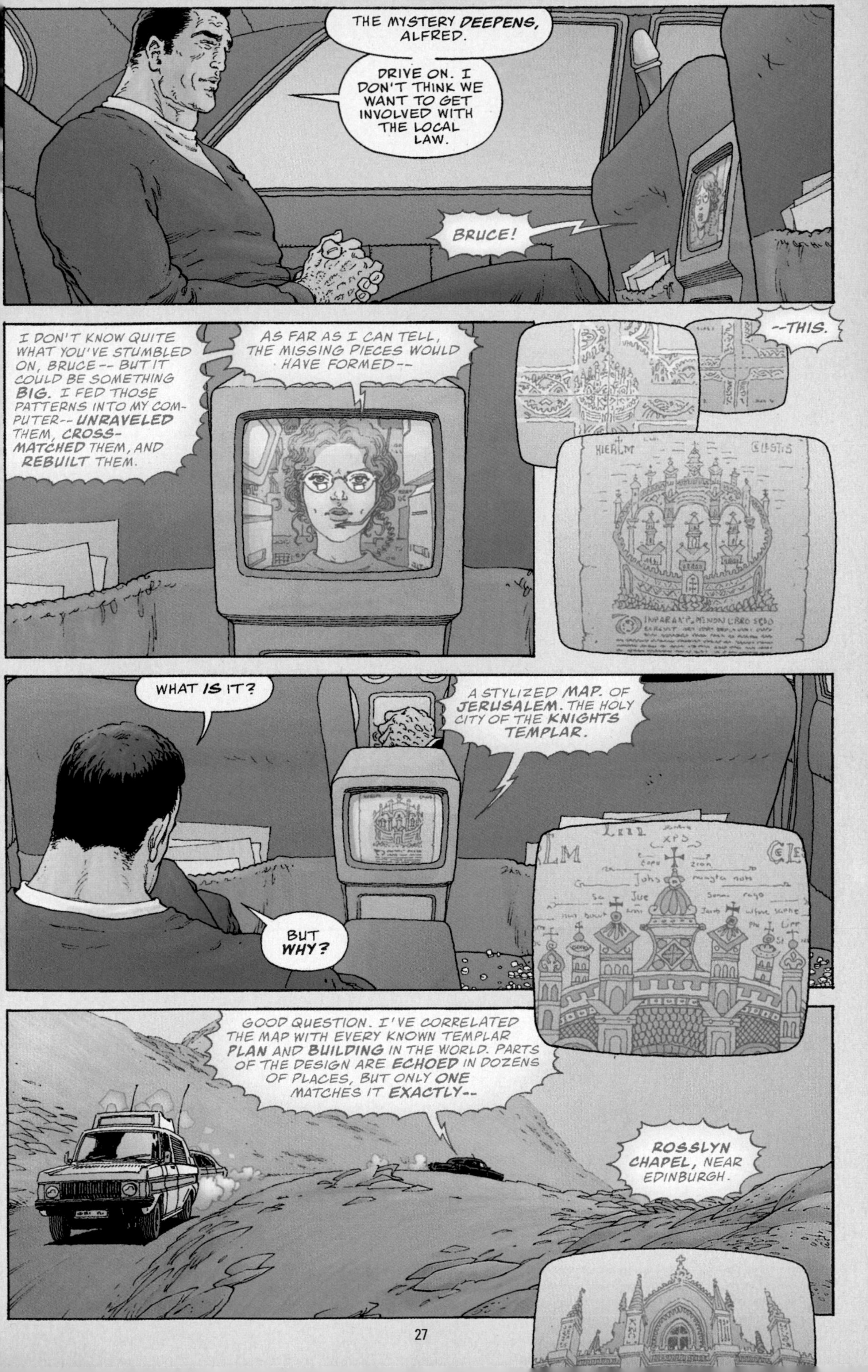
THE MYSTERY DEEPENS, ALFRED.
DRIVE ON. I DON'T THINK WE WANT TO GET INVOLVED WITH THE LOCAL LAW.
BRUCE!
I DON'T KNOW QUITE WHAT YOU'VE STUMBLED ON, BRUCE -- BUT IT COULD BE SOMETHING BIG. I FED THOSE PATTERNS INTO MY COMPUTER-- UNRAVELED THEM, CROSS-MATCHED THEM, AND REBUILT THEM.
AS FAR AS I CAN TELL, THE MISSING PIECES WOULD HAVE FORMED--
--THIS.
WHAT IS IT?
A STYLIZED MAP. OF JERUSALEM. THE HOLY CITY OF THE KNIGHTS TEMPLAR.
BUT WHY?
GOOD QUESTION. I'VE CORRELATED THE MAP WITH EVERY KNOWN TEMPLAR PLAN AND BUILDING IN THE WORLD. PARTS OF THE DESIGN ARE ECHOED IN DOZENS OF PLACES, BUT ONLY ONE MATCHES IT EXACTLY--
ROSSLYN CHAPEL, NEAR EDINBURGH.

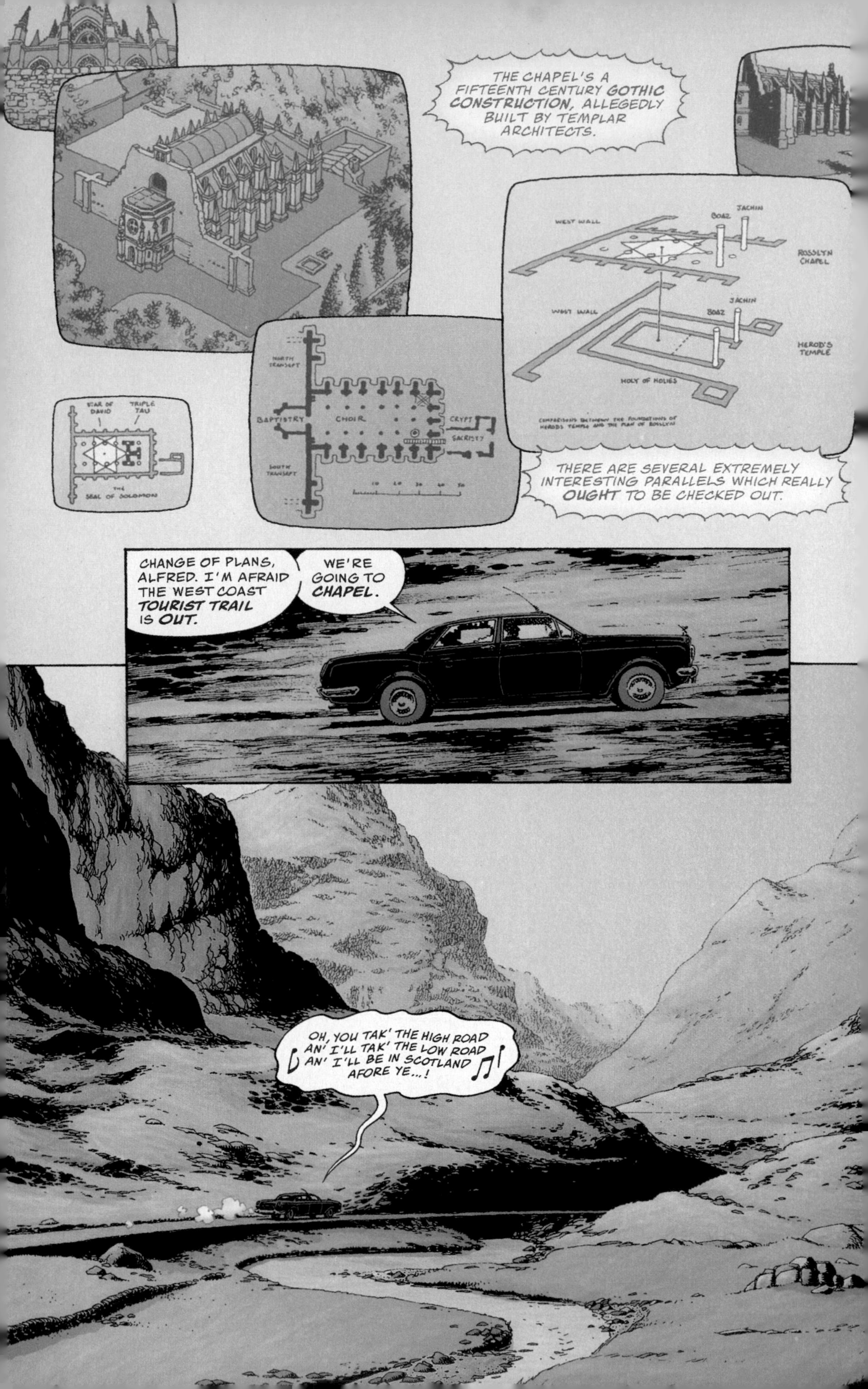
THE CHAPEL'S A FIFTEENTH CENTURY **GOTHIC CONSTRUCTION**, ALLEGEDLY BUILT BY TEMPLAR ARCHITECTS.
WEST WALL
BOAZ
JACHIN
ROSSLYN CHAPEL
WEST WALL
BOAZ
JACHIN
HEROD'S TEMPLE
HOLY OF HOLIES
STAR OF DAVID
TRIPLE TAU
THE SEAL OF SOLOMON
NORTH TRANSEPT
BAPTISTRY
CHOIR
CRYPT
SACRISTY
SOUTH TRANSEPT
10 20 30 40 50
THERE ARE SEVERAL EXTREMELY INTERESTING PARALLELS WHICH REALLY **OUGHT** TO BE CHECKED OUT.
CHANGE OF PLANS, ALFRED. I'M AFRAID THE WEST COAST **TOURIST TRAIL** IS **OUT**.
WE'RE GOING TO **CHAPEL**.
OH, YOU TAK' THE HIGH ROAD AN' I'LL TAK' THE LOW ROAD AN' I'LL BE IN SCOTLAND AFORE YE...!

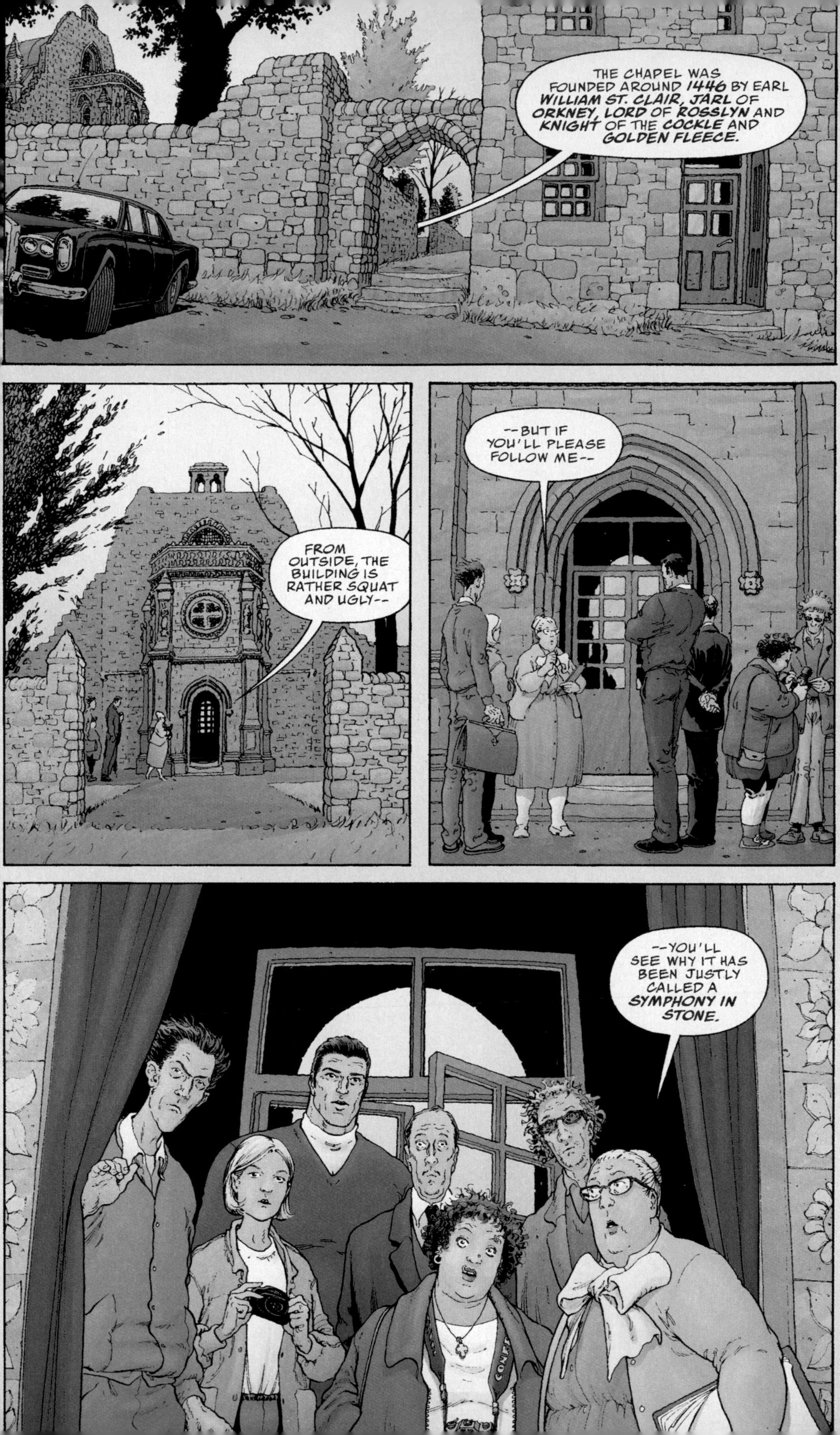
THE CHAPEL WAS FOUNDED AROUND 1446 BY EARL WILLIAM ST. CLAIR, JARL OF ORKNEY, LORD OF ROSSLYN AND KNIGHT OF THE COCKLE AND GOLDEN FLEECE.
FROM OUTSIDE, THE BUILDING IS RATHER SQUAT AND UGLY--
--BUT IF YOU'LL PLEASE FOLLOW ME--
--YOU'LL SEE WHY IT HAS BEEN JUSTLY CALLED A SYMPHONY IN STONE.

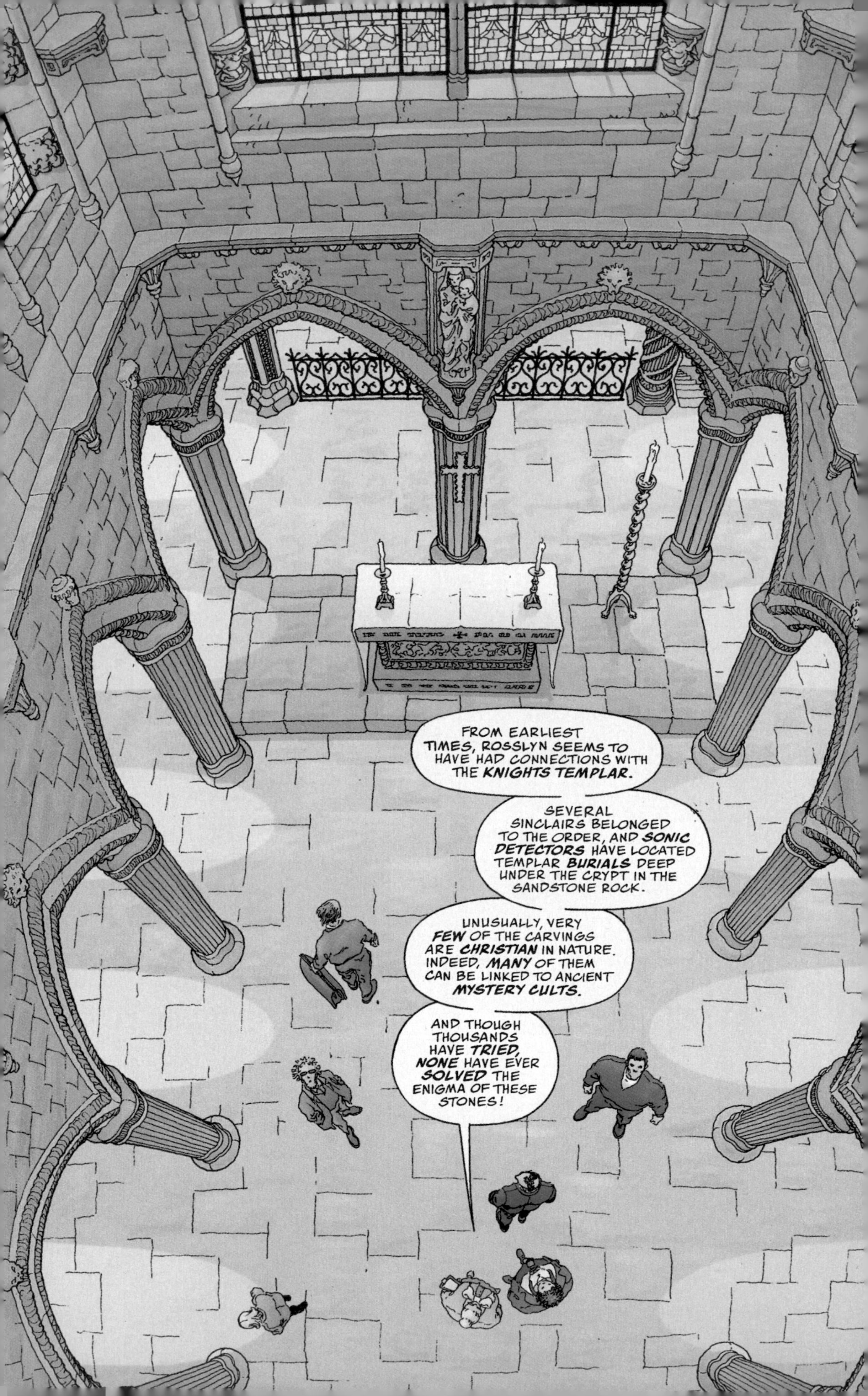
FROM EARLIEST TIMES, ROSSLYN SEEMS TO HAVE HAD CONNECTIONS WITH THE KNIGHTS TEMPLAR.
SEVERAL SINCLAIRS BELONGED TO THE ORDER, AND SONIC DETECTORS HAVE LOCATED TEMPLAR BURIALS DEEP UNDER THE CRYPT IN THE SANDSTONE ROCK.
UNUSUALLY, VERY FEW OF THE CARVINGS ARE CHRISTIAN IN NATURE. INDEED, MANY OF THEM CAN BE LINKED TO ANCIENT MYSTERY CULTS.
AND THOUGH THOUSANDS HAVE TRIED, NONE HAVE EVER SOLVED THE ENIGMA OF THESE STONES!

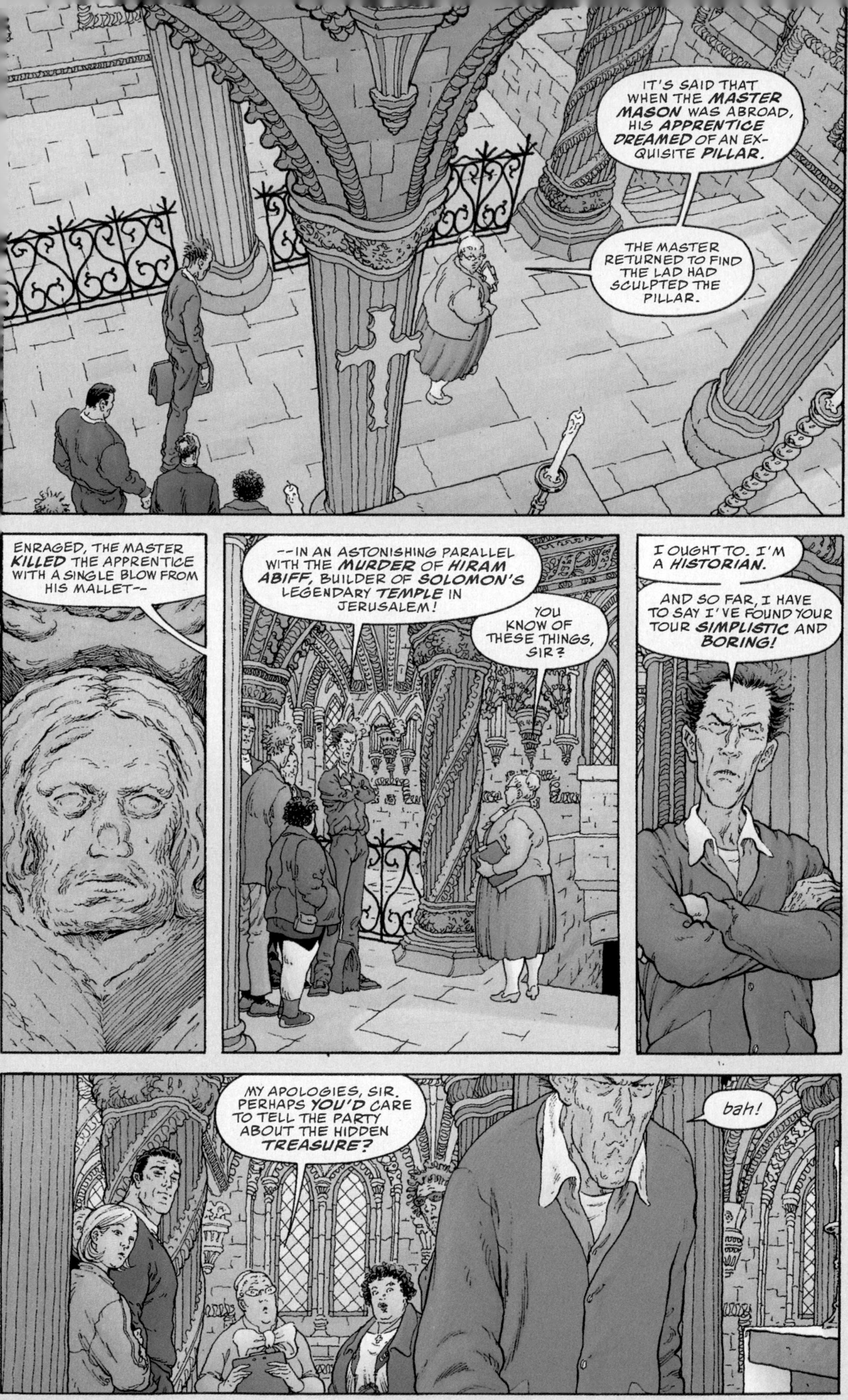
IT'S SAID THAT WHEN THE MASTER MASON WAS ABROAD, HIS APPRENTICE DREAMED OF AN EX-QUISITE PILLAR.
THE MASTER RETURNED TO FIND THE LAD HAD SCULPTED THE PILLAR.
ENRAGED, THE MASTER KILLED THE APPRENTICE WITH A SINGLE BLOW FROM HIS MALLET--
--IN AN ASTONISHING PARALLEL WITH THE MURDER OF HIRAM ABIFF, BUILDER OF SOLOMON'S LEGENDARY TEMPLE IN JERUSALEM!
YOU KNOW OF THESE THINGS, SIR?
I OUGHT TO. I'M A HISTORIAN.
AND SO FAR, I HAVE TO SAY I'VE FOUND YOUR TOUR SIMPLISTIC AND BORING!
MY APOLOGIES, SIR. PERHAPS YOU'D CARE TO TELL THE PARTY ABOUT THE HIDDEN TREASURE?
bah!

IT'S RUMORED THAT A GREAT **SECRET** IS BURIED HERE. SOME SAY IT IS THE **HOLY ROOD** OF SCOTLAND-- A FRAGMENT OF THE **CROSS** OF **CHRIST**.

OR IS IT THE LEGENDARY **TREASURE** OF **KING HEROD**, BROUGHT HERE BY THE **TEMPLARS**?

OR EVEN, AS SOME SAY, FORBIDDEN KNOWLEDGE THAT CAME FROM *THE DEVIL* HIMSELF?

MOST INTERESTING. THANK YOU.

THANK *YOU!*

WELL, SIR? ANY ANSWERS?

NO. BUT THE QUESTIONS *MULTIPLY!*

I'D LIKE A WORD WITH THAT *HISTORIAN*. HE SEEMED TO KNOW WHAT HE WAS TALKING ABOUT.

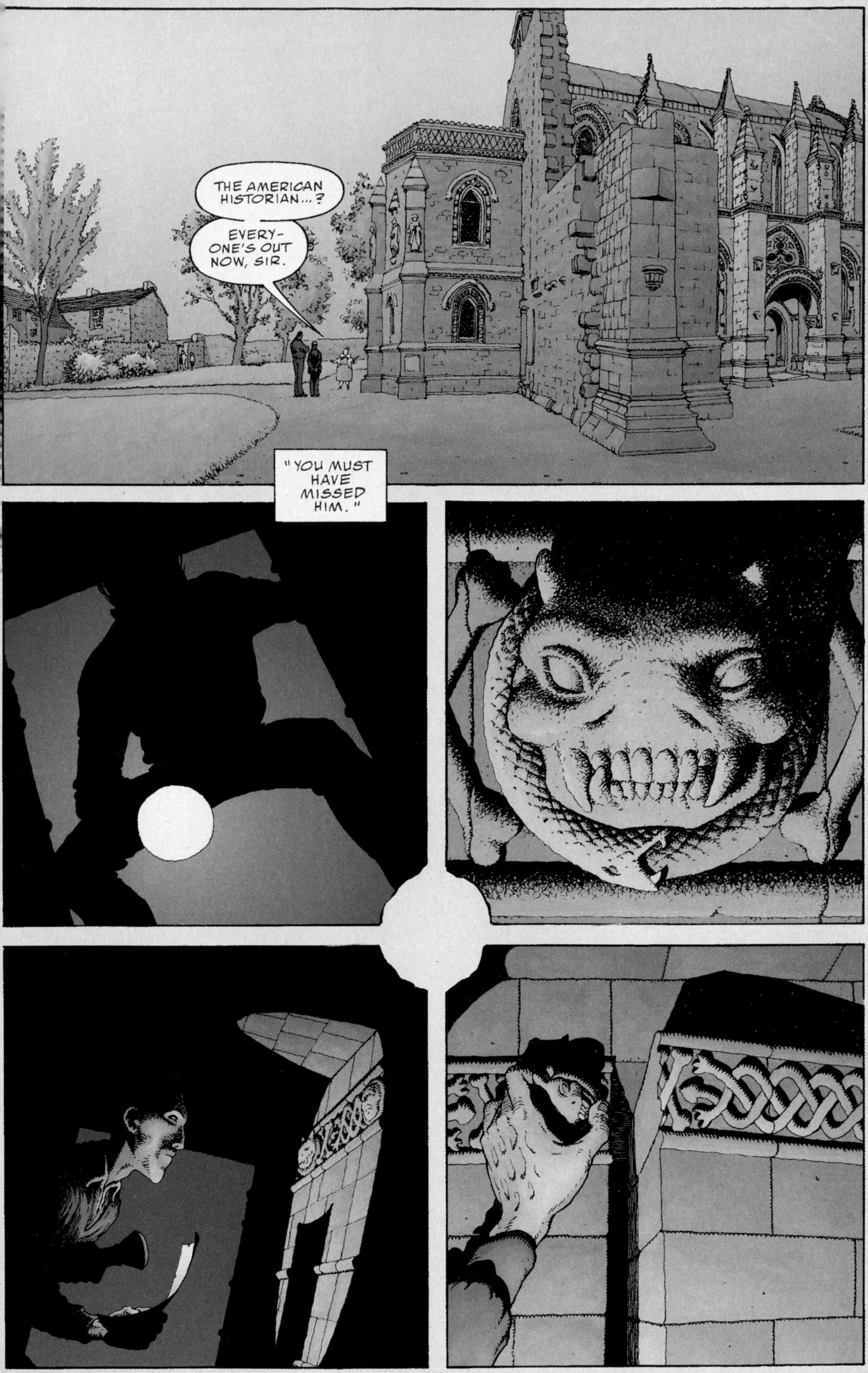
THE AMERICAN HISTORIAN...?
EVERY-ONE'S OUT NOW, SIR.
"YOU MUST HAVE MISSED HIM."

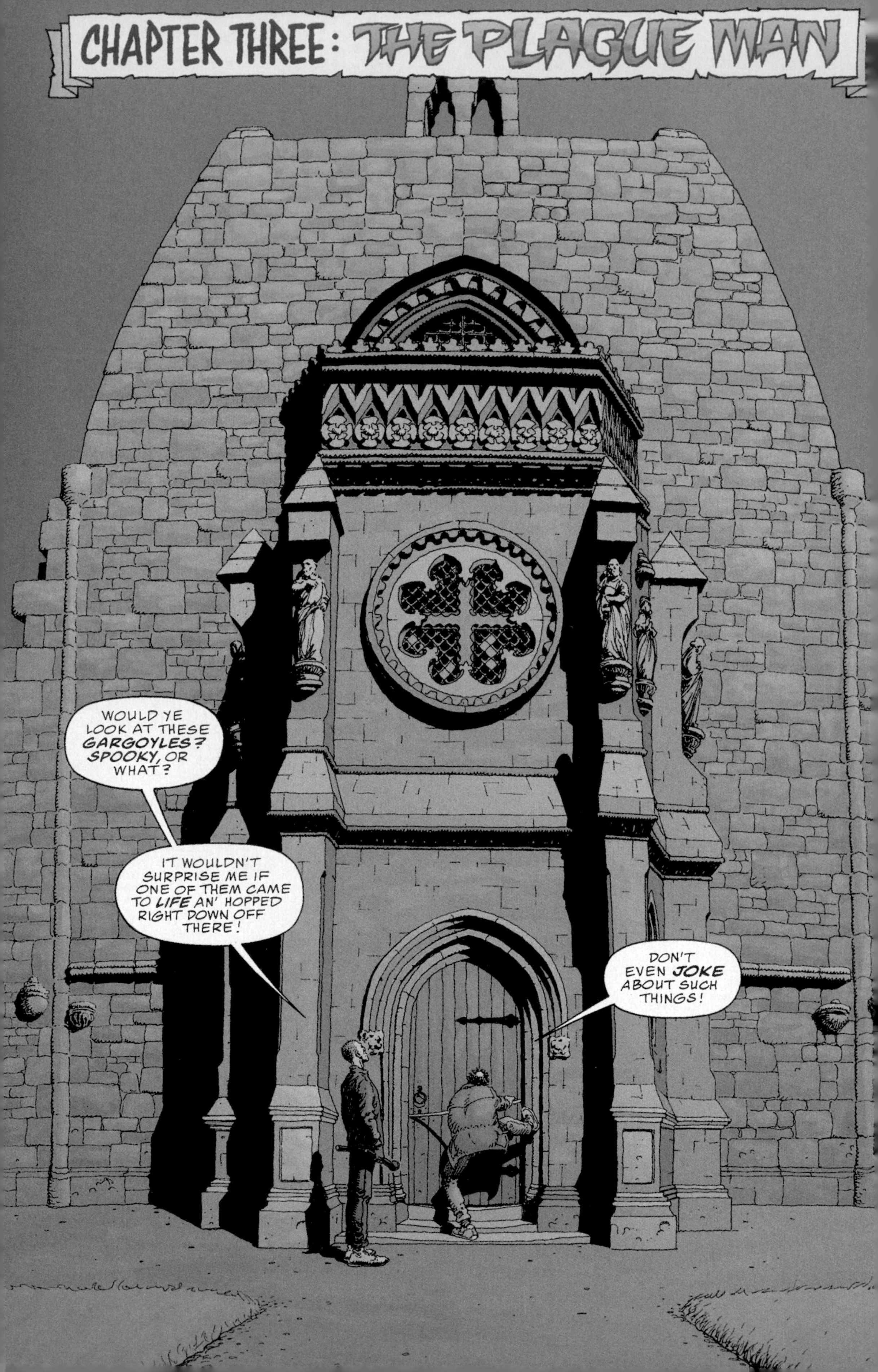
CHAPTER THREE: THE PLAGUE MAN
WOULD YE LOOK AT THESE GARGOYLES? SPOOKY, OR WHAT?
IT WOULDN'T SURPRISE ME IF ONE OF THEM CAME TO LIFE AN' HOPPED RIGHT DOWN OFF THERE!
DON'T EVEN JOKE ABOUT SUCH THINGS!

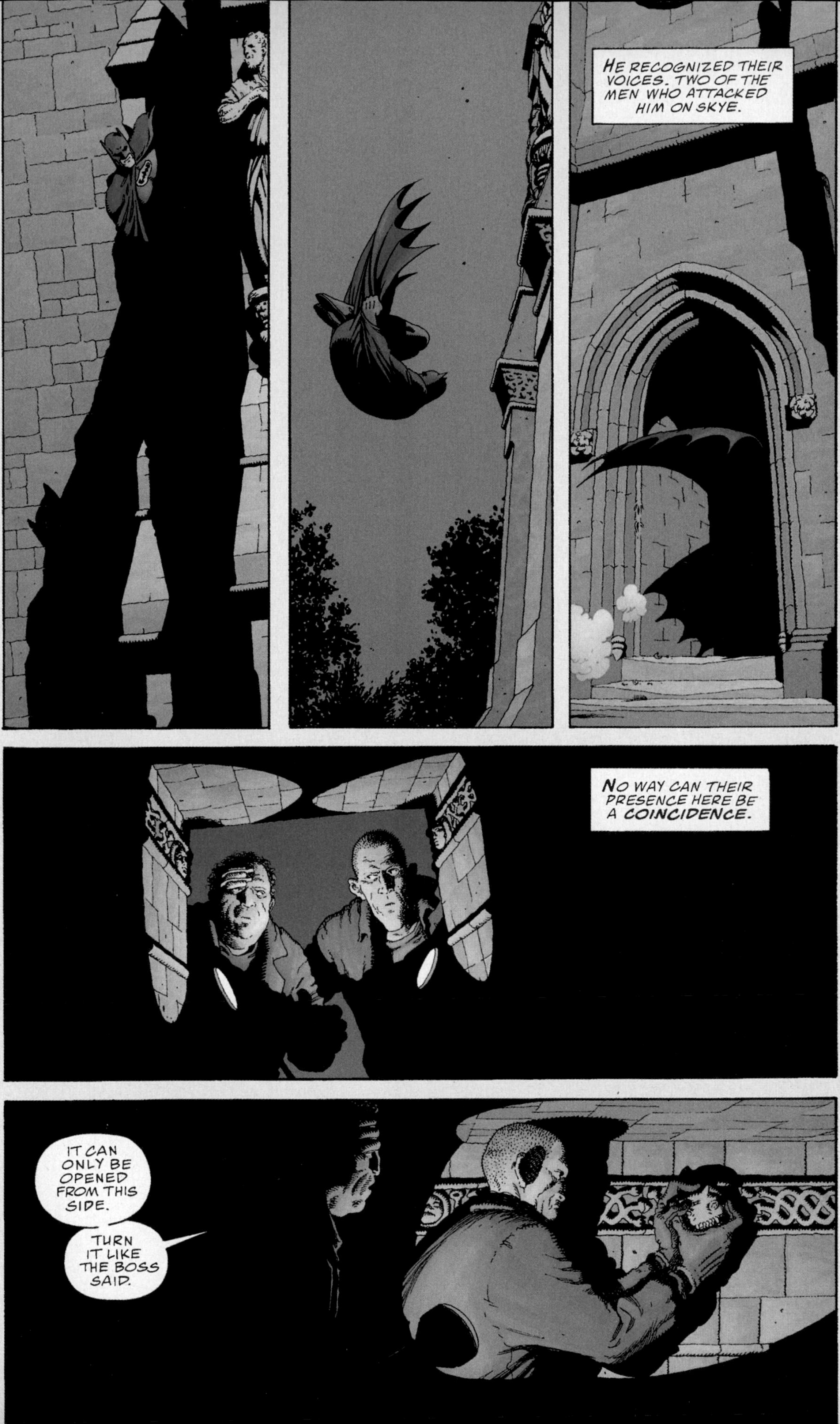
HE RECOGNIZED THEIR VOICES. TWO OF THE MEN WHO ATTACKED HIM ON SKYE.
NO WAY CAN THEIR PRESENCE HERE BE A COINCIDENCE.
IT CAN ONLY BE OPENED FROM THIS SIDE.
TURN IT LIKE THE BOSS SAID.

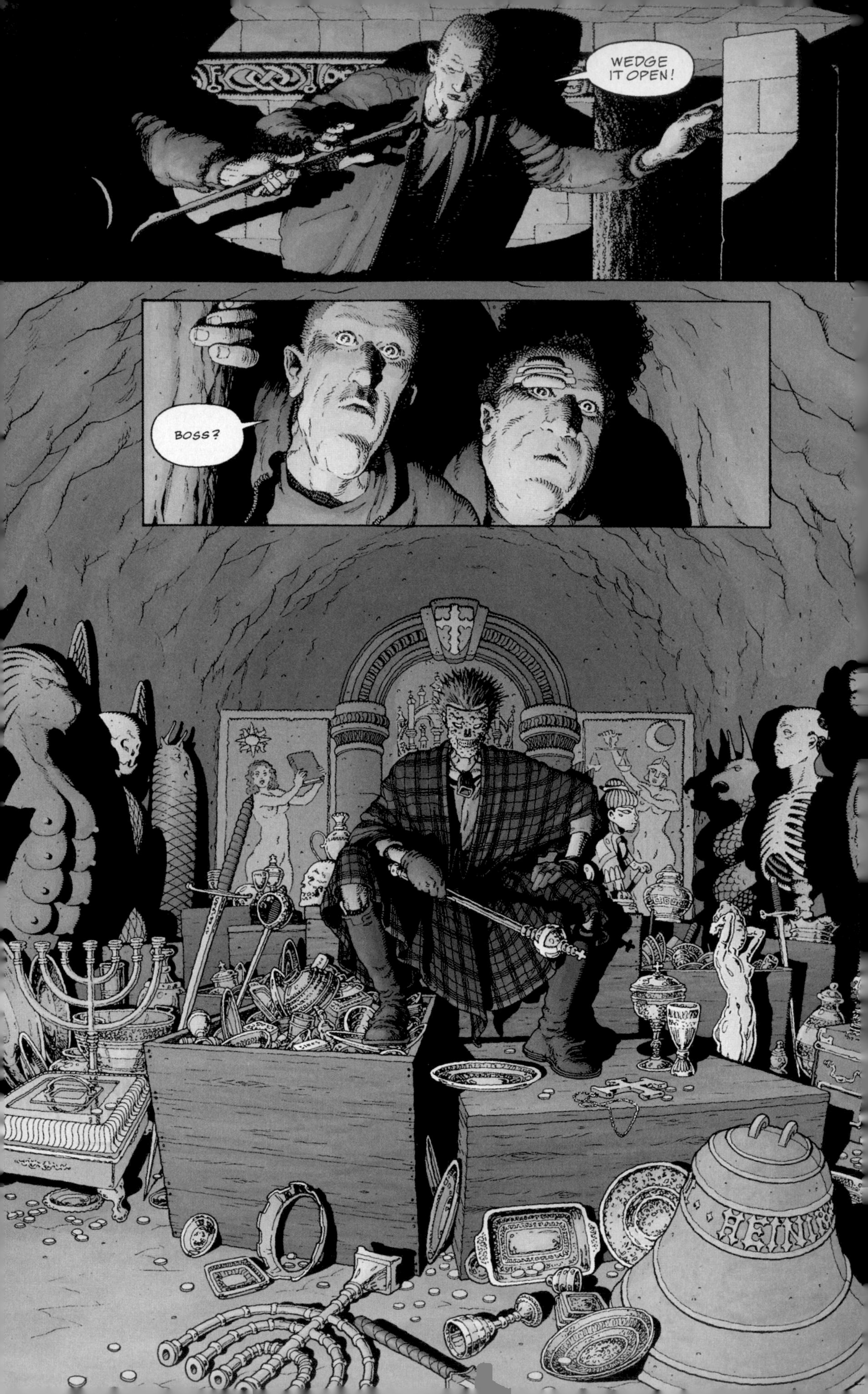
WEDGE IT OPEN!
BOSS?
HEIN

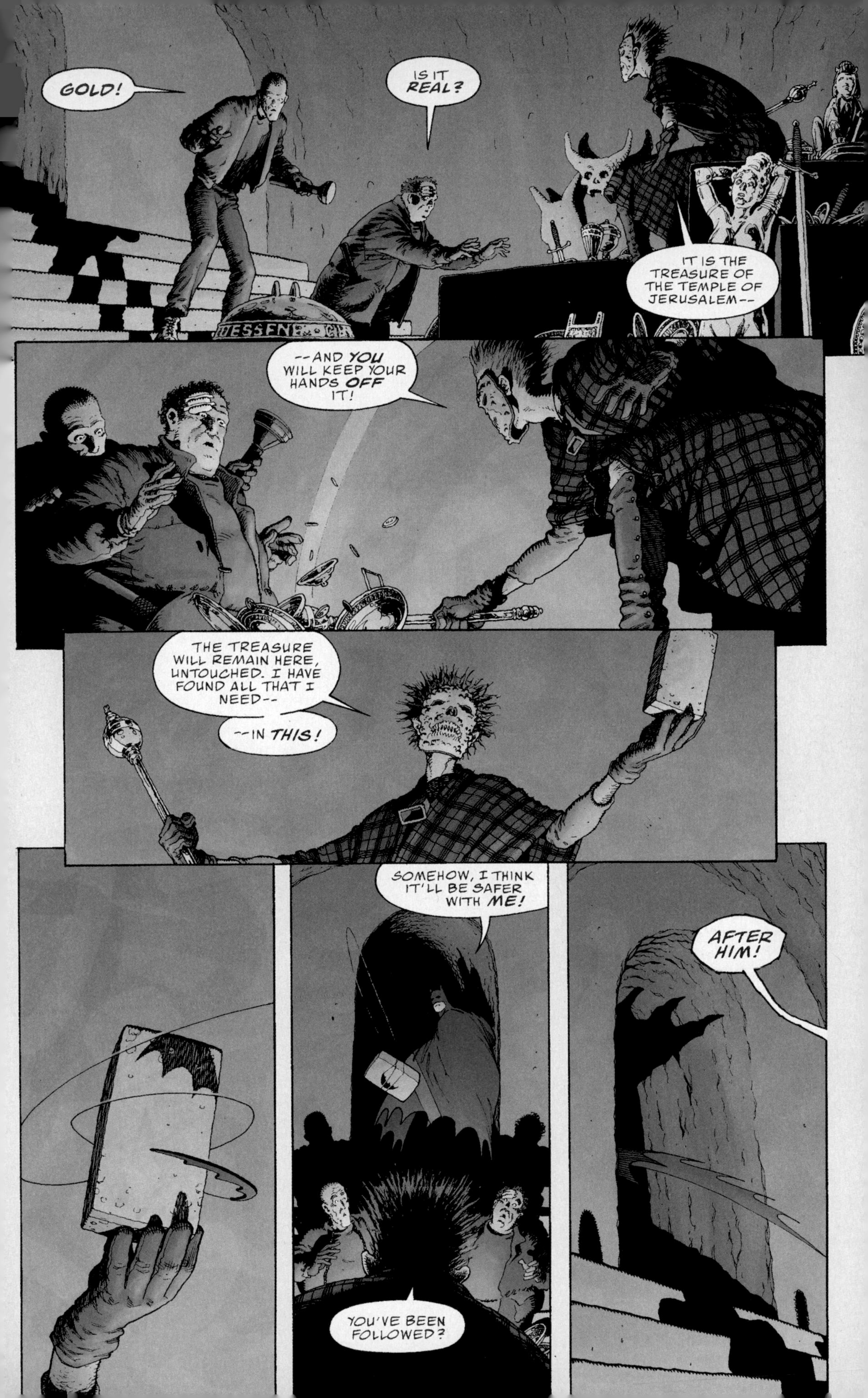
GOLD!
IS IT REAL?
IT IS THE TREASURE OF THE TEMPLE OF JERUSALEM--
--AND YOU WILL KEEP YOUR HANDS OFF IT!
THE TREASURE WILL REMAIN HERE, UNTOUCHED. I HAVE FOUND ALL THAT I NEED--
--IN THIS!
SOMEHOW, I THINK IT'LL BE SAFER WITH ME!
YOU'VE BEEN FOLLOWED?
AFTER HIM!

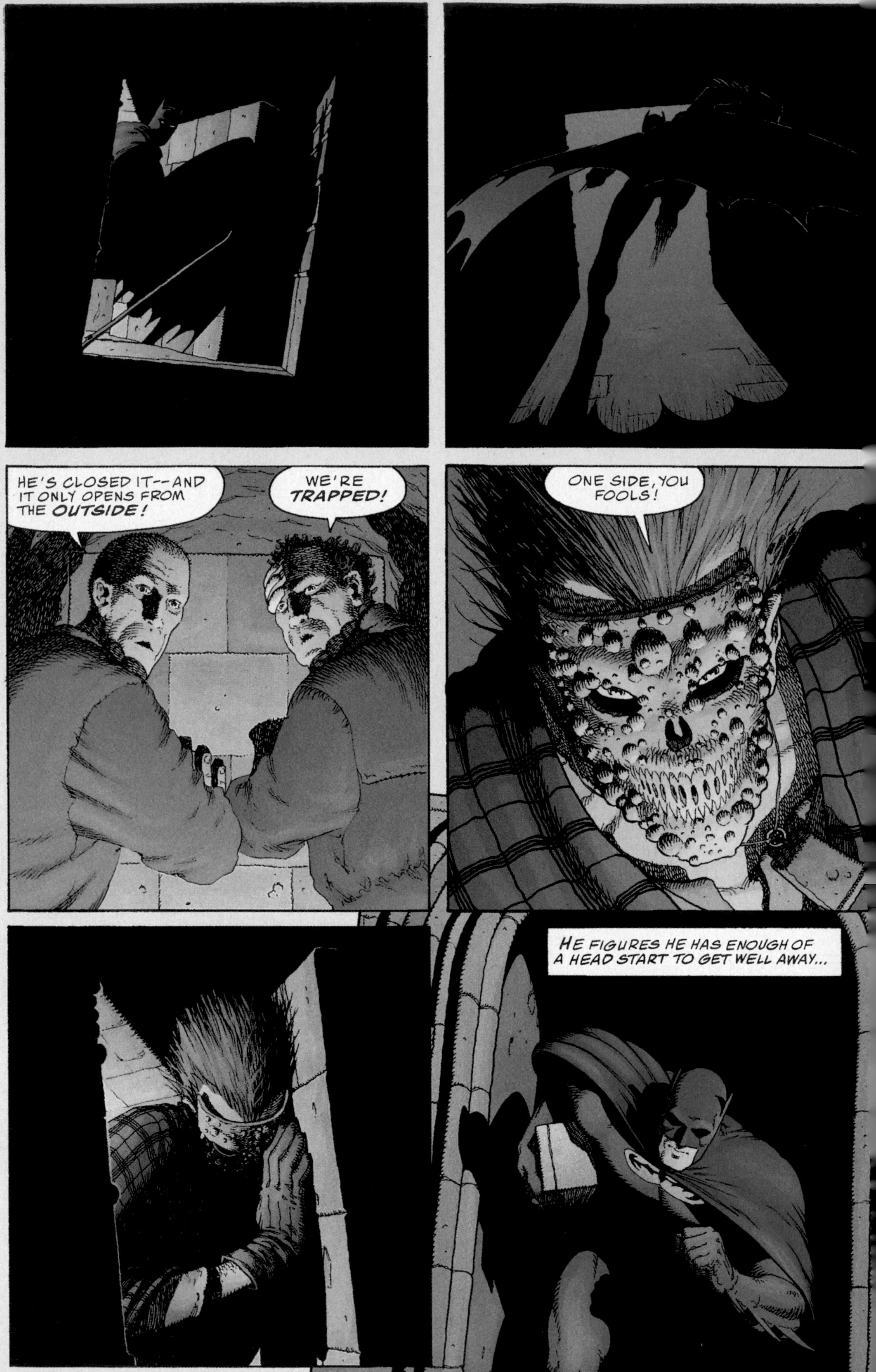
HE'S CLOSED IT--AND IT ONLY OPENS FROM THE *OUTSIDE*!
WE'RE *TRAPPED*!
ONE SIDE, YOU FOOLS!
HE FIGURES HE HAS ENOUGH OF A HEAD START TO GET WELL AWAY...

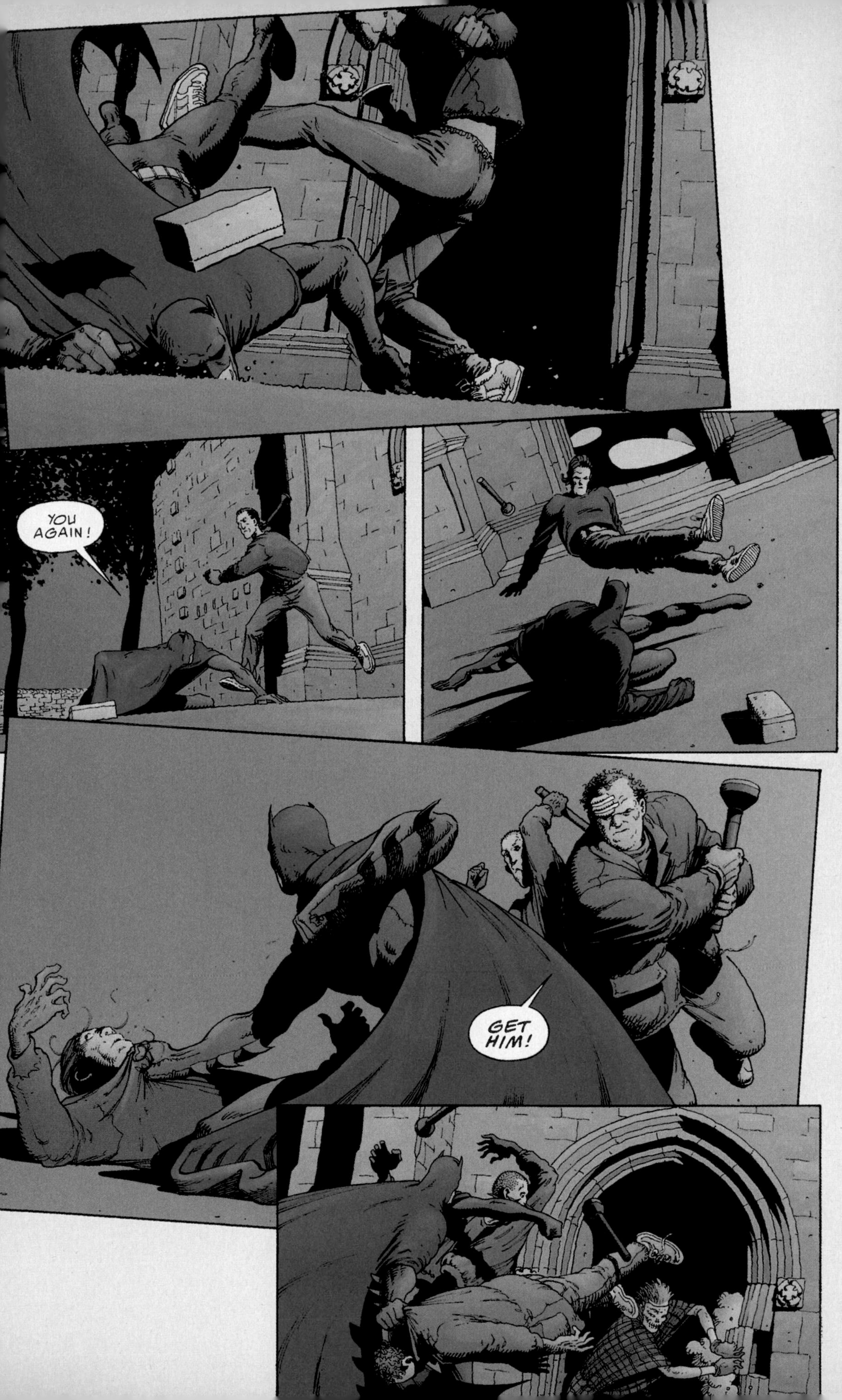
YOU AGAIN!
GET HIM!

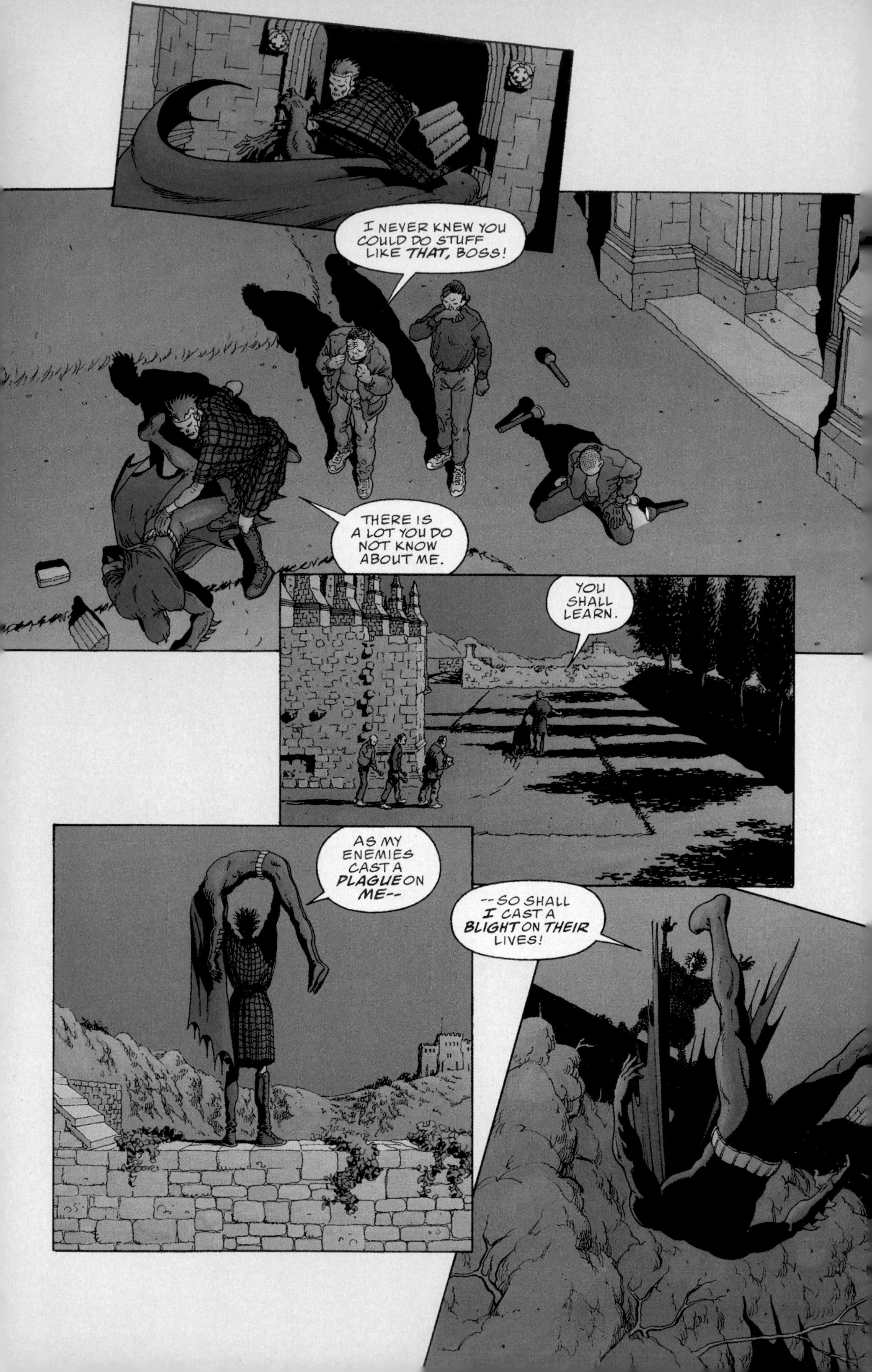
I NEVER KNEW YOU COULD DO STUFF LIKE THAT, BOSS!
THERE IS A LOT YOU DO NOT KNOW ABOUT ME.
YOU SHALL LEARN.
AS MY ENEMIES CAST A PLAGUE ON ME--
--SO SHALL I CAST A BLIGHT ON THEIR LIVES!

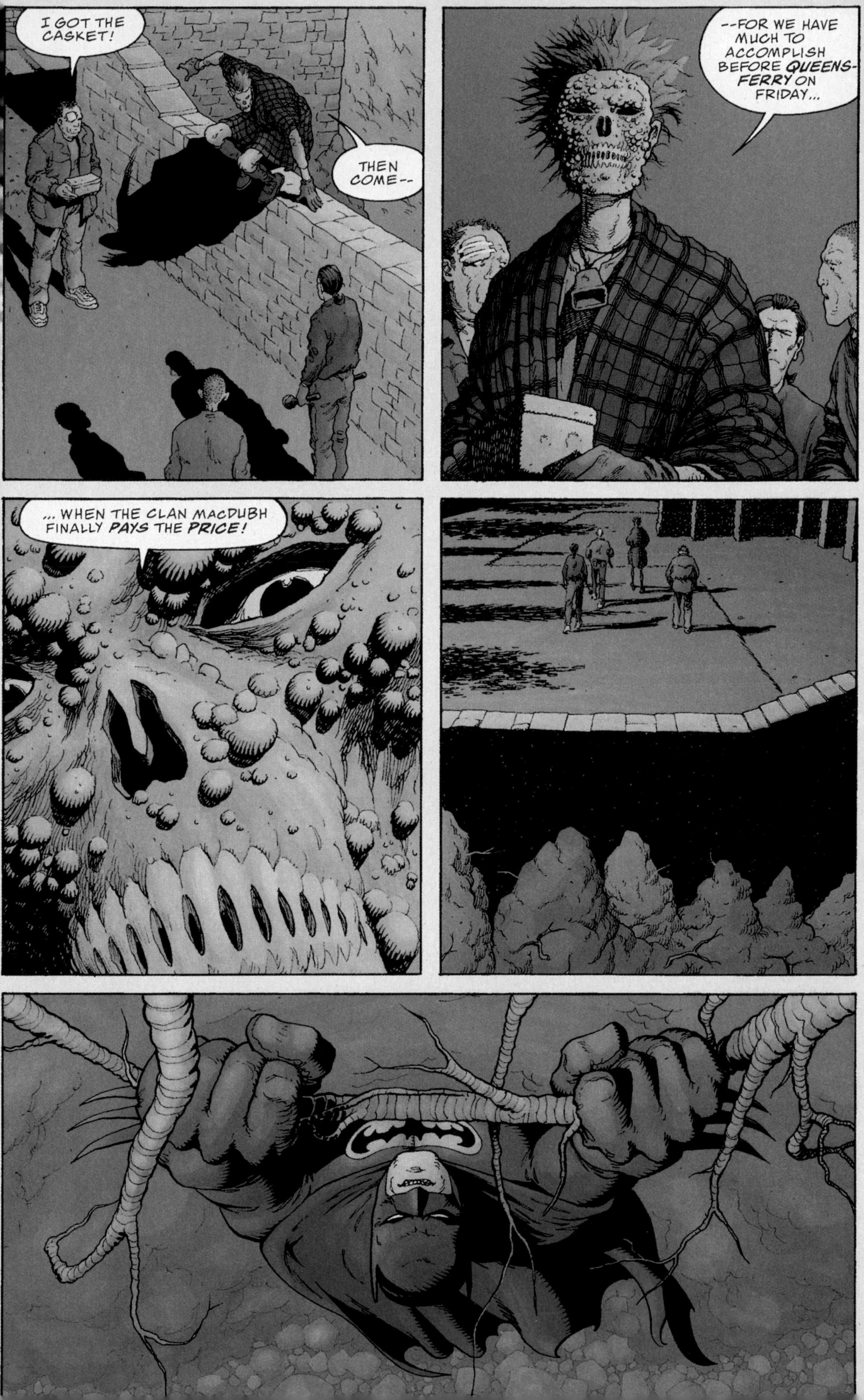
I GOT THE CASKET!
THEN COME--
--FOR WE HAVE MUCH TO ACCOMPLISH BEFORE QUEENSFERRY ON FRIDAY...
... WHEN THE CLAN MACDUBH FINALLY PAYS THE PRICE!

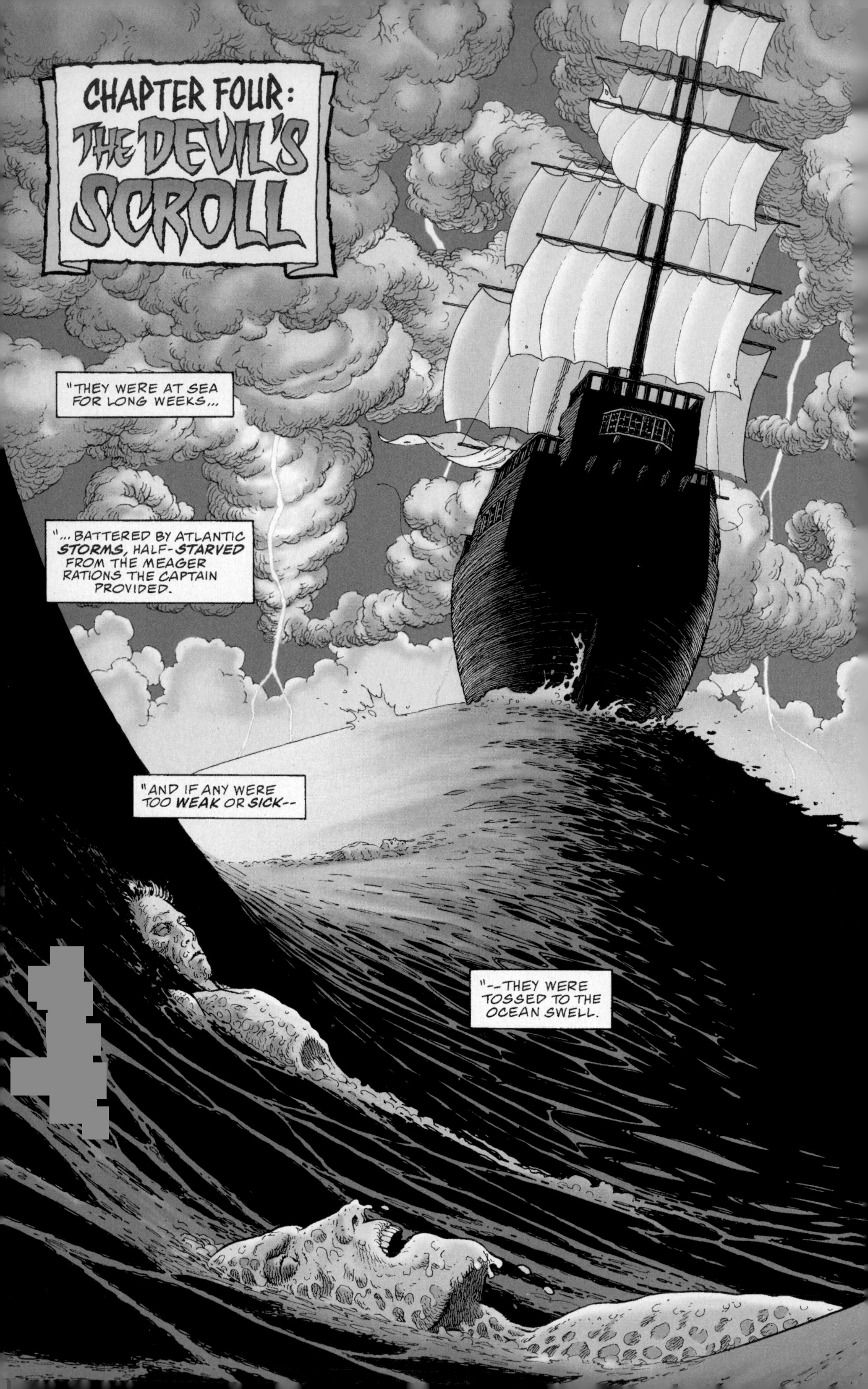
CHAPTER FOUR:
THE DEVIL'S SCROLL
"THEY WERE AT SEA FOR LONG WEEKS...
"...BATTERED BY ATLANTIC STORMS, HALF-STARVED FROM THE MEAGER RATIONS THE CAPTAIN PROVIDED.
"AND IF ANY WERE TOO WEAK OR SICK--
"--THEY WERE TOSSED TO THE OCEAN SWELL.

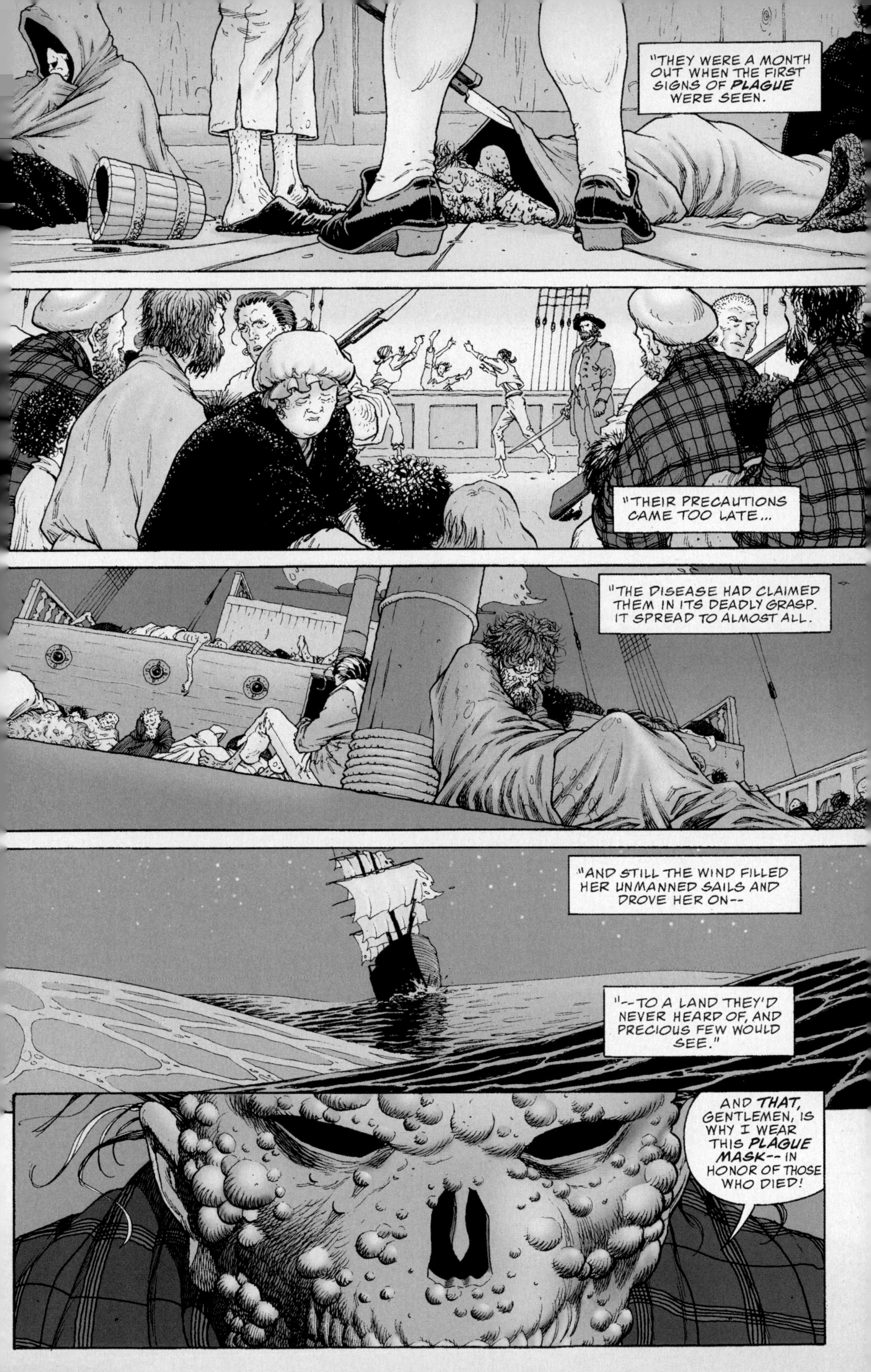
"THEY WERE A MONTH OUT WHEN THE FIRST SIGNS OF PLAGUE WERE SEEN.
"THEIR PRECAUTIONS CAME TOO LATE...
"THE DISEASE HAD CLAIMED THEM IN ITS DEADLY GRASP. IT SPREAD TO ALMOST ALL.
"AND STILL THE WIND FILLED HER UNMANNED SAILS AND DROVE HER ON--
"--TO A LAND THEY'D NEVER HEARD OF, AND PRECIOUS FEW WOULD SEE."
AND THAT, GENTLEMEN, IS WHY I WEAR THIS PLAGUE MASK-- IN HONOR OF THOSE WHO DIED!

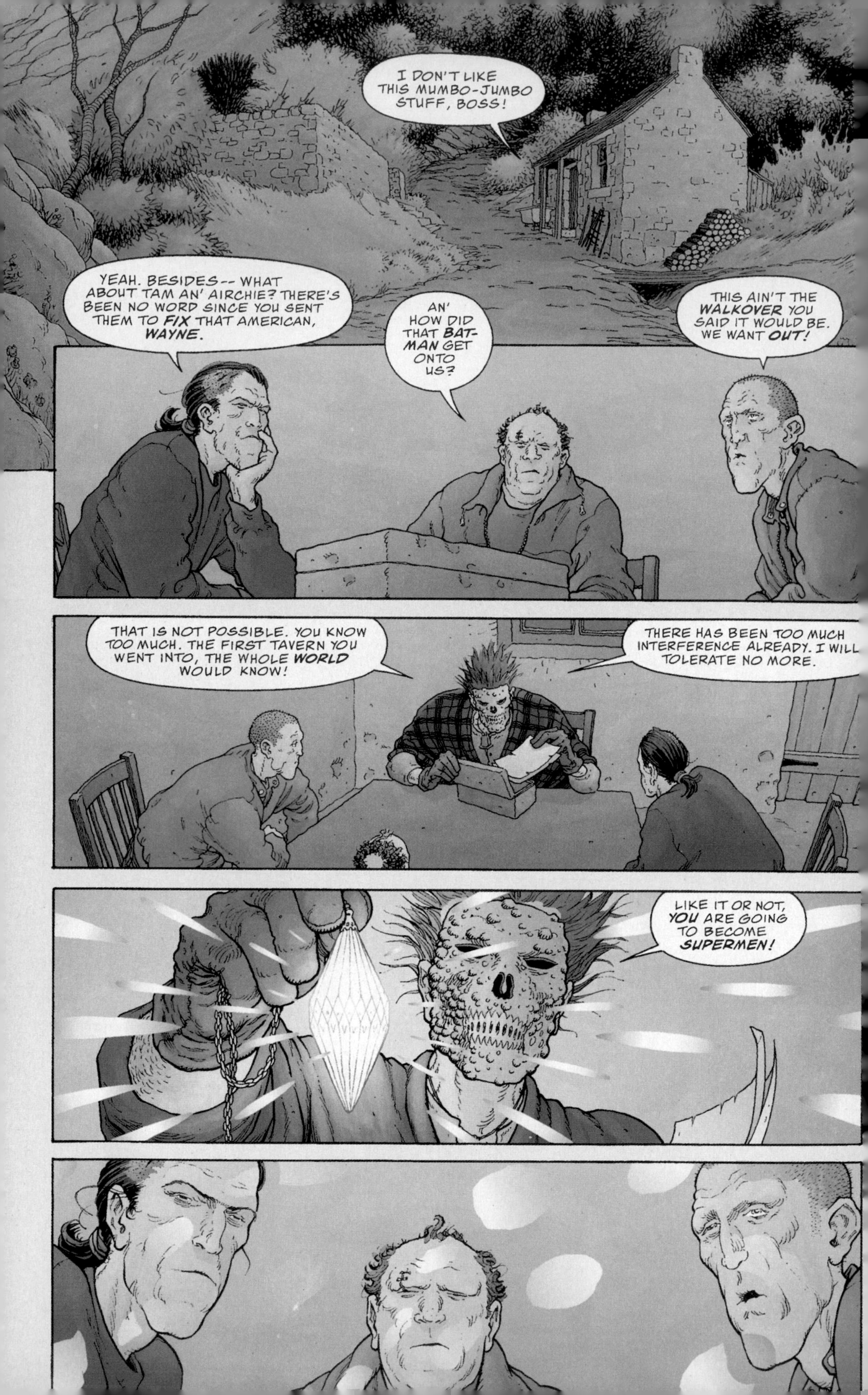
I DON'T LIKE THIS MUMBO-JUMBO STUFF, BOSS!
YEAH. BESIDES-- WHAT ABOUT TAM AN' AIRCHIE? THERE'S BEEN NO WORD SINCE YOU SENT THEM TO FIX THAT AMERICAN, WAYNE.
AN' HOW DID THAT BAT-MAN GET ONTO US?
THIS AIN'T THE WALKOVER YOU SAID IT WOULD BE. WE WANT OUT!
THAT IS NOT POSSIBLE. YOU KNOW TOO MUCH. THE FIRST TAVERN YOU WENT INTO, THE WHOLE WORLD WOULD KNOW!
THERE HAS BEEN TOO MUCH INTERFERENCE ALREADY. I WILL TOLERATE NO MORE.
LIKE IT OR NOT, YOU ARE GOING TO BECOME SUPERMEN!

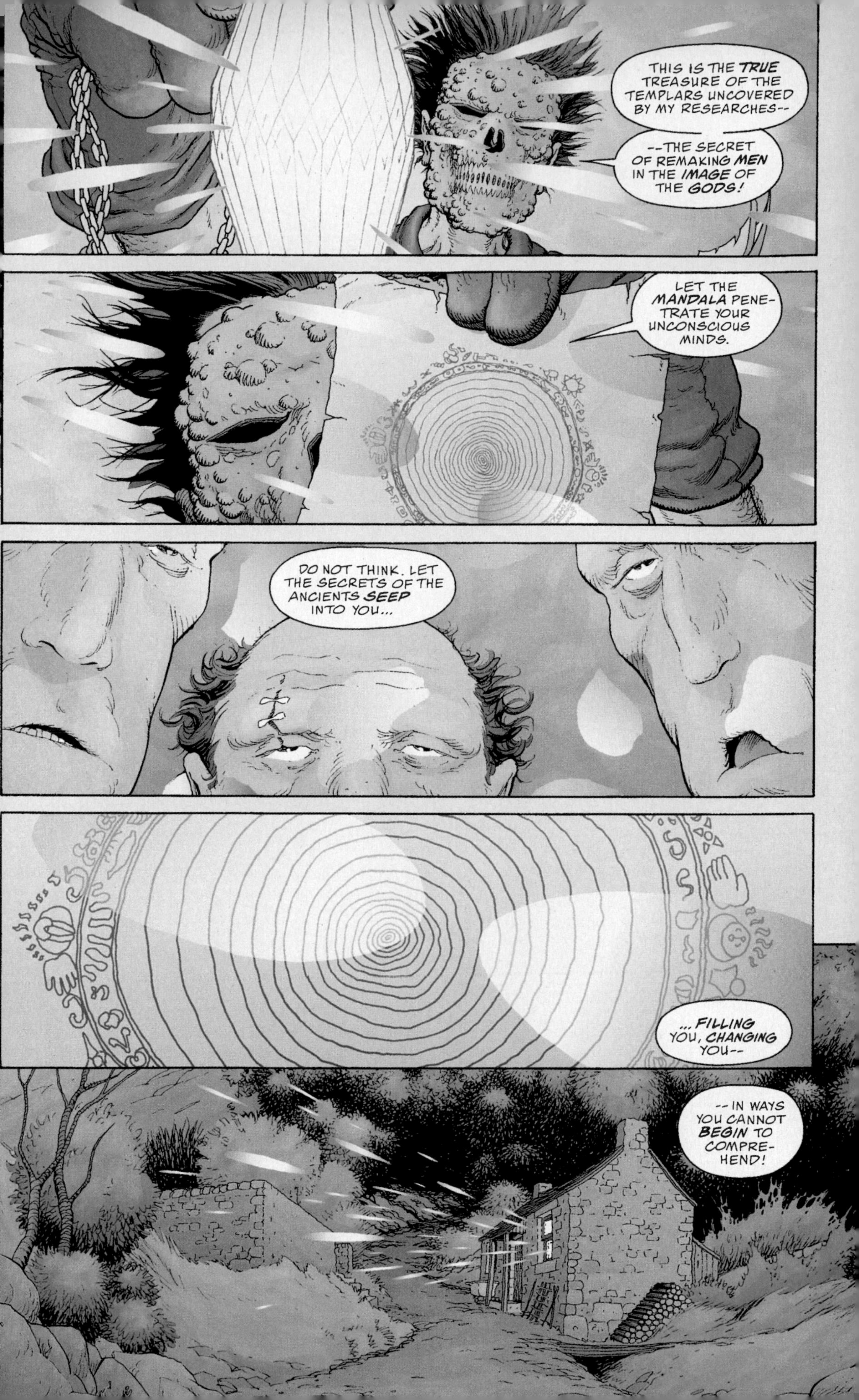
THIS IS THE TRUE TREASURE OF THE TEMPLARS UNCOVERED BY MY RESEARCHES--
--THE SECRET OF REMAKING MEN IN THE IMAGE OF THE GODS!
LET THE MANDALA PENETRATE YOUR UNCONSCIOUS MINDS.
DO NOT THINK. LET THE SECRETS OF THE ANCIENTS SEEP INTO YOU...
...FILLING YOU, CHANGING YOU--
--IN WAYS YOU CANNOT BEGIN TO COMPREHEND!

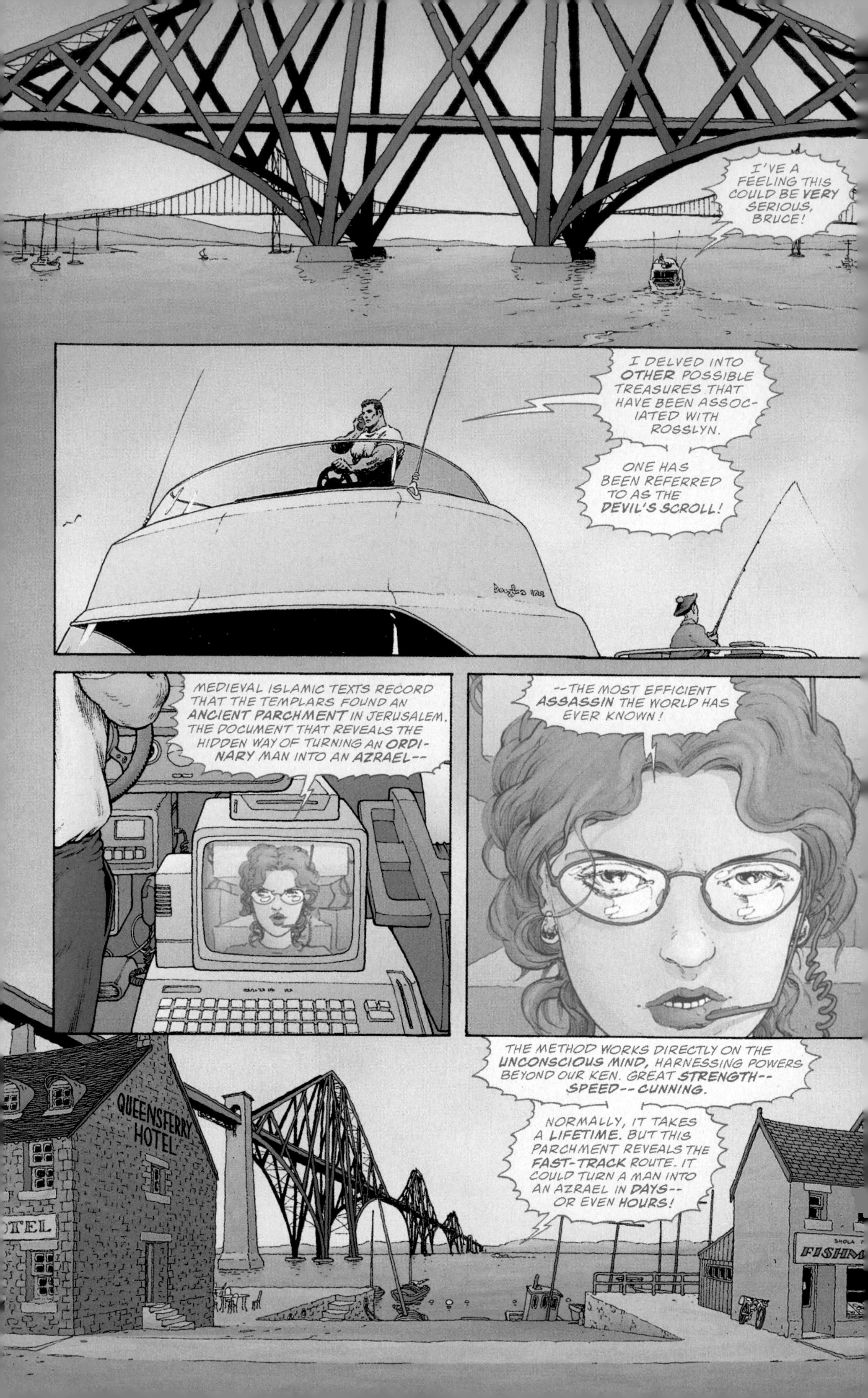
I'VE A FEELING THIS COULD BE VERY SERIOUS, BRUCE!
I DELVED INTO OTHER POSSIBLE TREASURES THAT HAVE BEEN ASSOCIATED WITH ROSSLYN.
ONE HAS BEEN REFERRED TO AS THE DEVIL'S SCROLL!
MEDIEVAL ISLAMIC TEXTS RECORD THAT THE TEMPLARS FOUND AN ANCIENT PARCHMENT IN JERUSALEM. THE DOCUMENT THAT REVEALS THE HIDDEN WAY OF TURNING AN ORDINARY MAN INTO AN AZRAEL--
--THE MOST EFFICIENT ASSASSIN THE WORLD HAS EVER KNOWN!
THE METHOD WORKS DIRECTLY ON THE UNCONSCIOUS MIND, HARNESSING POWERS BEYOND OUR KEN. GREAT STRENGTH--SPEED--CUNNING.
NORMALLY, IT TAKES A LIFETIME. BUT THIS PARCHMENT REVEALS THE FAST-TRACK ROUTE. IT COULD TURN A MAN INTO AN AZRAEL IN DAYS--OR EVEN HOURS!
QUEENSFERRY HOTEL
OTEL
FISHM

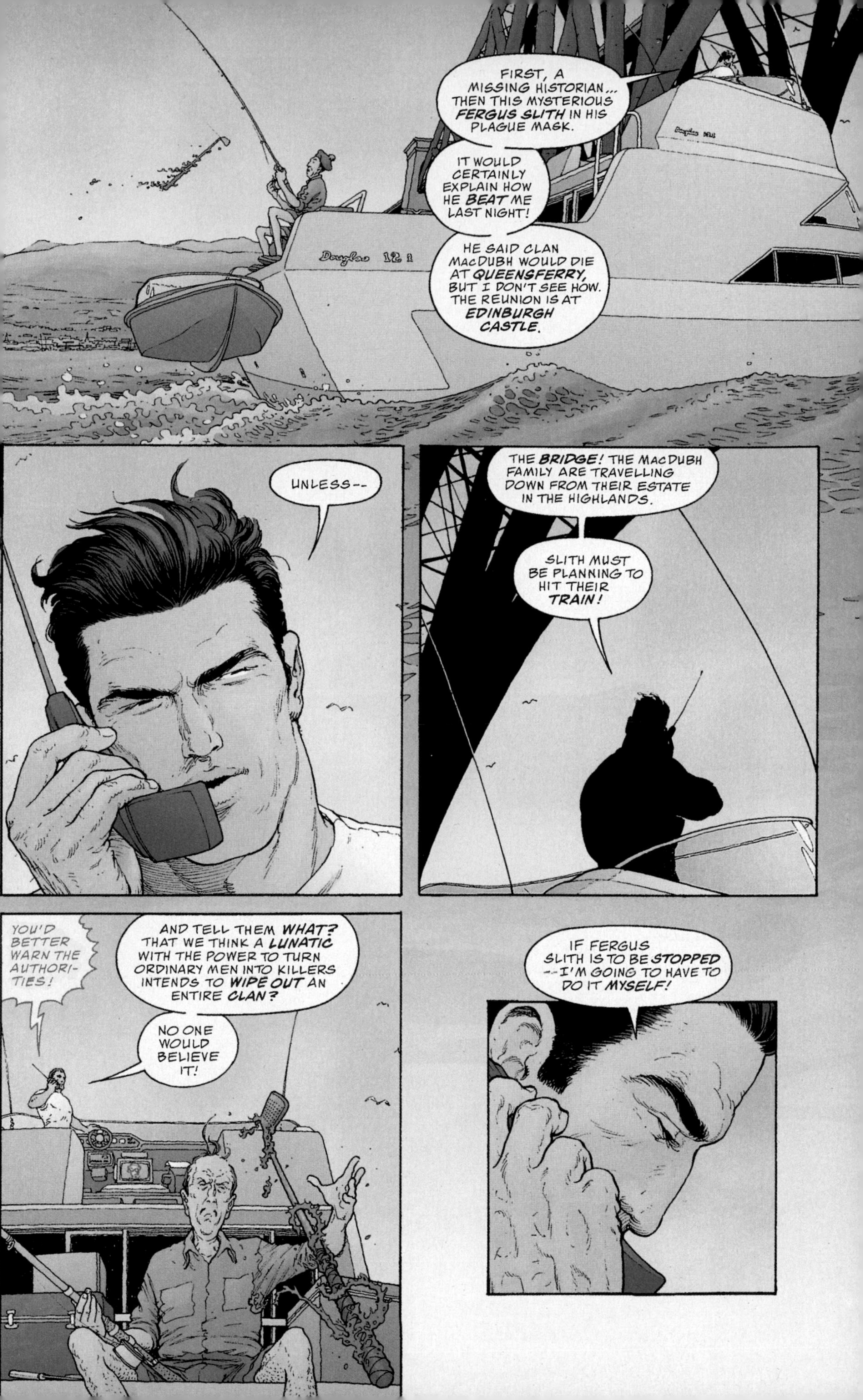
FIRST, A MISSING HISTORIAN... THEN THIS MYSTERIOUS FERGUS SLITH IN HIS PLAGUE MASK.
IT WOULD CERTAINLY EXPLAIN HOW HE BEAT ME LAST NIGHT!
HE SAID CLAN MacDUBH WOULD DIE AT QUEENSFERRY, BUT I DON'T SEE HOW. THE REUNION IS AT EDINBURGH CASTLE.
Douglas 12 1
UNLESS--
THE BRIDGE! THE MacDUBH FAMILY ARE TRAVELLING DOWN FROM THEIR ESTATE IN THE HIGHLANDS.
SLITH MUST BE PLANNING TO HIT THEIR TRAIN!
YOU'D BETTER WARN THE AUTHORITIES!
AND TELL THEM WHAT? THAT WE THINK A LUNATIC WITH THE POWER TO TURN ORDINARY MEN INTO KILLERS INTENDS TO WIPE OUT AN ENTIRE CLAN?
NO ONE WOULD BELIEVE IT!
IF FERGUS SLITH IS TO BE STOPPED --I'M GOING TO HAVE TO DO IT MYSELF!

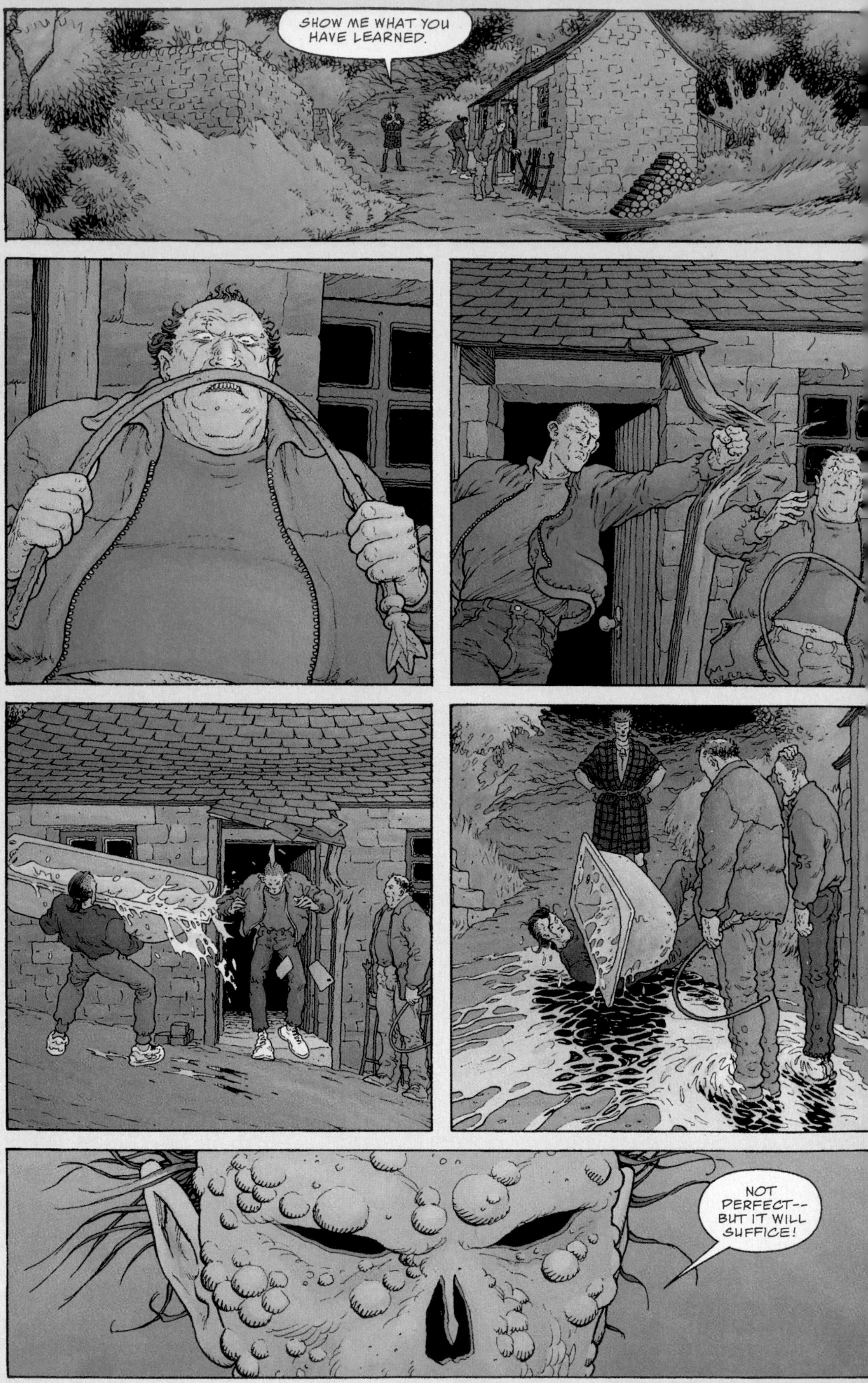
SHOW ME WHAT YOU HAVE LEARNED.
NOT PERFECT-- BUT IT WILL SUFFICE!

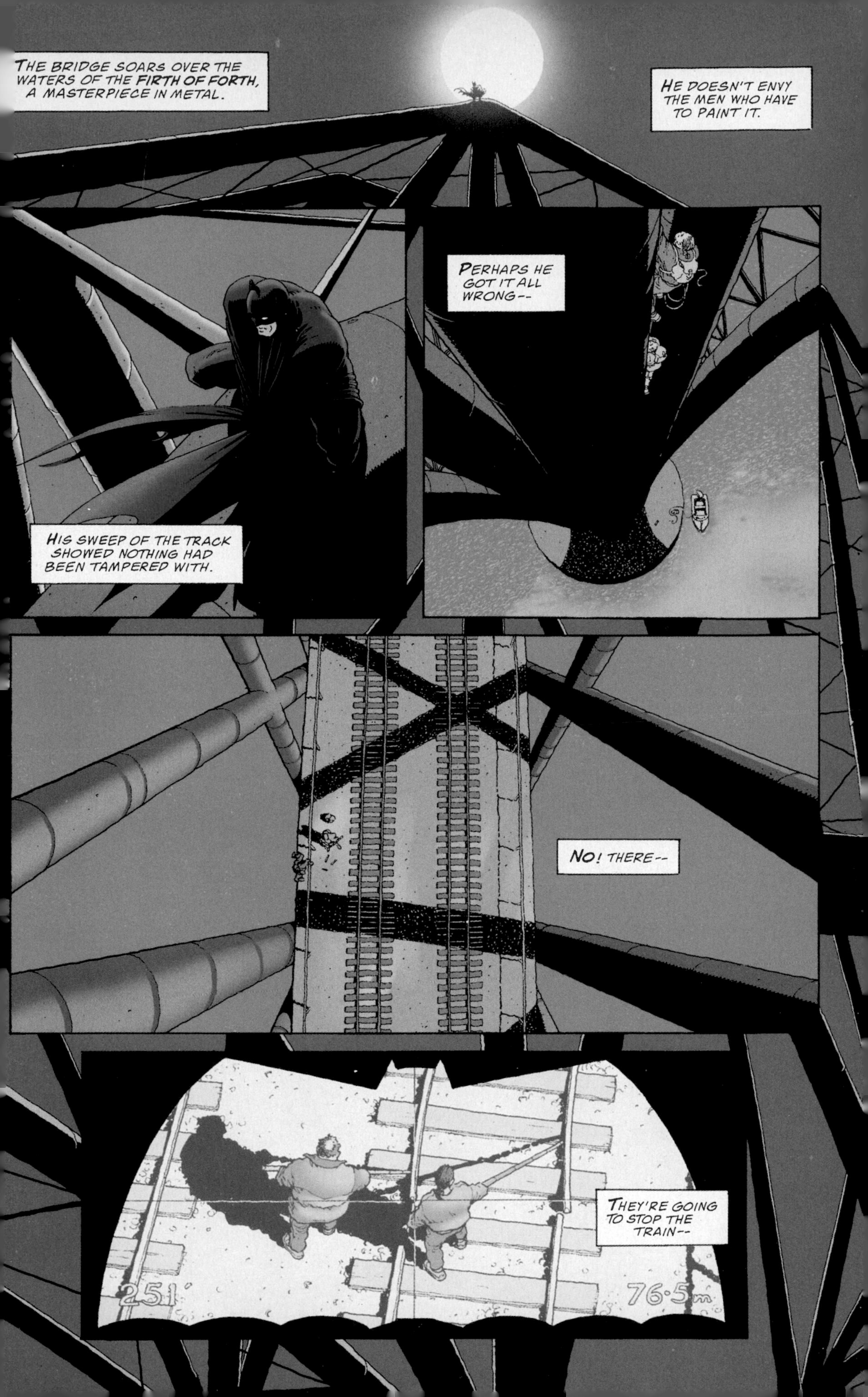
THE BRIDGE SOARS OVER THE WATERS OF THE FIRTH OF FORTH, A MASTERPIECE IN METAL.
HE DOESN'T ENVY THE MEN WHO HAVE TO PAINT IT.
HIS SWEEP OF THE TRACK SHOWED NOTHING HAD BEEN TAMPERED WITH.
PERHAPS HE GOT IT ALL WRONG--
NO! THERE--
251
76·5m
THEY'RE GOING TO STOP THE TRAIN--

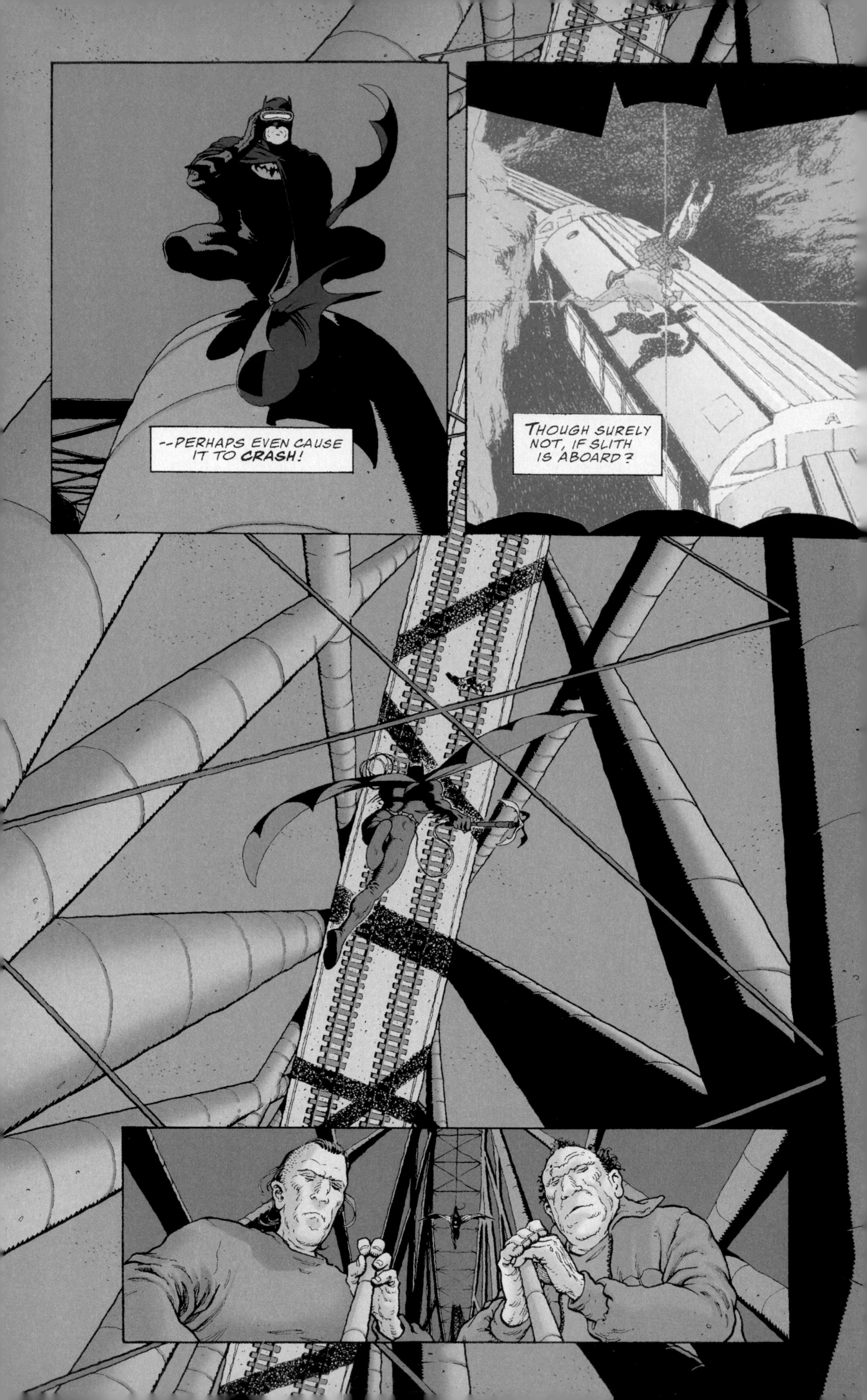
--PERHAPS EVEN CAUSE IT TO CRASH!
THOUGH SURELY NOT, IF SLITH IS ABOARD?

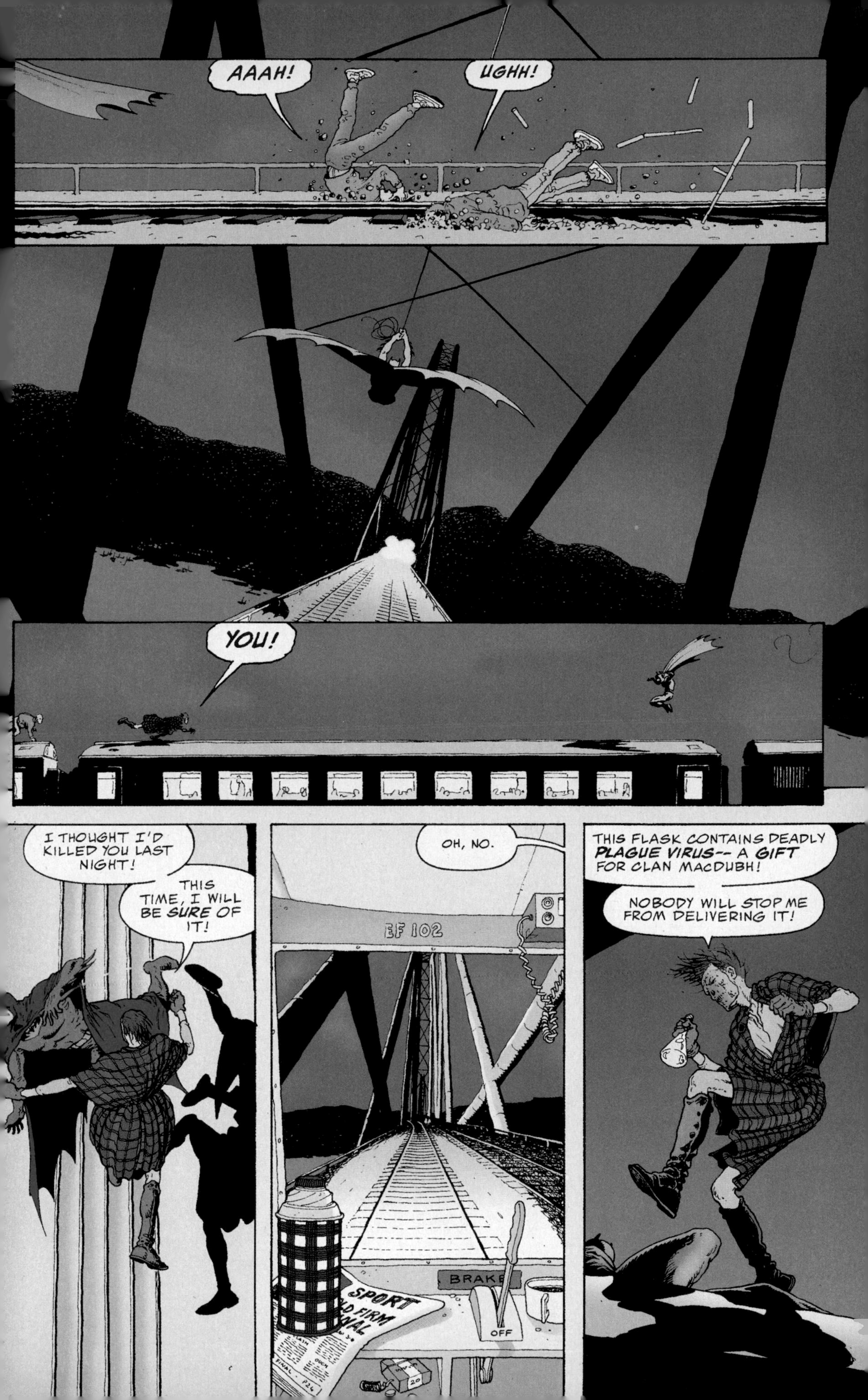
AAAH!
UGHH!
YOU!
I THOUGHT I'D KILLED YOU LAST NIGHT!
THIS TIME, I WILL BE SURE OF IT!
OH, NO.
EF 102
BRAKE
OFF
SPORT
THIS FLASK CONTAINS DEADLY PLAGUE VIRUS-- A GIFT FOR CLAN MACDUBH!
NOBODY WILL STOP ME FROM DELIVERING IT!

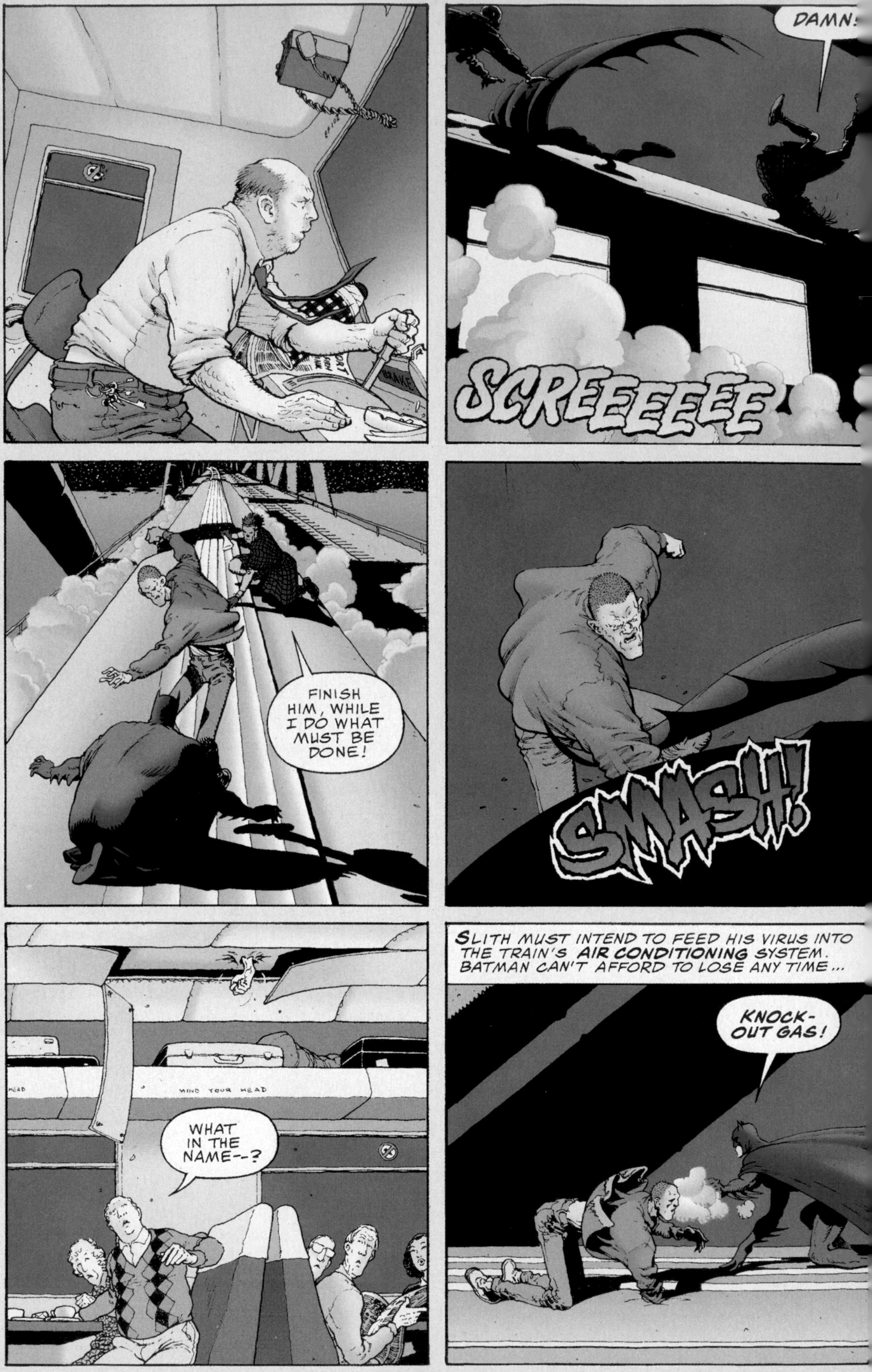
DAMN!
SCREEEEEEE
FINISH HIM, WHILE I DO WHAT MUST BE DONE!
SMASH!
MIND YOUR HEAD
WHAT IN THE NAME--?
SLITH MUST INTEND TO FEED HIS VIRUS INTO THE TRAIN'S AIR CONDITIONING SYSTEM. BATMAN CAN'T AFFORD TO LOSE ANY TIME...
KNOCK-OUT GAS!

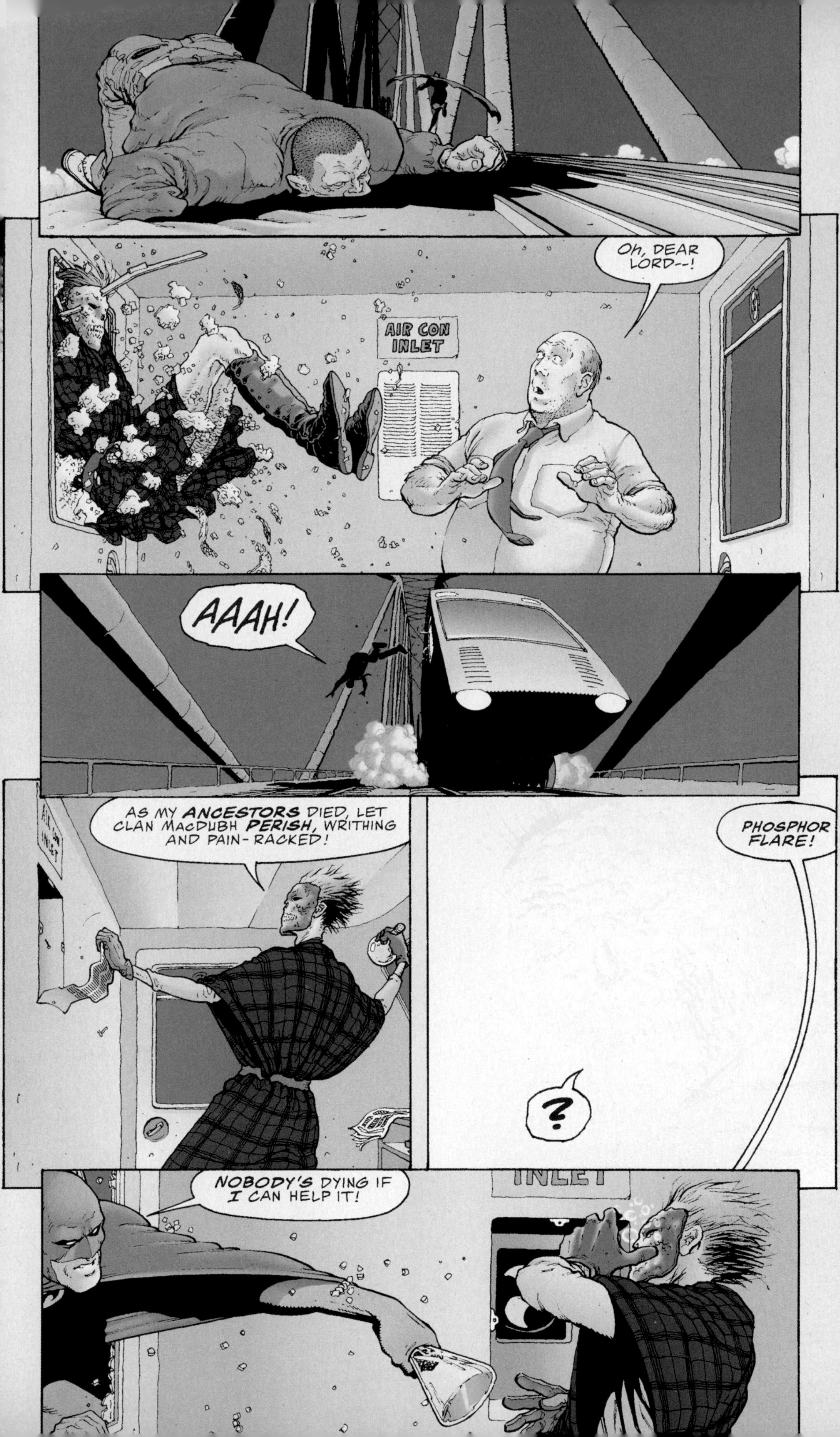
Oh, DEAR LORD--!
AIR CON INLET
AAAH!
AS MY ANCESTORS DIED, LET CLAN MacDUBH PERISH, WRITHING AND PAIN-RACKED!
PHOSPHOR FLARE!
?
NOBODY'S DYING IF I CAN HELP IT!
INLET

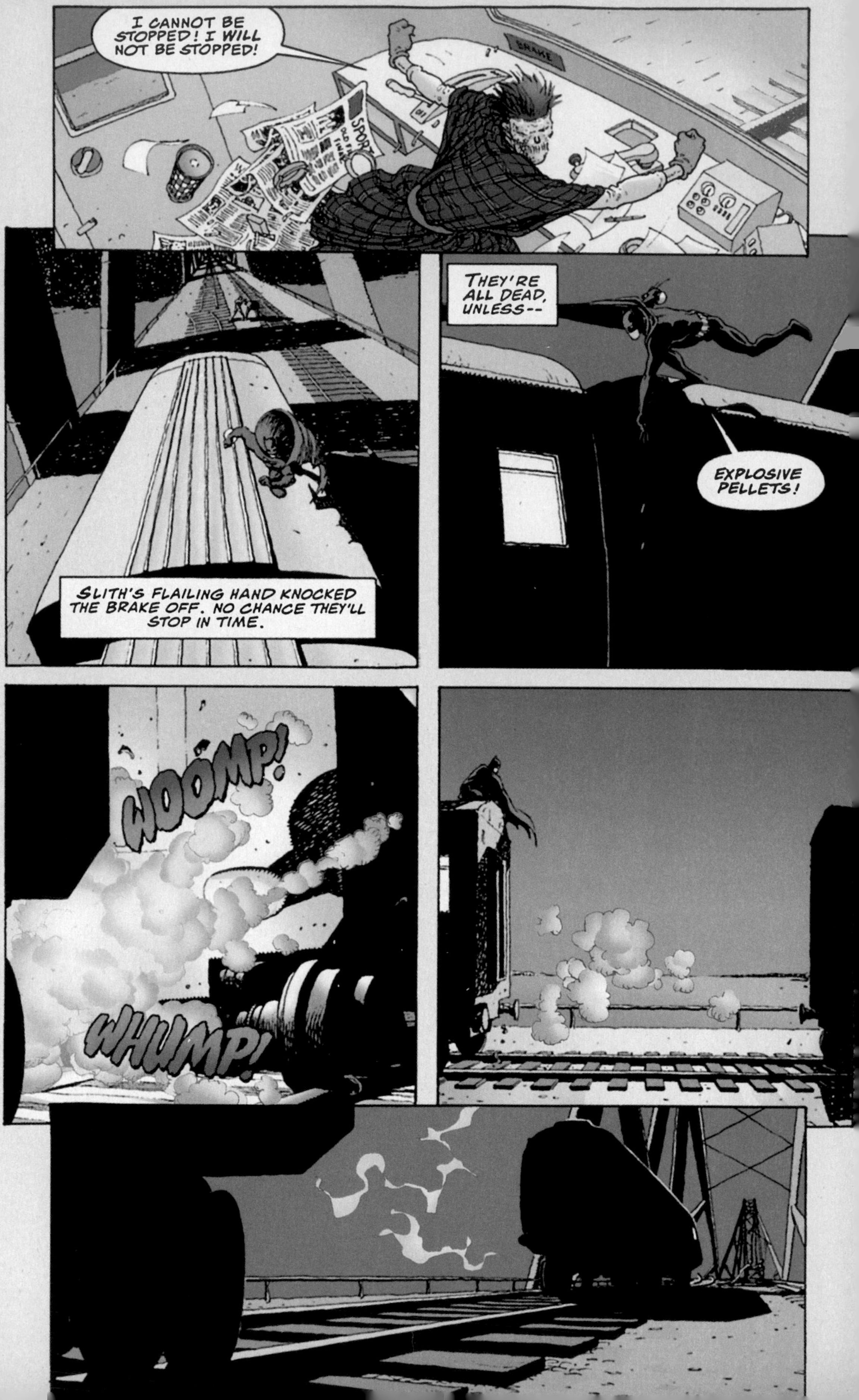
I CANNOT BE STOPPED! I WILL NOT BE STOPPED!
BRAKE
SLITH'S FLAILING HAND KNOCKED THE BRAKE OFF. NO CHANCE THEY'LL STOP IN TIME.
THEY'RE ALL DEAD, UNLESS--
EXPLOSIVE PELLETS!
WOOMP!
WHUMP!

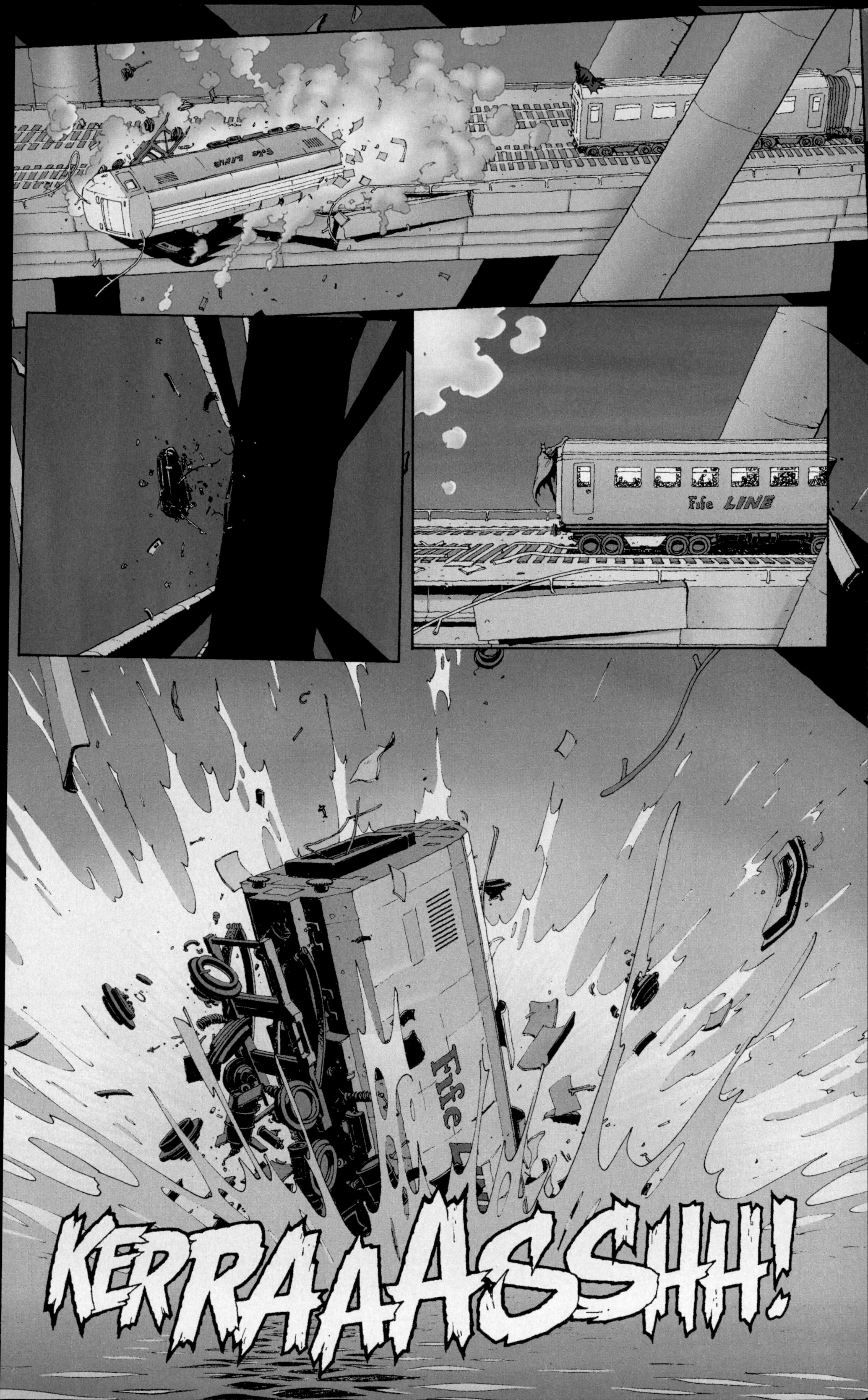
Fife LINE
KERRAASSH!

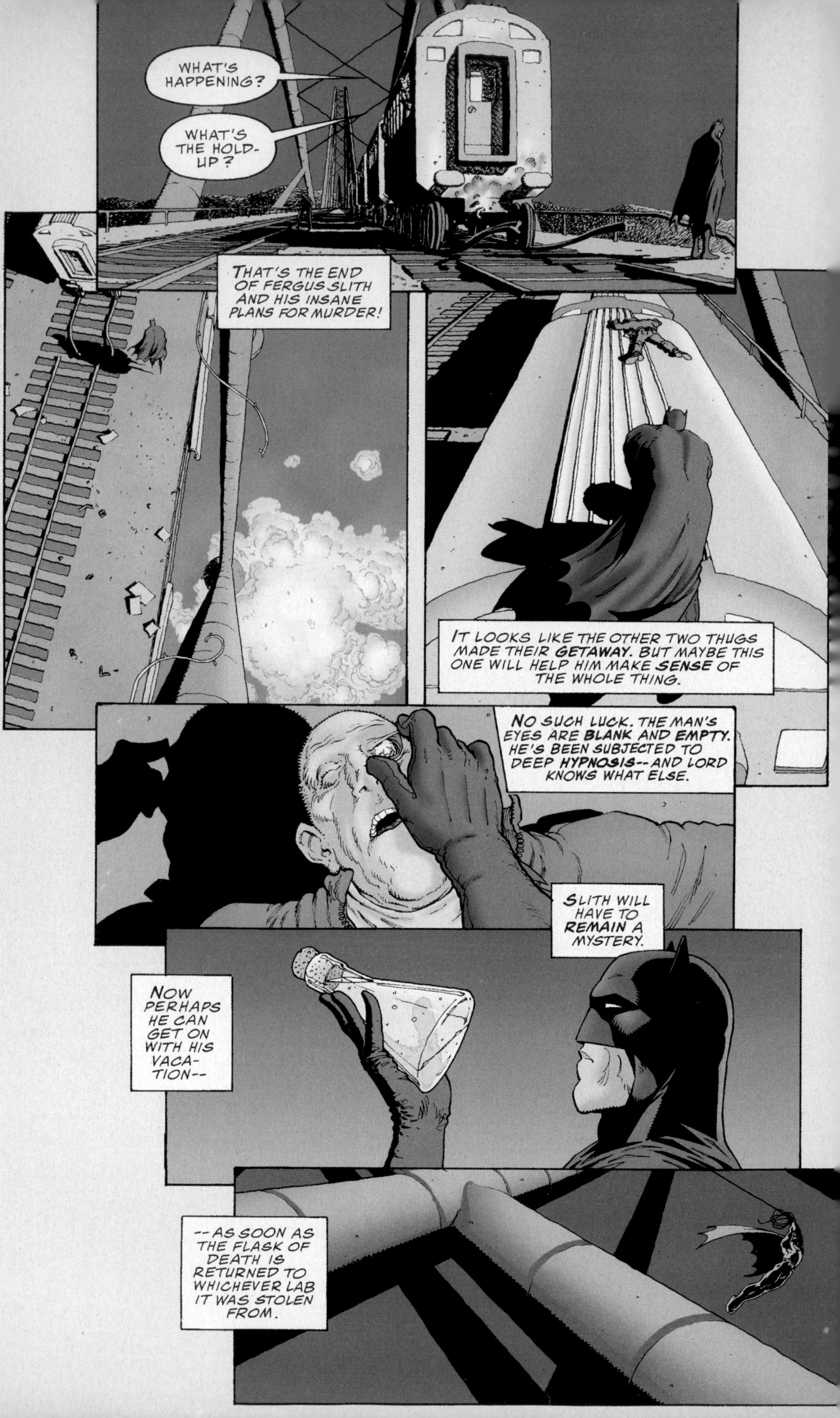
WHAT'S HAPPENING?
WHAT'S THE HOLD-UP?
THAT'S THE END OF FERGUS SLITH AND HIS INSANE PLANS FOR MURDER!
IT LOOKS LIKE THE OTHER TWO THUGS MADE THEIR GETAWAY. BUT MAYBE THIS ONE WILL HELP HIM MAKE SENSE OF THE WHOLE THING.
NO SUCH LUCK. THE MAN'S EYES ARE BLANK AND EMPTY. HE'S BEEN SUBJECTED TO DEEP HYPNOSIS--AND LORD KNOWS WHAT ELSE.
SLITH WILL HAVE TO REMAIN A MYSTERY.
NOW PERHAPS HE CAN GET ON WITH HIS VACATION--
--AS SOON AS THE FLASK OF DEATH IS RETURNED TO WHICHEVER LAB IT WAS STOLEN FROM.

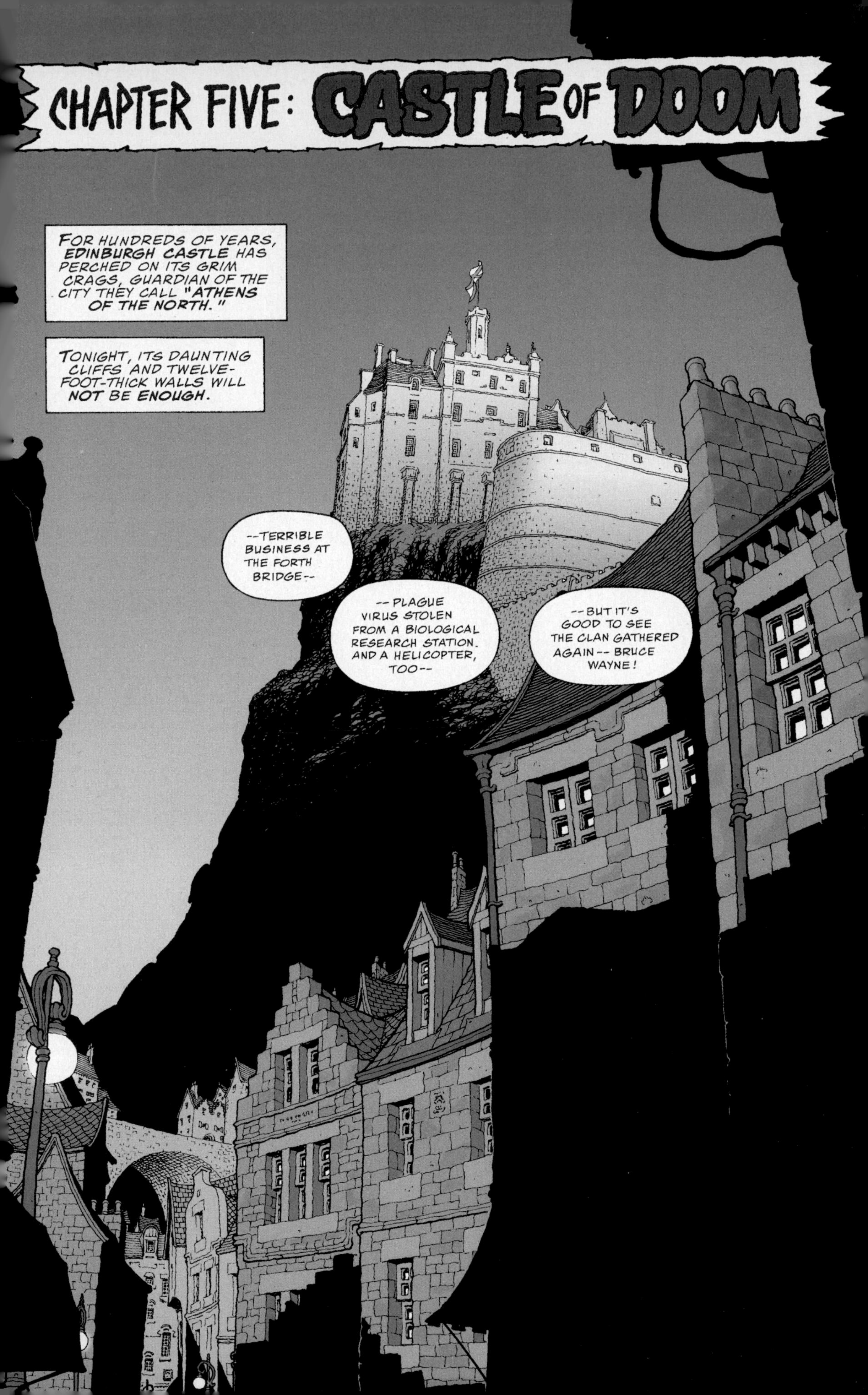

CHAPTER FIVE: CASTLE OF DOOM
FOR HUNDREDS OF YEARS, EDINBURGH CASTLE HAS PERCHED ON ITS GRIM CRAGS, GUARDIAN OF THE CITY THEY CALL "ATHENS OF THE NORTH."
TONIGHT, ITS DAUNTING CLIFFS AND TWELVE-FOOT-THICK WALLS WILL NOT BE ENOUGH.
--TERRIBLE BUSINESS AT THE FORTH BRIDGE--
--PLAGUE VIRUS STOLEN FROM A BIOLOGICAL RESEARCH STATION. AND A HELICOPTER, TOO--
--BUT IT'S GOOD TO SEE THE CLAN GATHERED AGAIN-- BRUCE WAYNE!

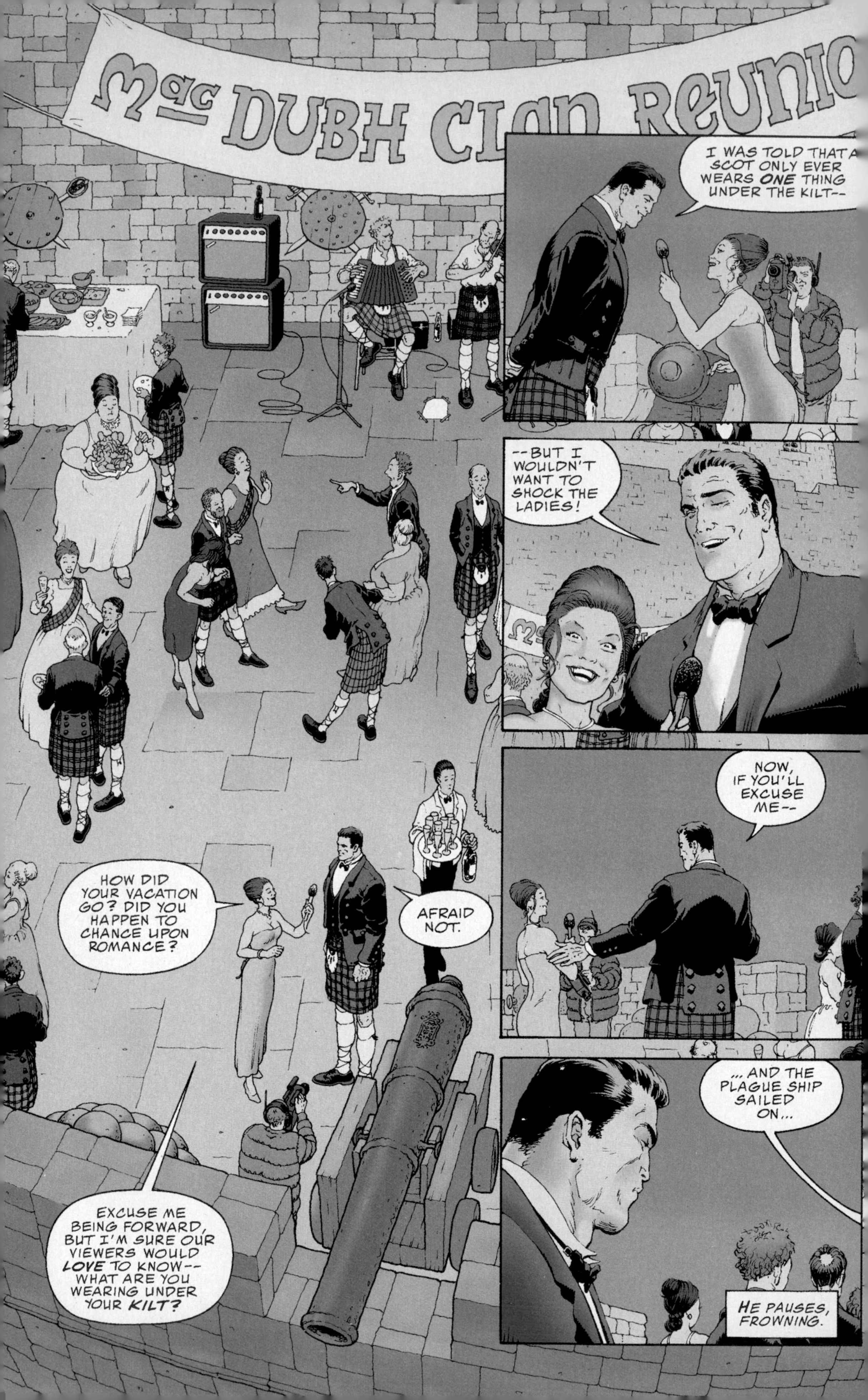
MacDUBH CLAN REUNIO
I WAS TOLD THAT A SCOT ONLY EVER WEARS ONE THING UNDER THE KILT--
--BUT I WOULDN'T WANT TO SHOCK THE LADIES!
HOW DID YOUR VACATION GO? DID YOU HAPPEN TO CHANCE UPON ROMANCE?
AFRAID NOT.
NOW, IF YOU'LL EXCUSE ME--
EXCUSE ME BEING FORWARD, BUT I'M SURE OUR VIEWERS WOULD LOVE TO KNOW--WHAT ARE YOU WEARING UNDER YOUR KILT?
... AND THE PLAGUE SHIP SAILED ON...
HE PAUSES, FROWNING.

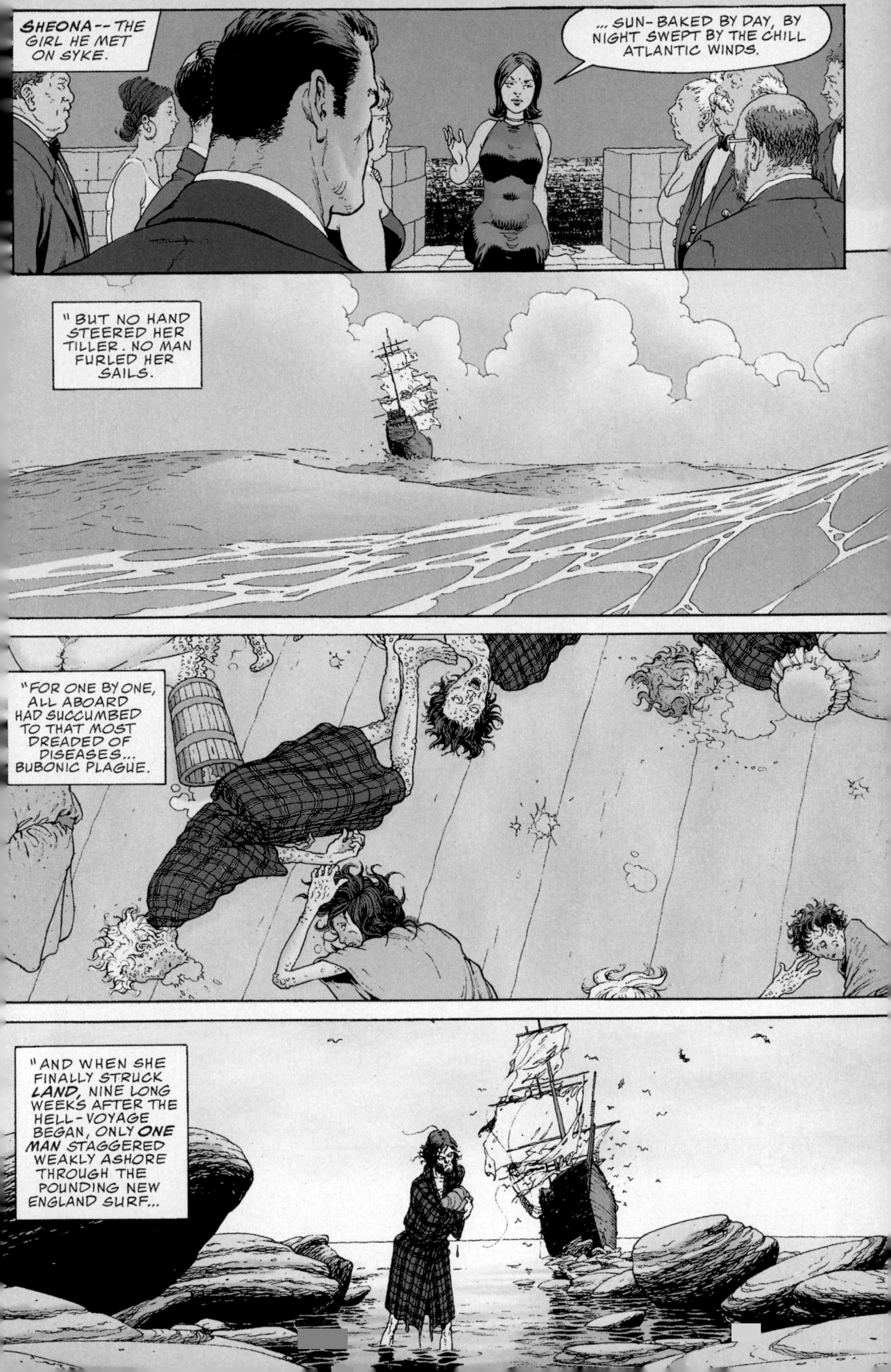
SHEONA--THE GIRL HE MET ON SYKE.
...SUN-BAKED BY DAY, BY NIGHT SWEPT BY THE CHILL ATLANTIC WINDS.
"BUT NO HAND STEERED HER TILLER. NO MAN FURLED HER SAILS.
"FOR ONE BY ONE, ALL ABOARD HAD SUCCUMBED TO THAT MOST DREADED OF DISEASES... BUBONIC PLAGUE.
"AND WHEN SHE FINALLY STRUCK LAND, NINE LONG WEEKS AFTER THE HELL-VOYAGE BEGAN, ONLY ONE MAN STAGGERED WEAKLY ASHORE THROUGH THE POUNDING NEW ENGLAND SURF...

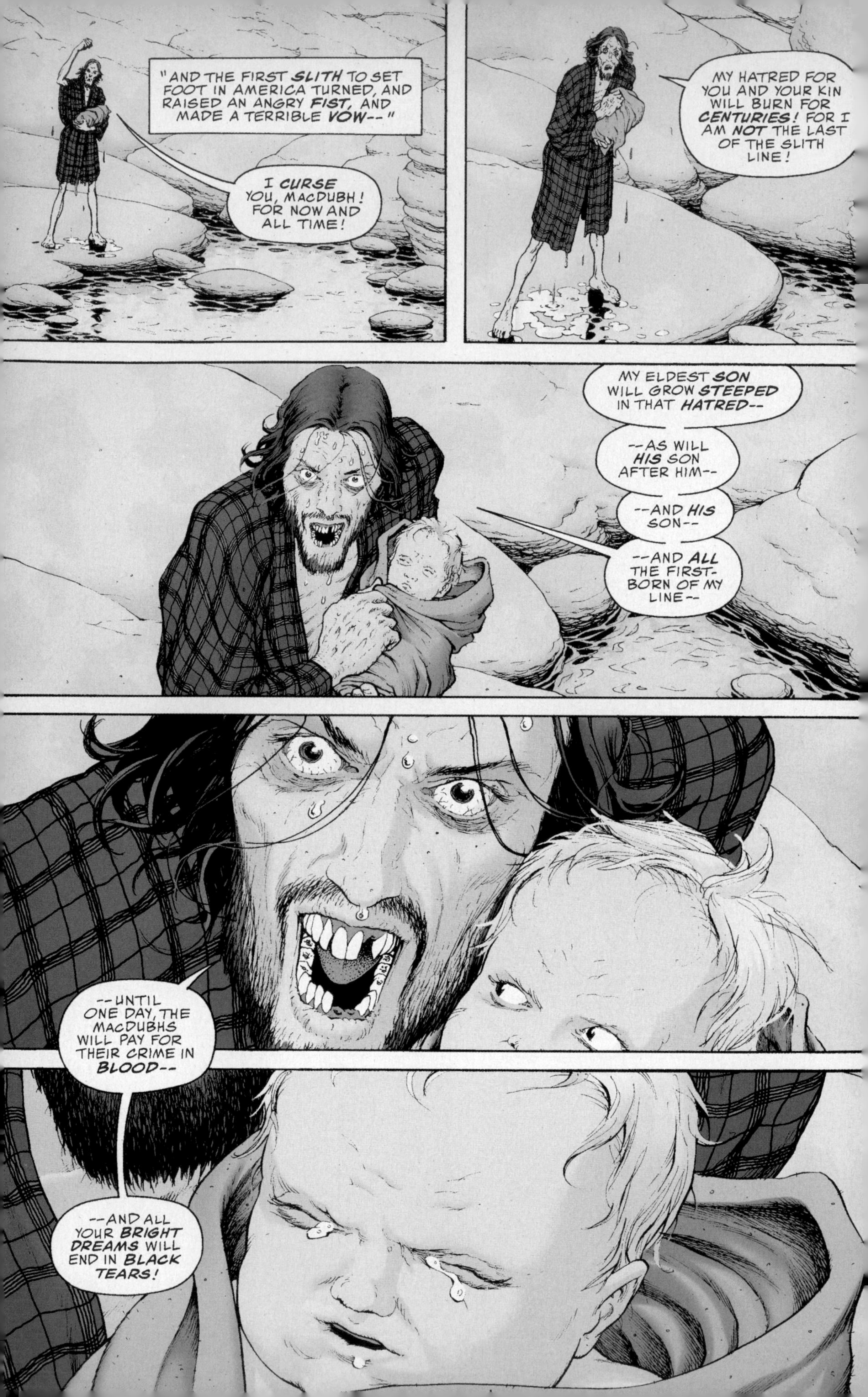
"AND THE FIRST SLITH TO SET FOOT IN AMERICA TURNED, AND RAISED AN ANGRY FIST, AND MADE A TERRIBLE VOW--"
I CURSE YOU, MACDUBH! FOR NOW AND ALL TIME!
MY HATRED FOR YOU AND YOUR KIN WILL BURN FOR CENTURIES! FOR I AM NOT THE LAST OF THE SLITH LINE!
MY ELDEST SON WILL GROW STEEPED IN THAT HATRED--
--AS WILL HIS SON AFTER HIM--
--AND HIS SON--
--AND ALL THE FIRST-BORN OF MY LINE--
--UNTIL ONE DAY, THE MACDUBHS WILL PAY FOR THEIR CRIME IN BLOOD--
--AND ALL YOUR BRIGHT DREAMS WILL END IN BLACK TEARS!

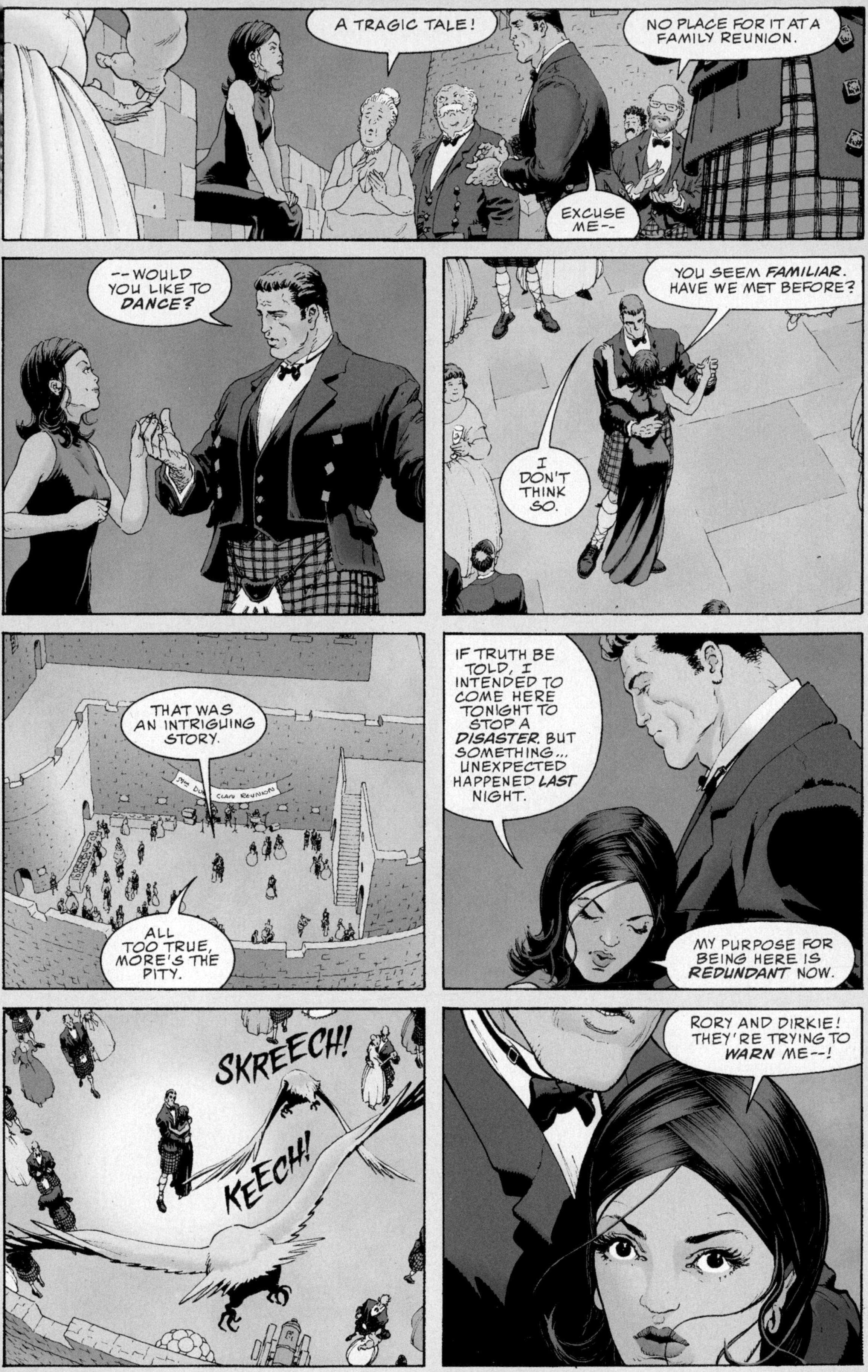
A TRAGIC TALE!
NO PLACE FOR IT AT A FAMILY REUNION.
EXCUSE ME--
--WOULD YOU LIKE TO DANCE?
YOU SEEM FAMILIAR. HAVE WE MET BEFORE?
I DON'T THINK SO.
THAT WAS AN INTRIGUING STORY.
ALL TOO TRUE, MORE'S THE PITY.
IF TRUTH BE TOLD, I INTENDED TO COME HERE TONIGHT TO STOP A DISASTER. BUT SOMETHING... UNEXPECTED HAPPENED LAST NIGHT.
MY PURPOSE FOR BEING HERE IS REDUNDANT NOW.
SKREECH!
KEECH!
RORY AND DIRKIE! THEY'RE TRYING TO WARN ME--!

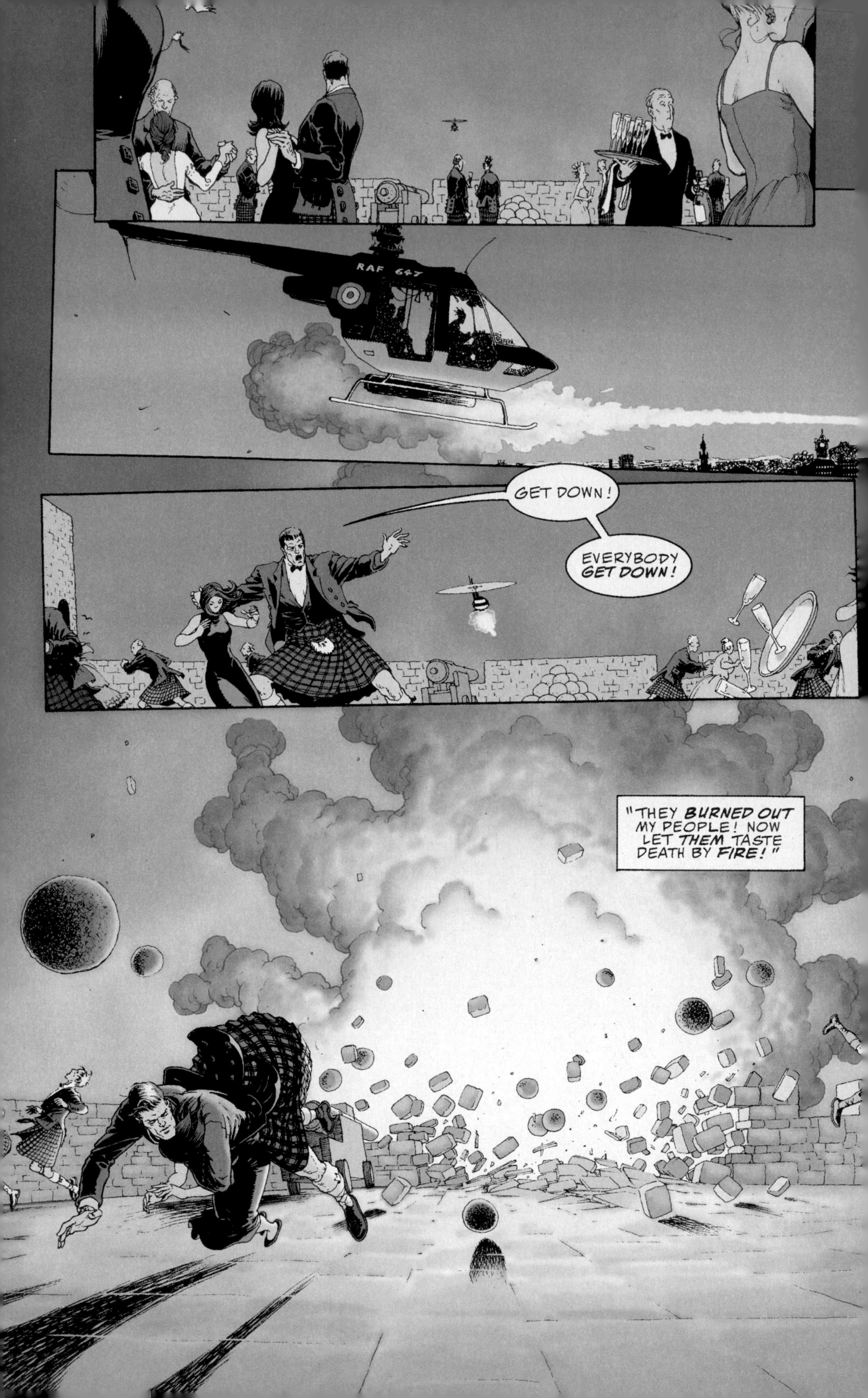
RAF 647
GET DOWN!
EVERYBODY GET DOWN!
"THEY BURNED OUT MY PEOPLE! NOW LET THEM TASTE DEATH BY FIRE!"

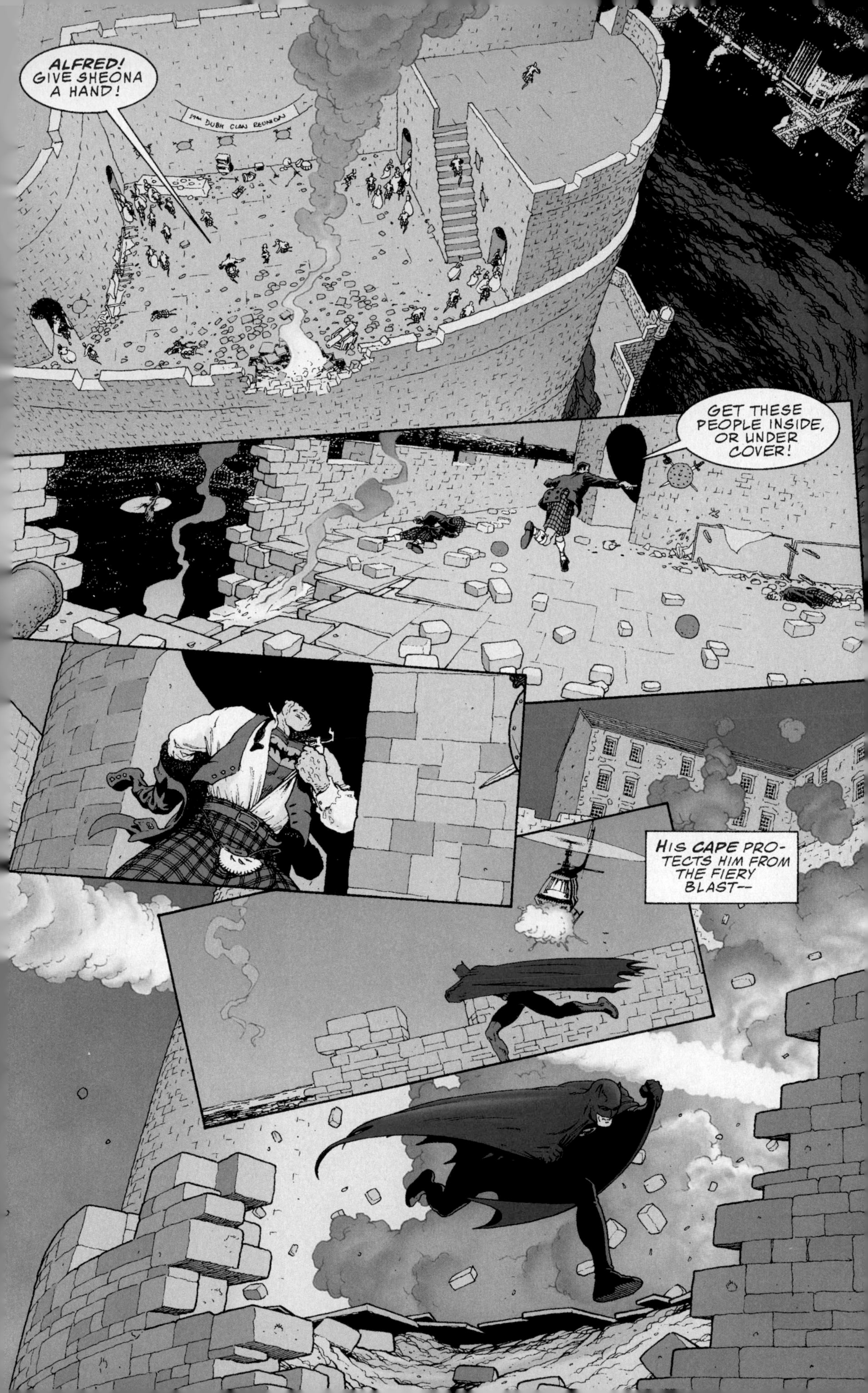
ALFRED! GIVE SHEONA A HAND!
GET THESE PEOPLE INSIDE, OR UNDER COVER!
HIS CAPE PROTECTS HIM FROM THE FIERY BLAST--

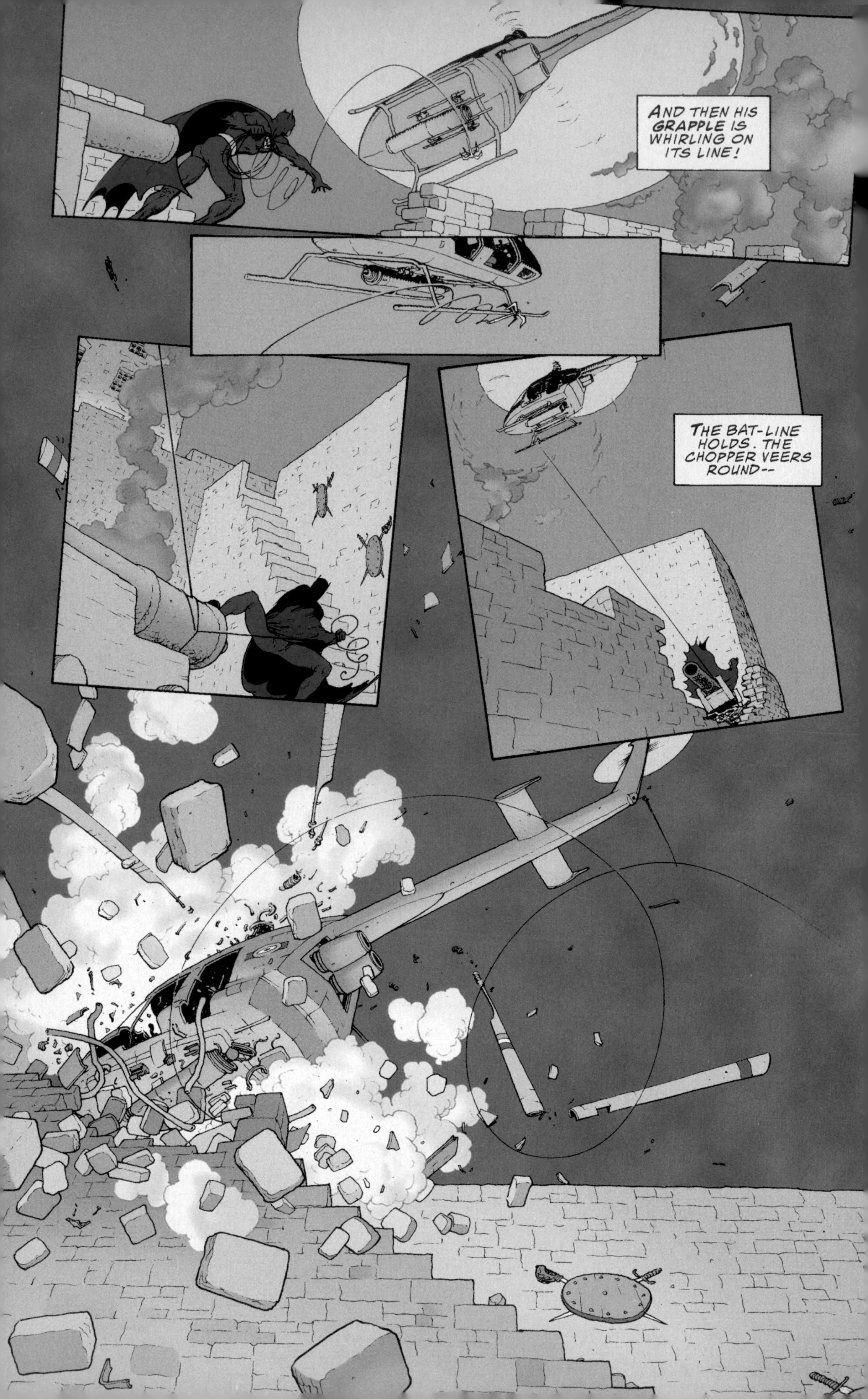
AND THEN HIS GRAPPLE IS WHIRLING ON ITS LINE!
THE BAT-LINE HOLDS. THE CHOPPER VEERS ROUND--

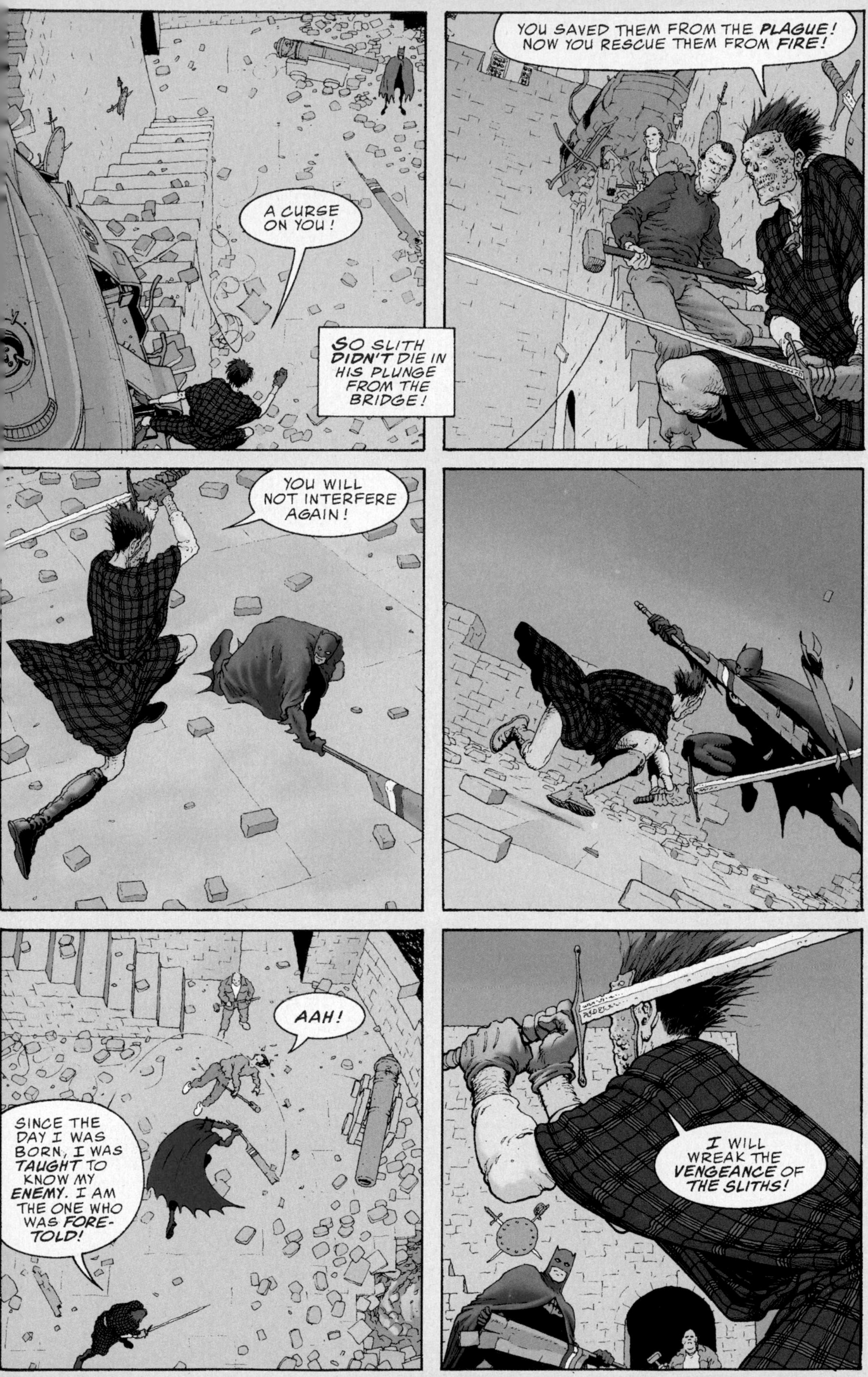
A CURSE ON YOU!
SO SLITH DIDN'T DIE IN HIS PLUNGE FROM THE BRIDGE!
YOU SAVED THEM FROM THE PLAGUE! NOW YOU RESCUE THEM FROM FIRE!
YOU WILL NOT INTERFERE AGAIN!
AAH!
SINCE THE DAY I WAS BORN, I WAS TAUGHT TO KNOW MY ENEMY. I AM THE ONE WHO WAS FORETOLD!
I WILL WREAK THE VENGEANCE OF THE SLITHS!

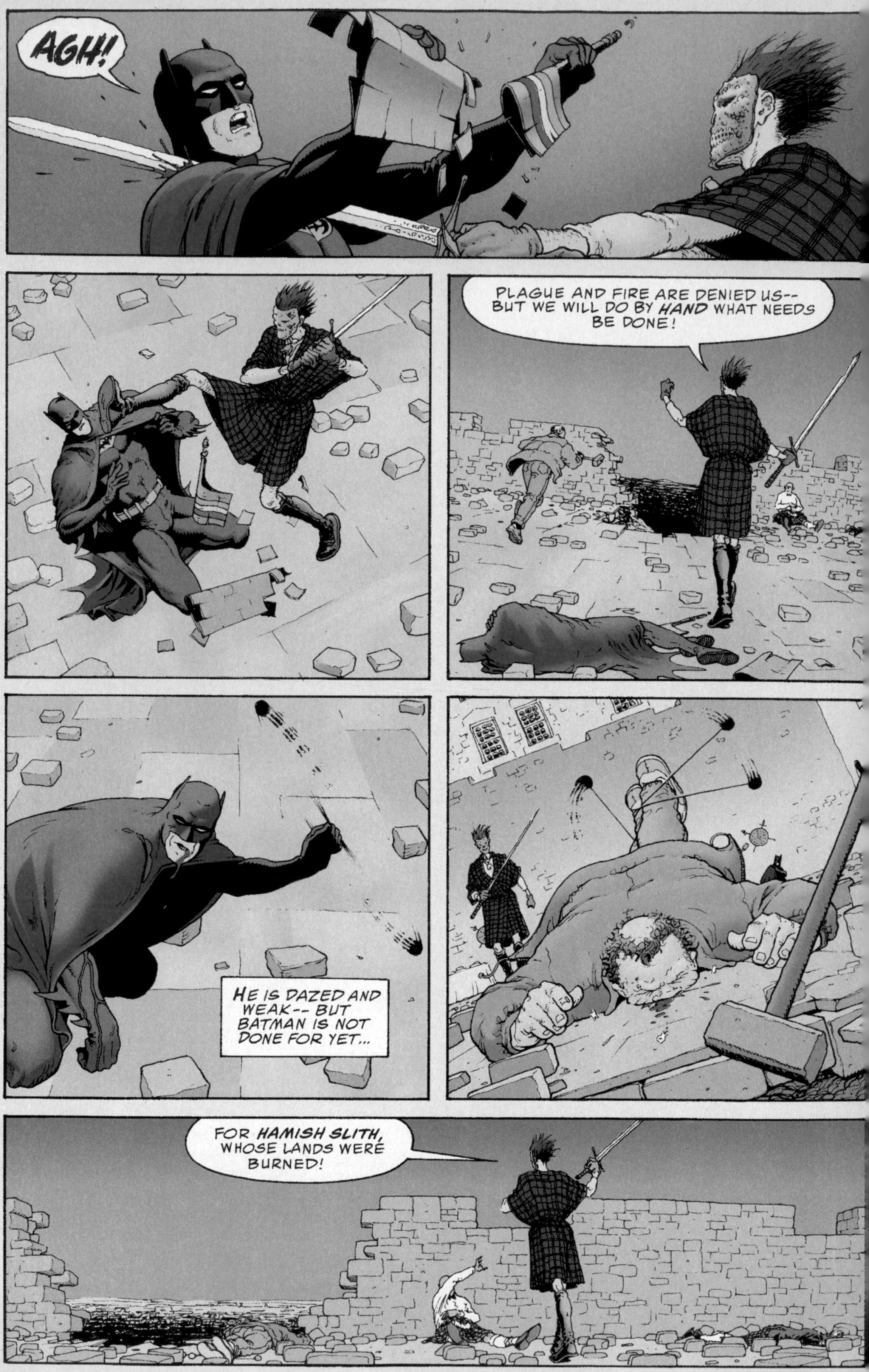
AGH!
PLAGUE AND FIRE ARE DENIED US-- BUT WE WILL DO BY HAND WHAT NEEDS BE DONE!
HE IS DAZED AND WEAK-- BUT BATMAN IS NOT DONE FOR YET...
FOR HAMISH SLITH, WHOSE LANDS WERE BURNED!

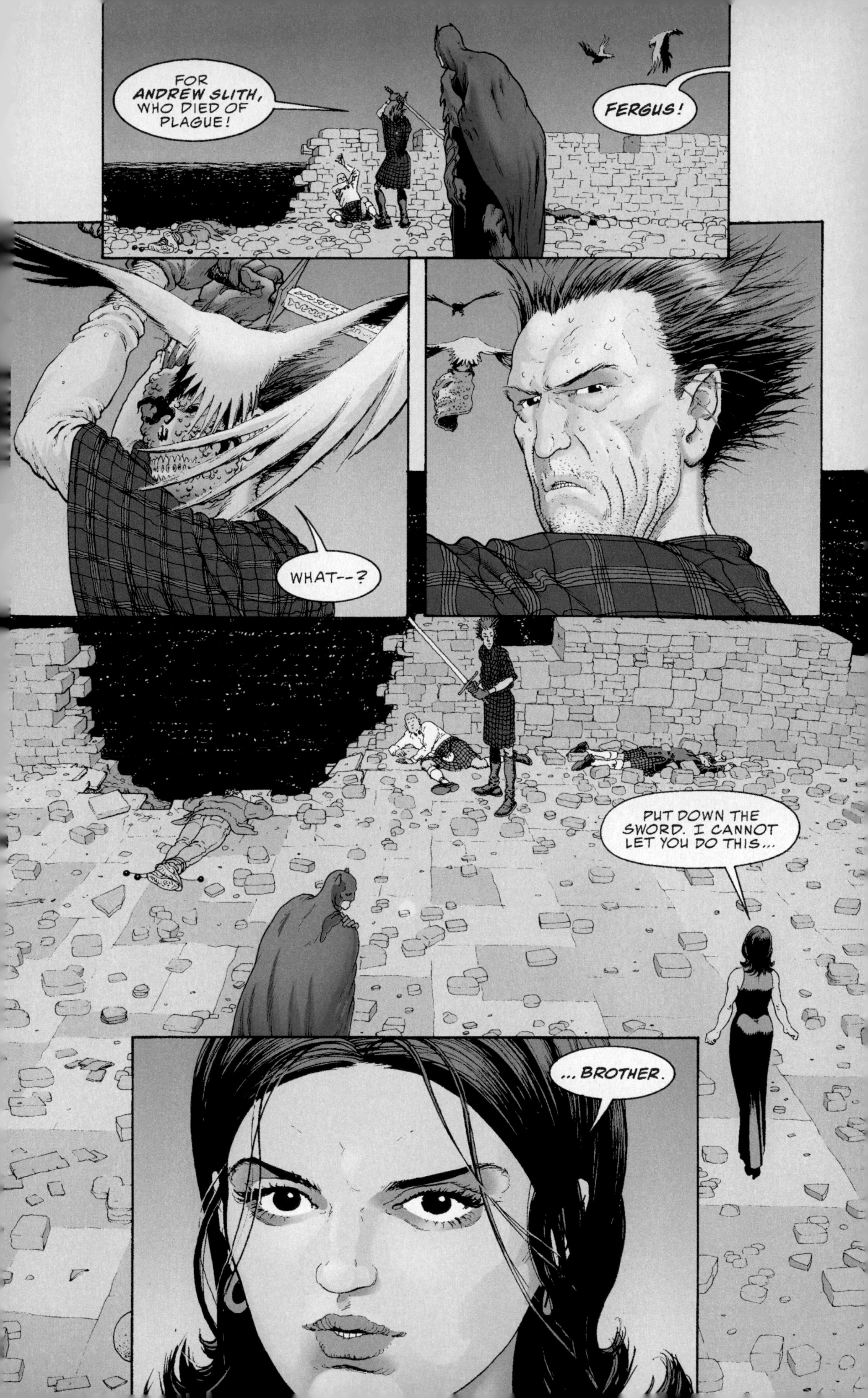
FOR ANDREW SLITH, WHO DIED OF PLAGUE!
FERGUS!
WHAT--?
PUT DOWN THE SWORD. I CANNOT LET YOU DO THIS...
...BROTHER.

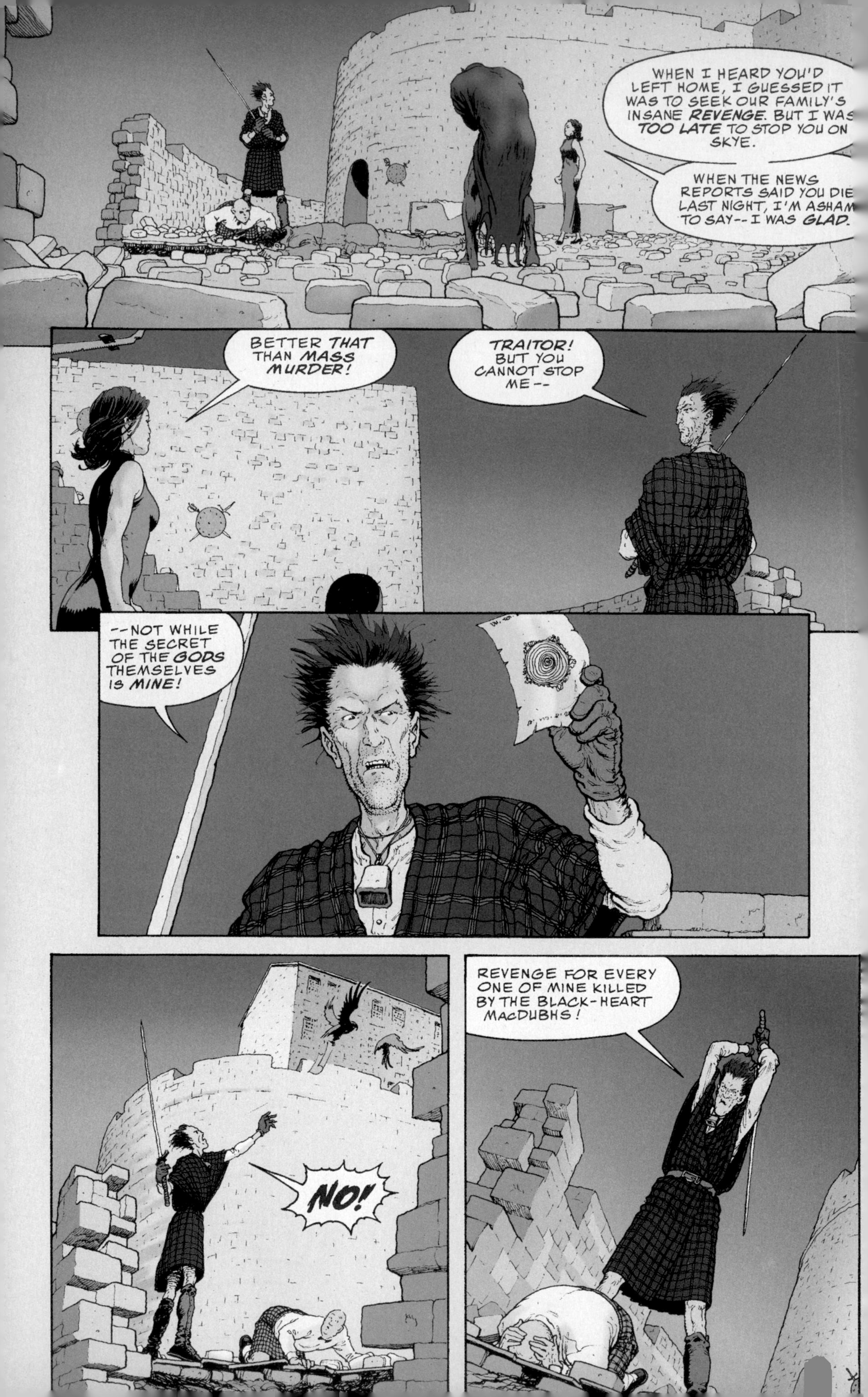
WHEN I HEARD YOU'D LEFT HOME, I GUESSED IT WAS TO SEEK OUR FAMILY'S INSANE REVENGE. BUT I WAS TOO LATE TO STOP YOU ON SKYE.
WHEN THE NEWS REPORTS SAID YOU DIE LAST NIGHT, I'M ASHAM TO SAY--I WAS GLAD.
BETTER THAT THAN MASS MURDER!
TRAITOR! BUT YOU CANNOT STOP ME--
--NOT WHILE THE SECRET OF THE GODS THEMSELVES IS MINE!
NO!
REVENGE FOR EVERY ONE OF MINE KILLED BY THE BLACK-HEART MacDUBHS!

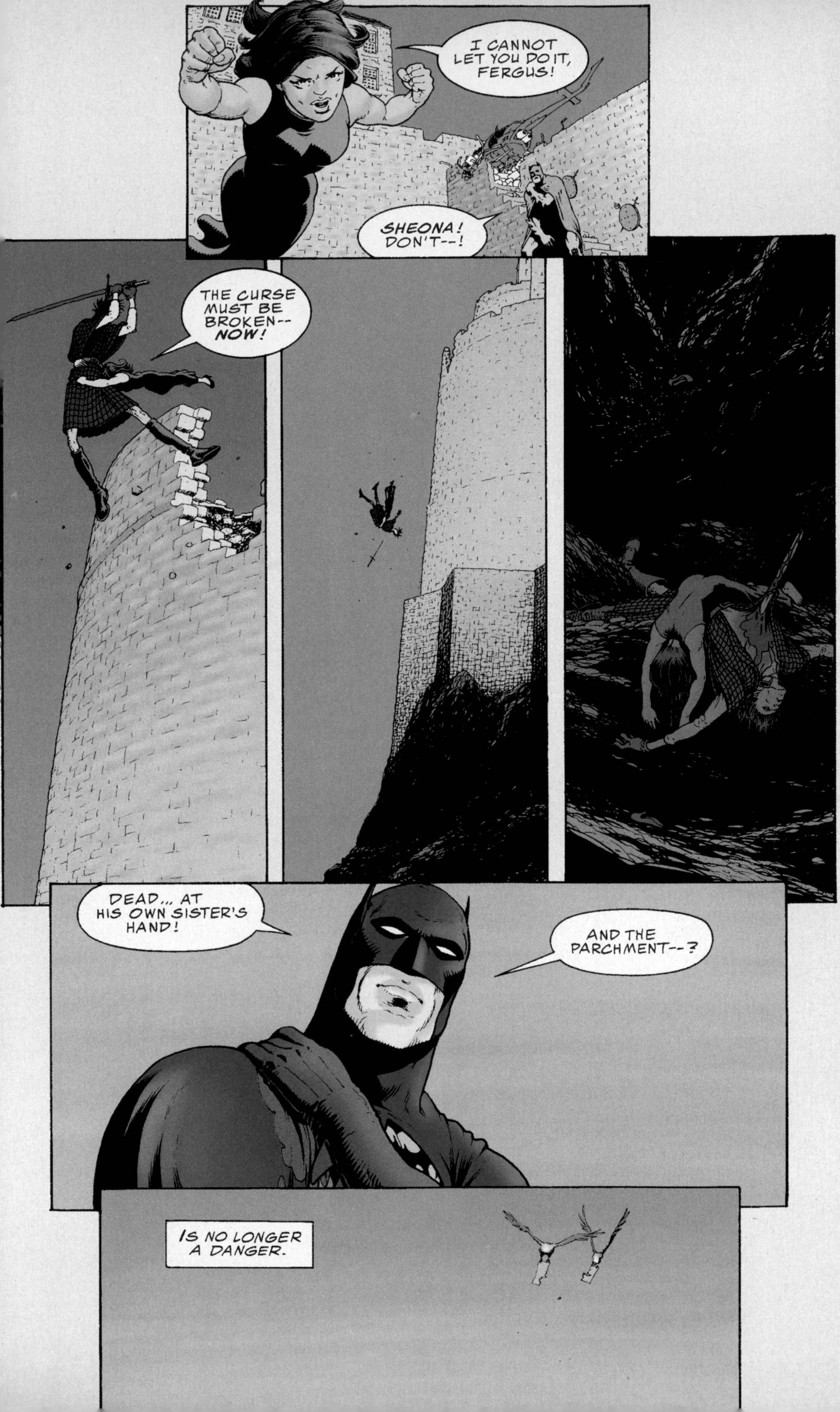
I CANNOT LET YOU DO IT, FERGUS!
SHEONA! DON'T--!
THE CURSE MUST BE BROKEN-- NOW!
DEAD... AT HIS OWN SISTER'S HAND!
AND THE PARCHMENT--?
IS NO LONGER A DANGER.

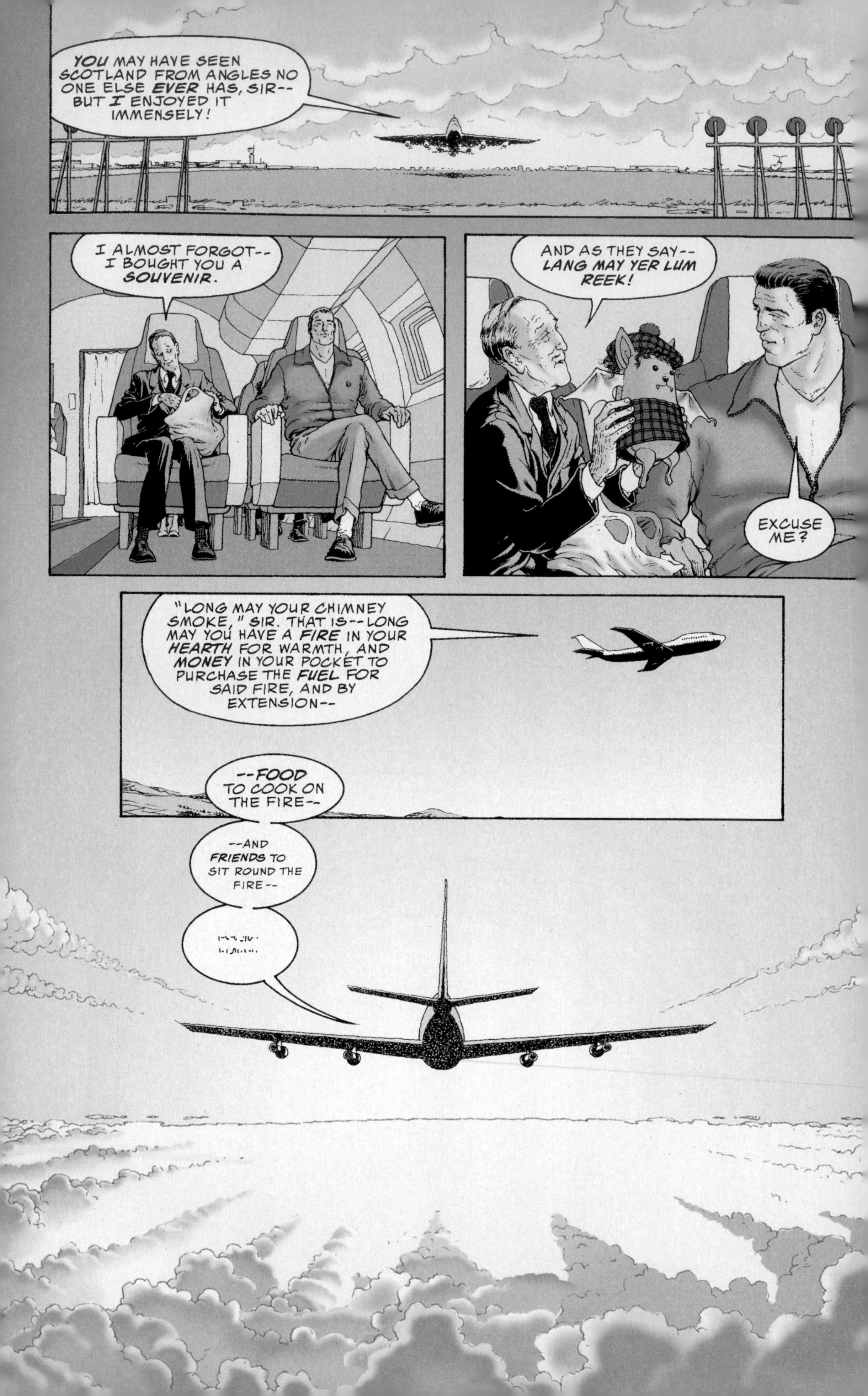
YOU MAY HAVE SEEN SCOTLAND FROM ANGLES NO ONE ELSE EVER HAS, SIR-- BUT I ENJOYED IT IMMENSELY!
I ALMOST FORGOT-- I BOUGHT YOU A SOUVENIR.
AND AS THEY SAY-- LANG MAY YER LUM REEK!
EXCUSE ME?
"LONG MAY YOUR CHIMNEY SMOKE," SIR. THAT IS--LONG MAY YOU HAVE A FIRE IN YOUR HEARTH FOR WARMTH, AND MONEY IN YOUR POCKET TO PURCHASE THE FUEL FOR SAID FIRE, AND BY EXTENSION--
--FOOD TO COOK ON THE FIRE--
--AND FRIENDS TO SIT ROUND THE FIRE--

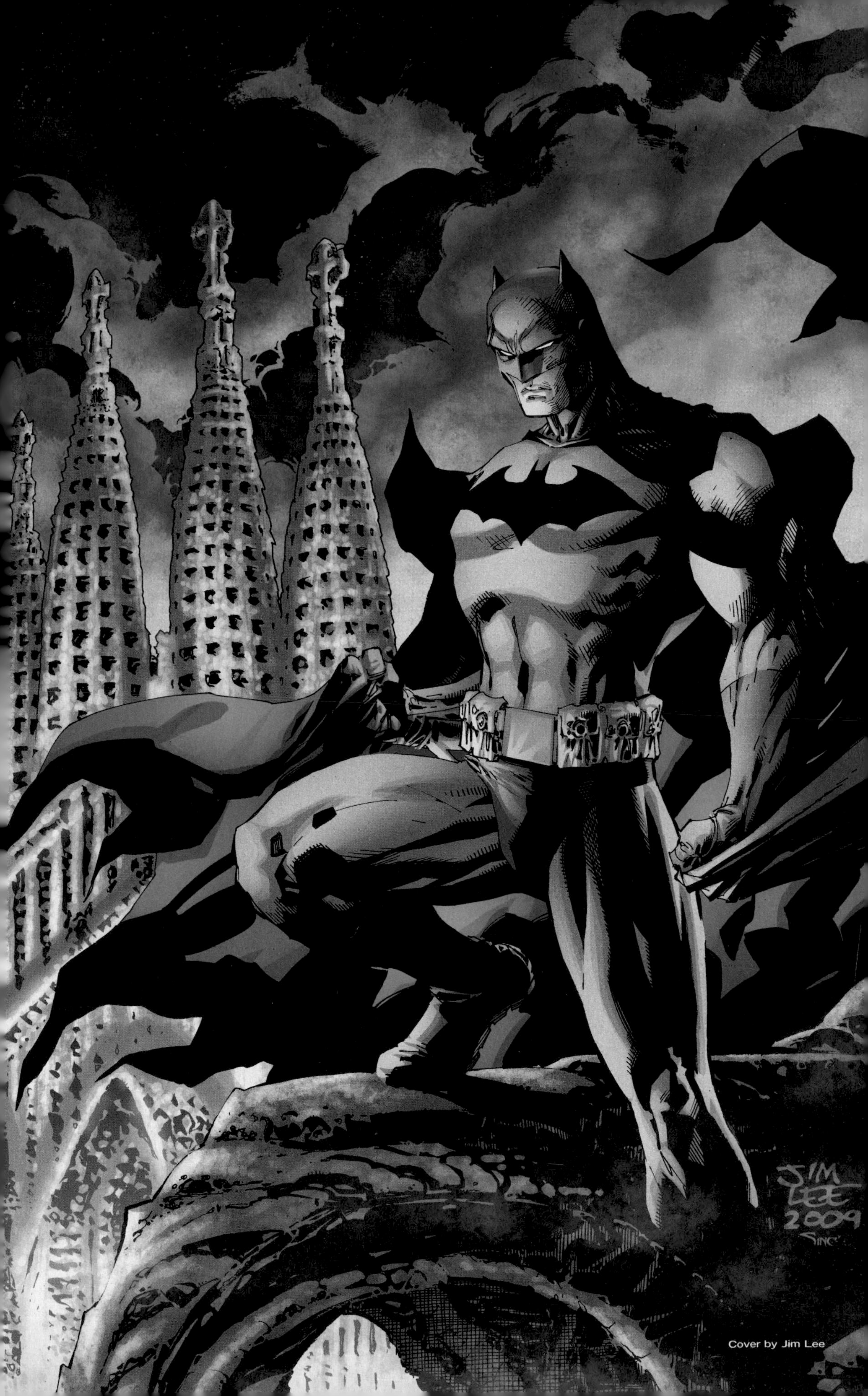
JIM LEE 2009

Cover by Jim Lee

BATMAN IN BARCELONA: DRAGON'S KNIGHT

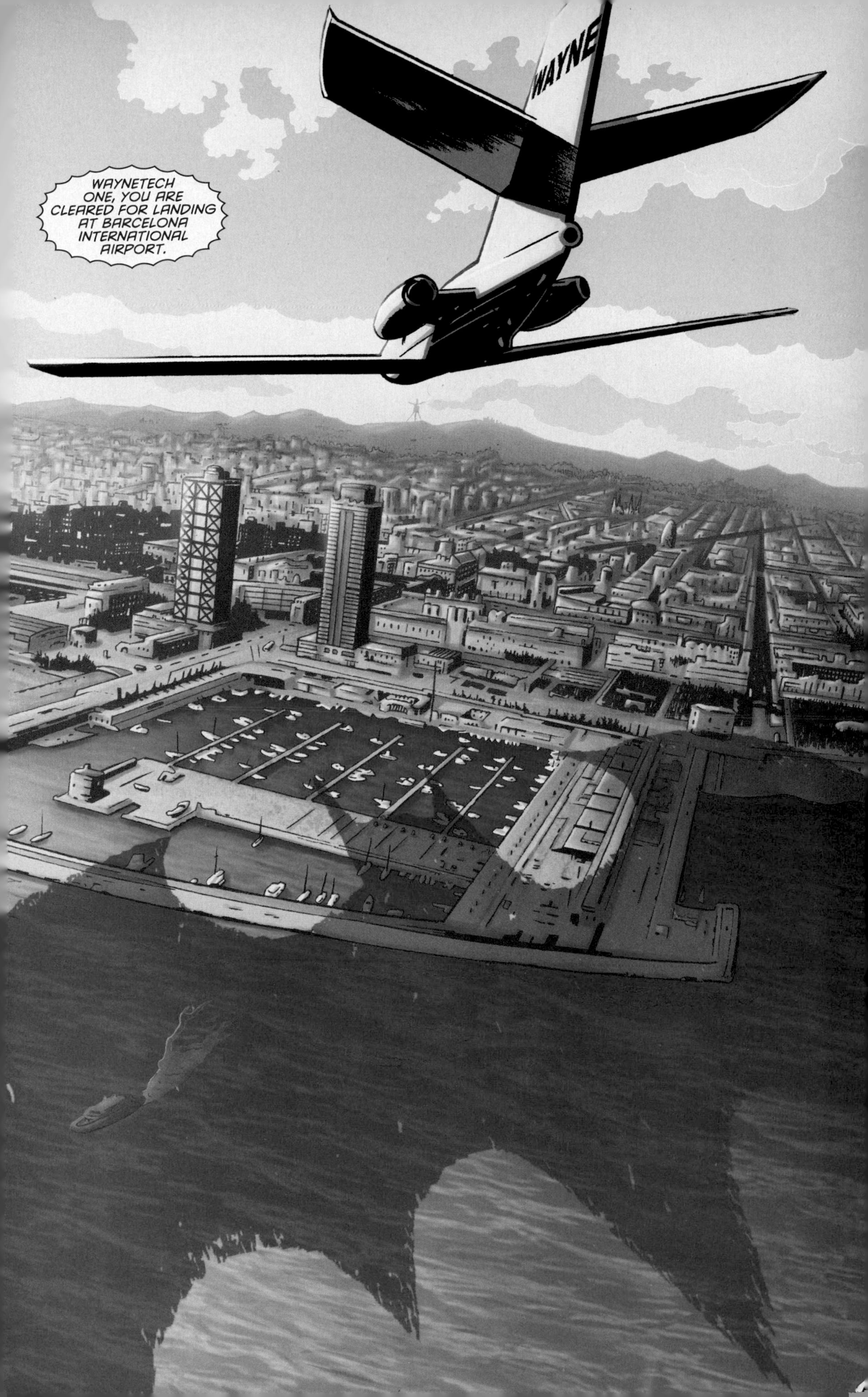
WAYNE
WAYNETECH ONE, YOU ARE CLEARED FOR LANDING AT BARCELONA INTERNATIONAL AIRPORT.

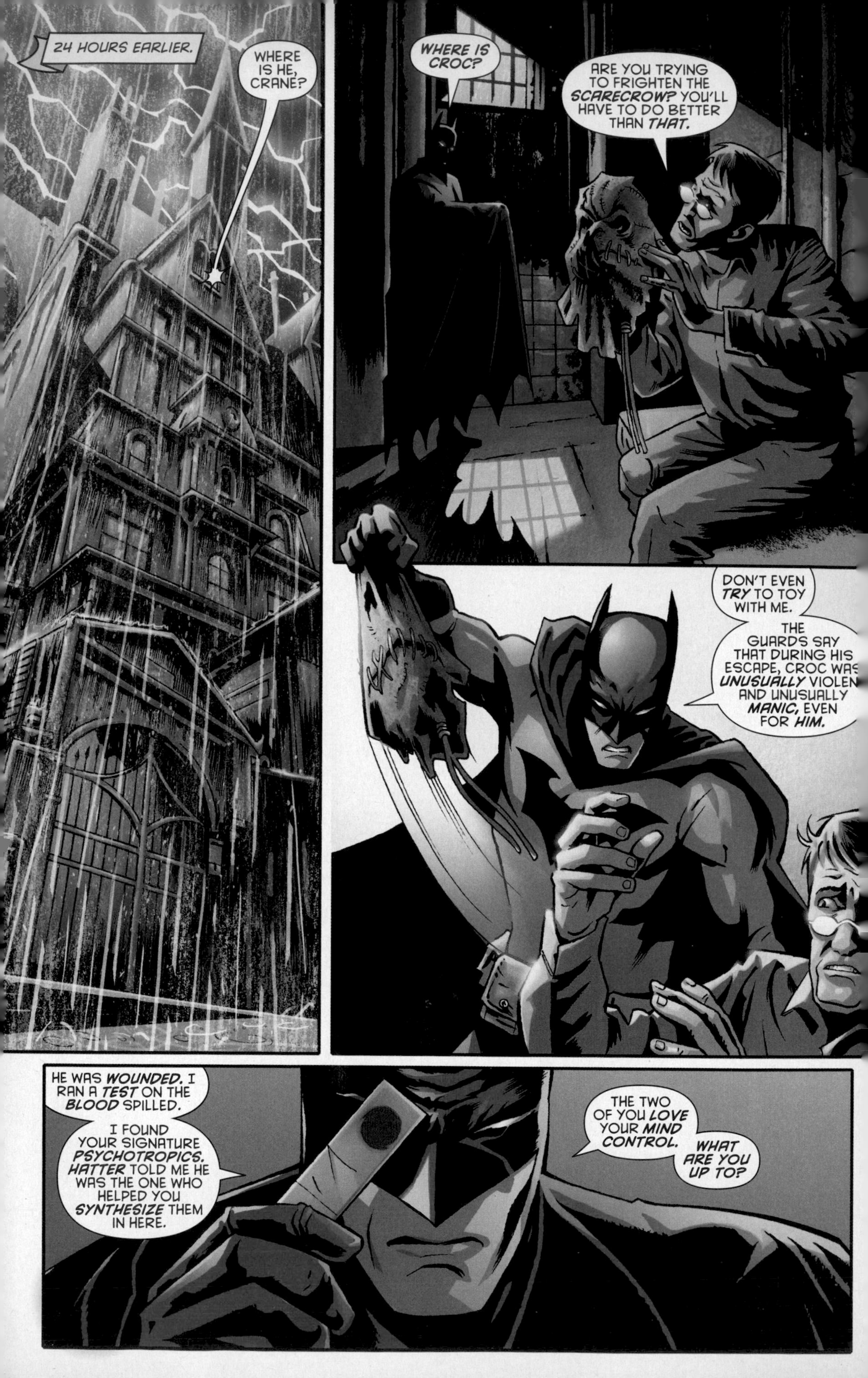
24 HOURS EARLIER.
WHERE IS HE, CRANE?
WHERE IS CROC?
ARE YOU TRYING TO FRIGHTEN THE SCARECROW? YOU'LL HAVE TO DO BETTER THAN THAT.
DON'T EVEN TRY TO TOY WITH ME.
THE GUARDS SAY THAT DURING HIS ESCAPE, CROC WAS UNUSUALLY VIOLEN AND UNUSUALLY MANIC, EVEN FOR HIM.
HE WAS WOUNDED. I RAN A TEST ON THE BLOOD SPILLED.
I FOUND YOUR SIGNATURE PSYCHOTROPICS. HATTER TOLD ME HE WAS THE ONE WHO HELPED YOU SYNTHESIZE THEM IN HERE.
THE TWO OF YOU LOVE YOUR MIND CONTROL.
WHAT ARE YOU UP TO?

TCH. POOR WAYLON. LITTLE SIDESHOW FREAK. HE'S NOT LIKE THE *REST* OF US.

JOKER, RIDDLER, *ME*... WE ARE *LEGENDS*. CROC IS JUST ANOTHER COMMON *GROTESQUERIE*. AND HE KNOWS IT.

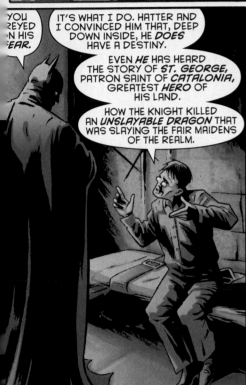

YOU REYED N HIS EAR.

IT'S WHAT I DO. HATTER AND I CONVINCED HIM THAT, DEEP DOWN INSIDE, HE *DOES* HAVE A DESTINY.

EVEN *HE* HAS HEARD THE STORY OF *ST. GEORGE*, PATRON SAINT OF *CATALONIA*, GREATEST *HERO* OF HIS LAND.

HOW THE KNIGHT KILLED AN *UNSLAYABLE DRAGON* THAT WAS SLAYING THE FAIR MAIDENS OF THE REALM.

"HATTER AND I... *SUGGESTED* TO WAYLON THAT HE WAS THE DRAGON *REINCARNATE*...

"...AND THAT HIS PATH TO GREATNESS WAS TO FINALLY *AVENGE* HIMSELF AGAINST HIS AVOWED *KNIGHT-ENEMY*."

IF YOU *WANT* CROC, I UNDERSTAND THAT IN *MODERN-DAY* CATALONIA-- BARCELONA--THEY'RE CURRENTLY DEALING WITH A LIZARD-LIKE *SERIAL KILLER*.

ONE WHO MURDERS A MAIDEN A *DAY*.

GOOD *HUNTING*.

BY THE WAY... THEY TELL ME HATTER RAN *AFOUL* OF CROC WHEN HE TRIED TO *PIGGYBACK* THE *ESCAPE*.

HOW *IS* THE LITTLE FELLOW?

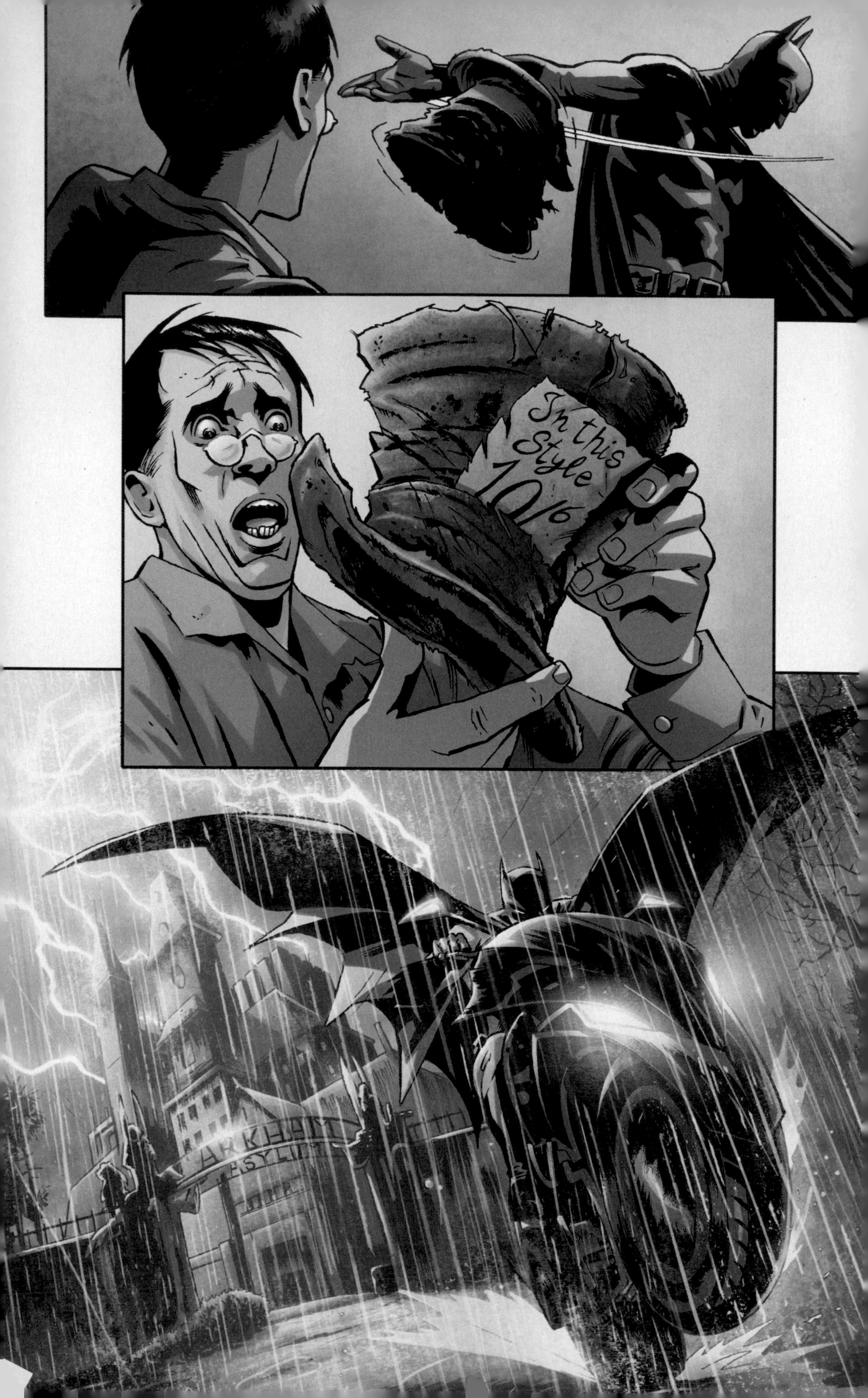
In this Style 10/6

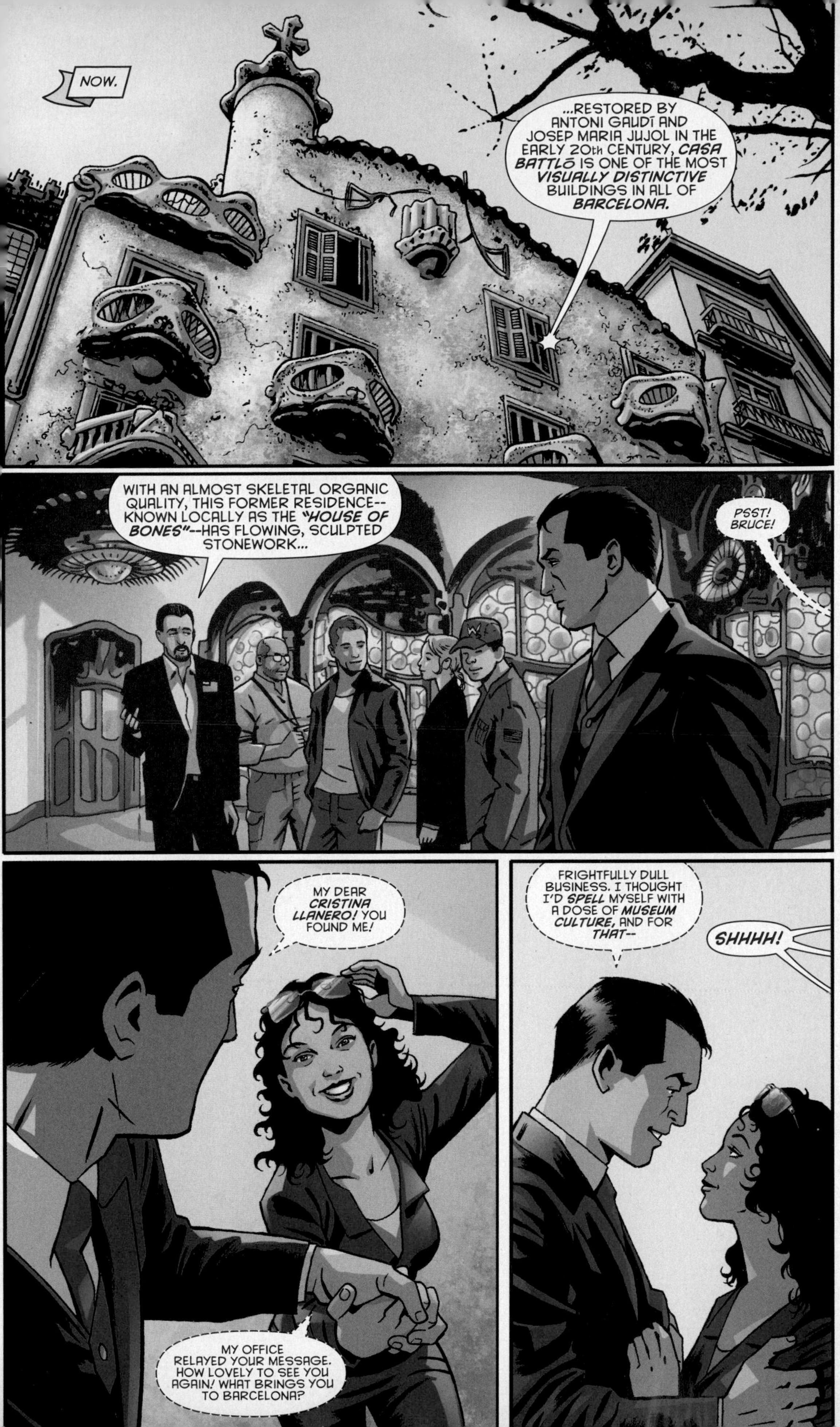
NOW.
...RESTORED BY ANTONI GAUDÍ AND JOSEP MARIA JUJOL IN THE EARLY 20th CENTURY, CASA BATLLÓ IS ONE OF THE MOST VISUALLY DISTINCTIVE BUILDINGS IN ALL OF BARCELONA.
WITH AN ALMOST SKELETAL ORGANIC QUALITY, THIS FORMER RESIDENCE--KNOWN LOCALLY AS THE "HOUSE OF BONES"--HAS FLOWING, SCULPTED STONEWORK...
PSST! BRUCE!
MY DEAR CRISTINA LLANERO! YOU FOUND ME!
MY OFFICE RELAYED YOUR MESSAGE. HOW LOVELY TO SEE YOU AGAIN! WHAT BRINGS YOU TO BARCELONA?
FRIGHTFULLY DULL BUSINESS. I THOUGHT I'D SPELL MYSELF WITH A DOSE OF MUSEUM CULTURE, AND FOR THAT--
SHHHH!

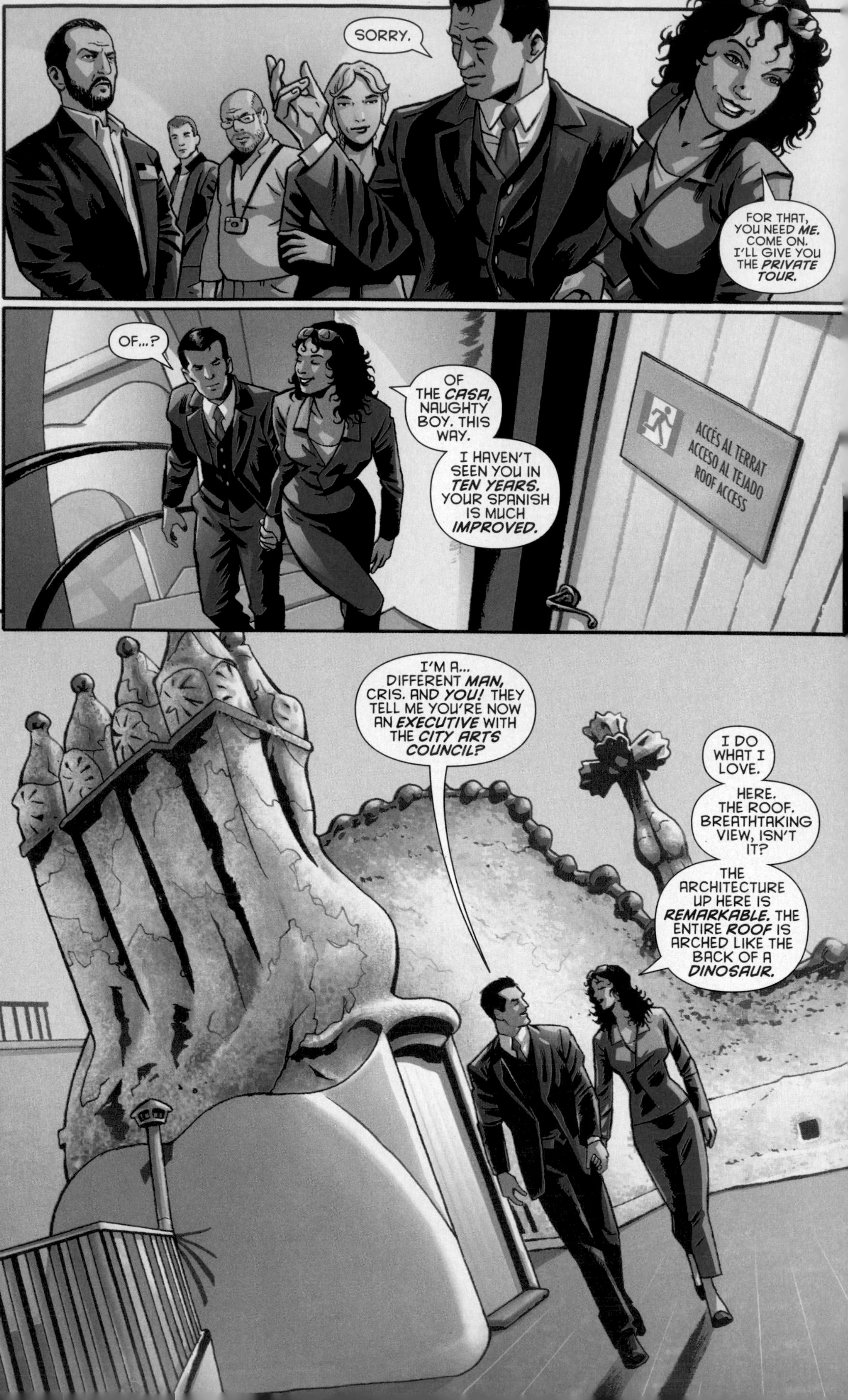
SORRY.
FOR THAT, YOU NEED *ME.* COME ON. I'LL GIVE YOU THE *PRIVATE TOUR.*
OF...?
OF THE *CASA,* NAUGHTY BOY. THIS WAY.
I HAVEN'T SEEN YOU IN *TEN YEARS.* YOUR SPANISH IS MUCH *IMPROVED.*
ACCÉS AL TERRAT
ACCESO AL TEJADO
ROOF ACCESS
I'M A... DIFFERENT *MAN,* CRIS. AND *YOU!* THEY TELL ME YOU'RE NOW AN *EXECUTIVE* WITH THE *CITY ARTS COUNCIL?*
I DO WHAT I LOVE.
HERE. THE ROOF. BREATHTAKING VIEW, ISN'T IT?
THE ARCHITECTURE UP HERE IS *REMARKABLE.* THE ENTIRE *ROOF* IS ARCHED LIKE THE BACK OF A *DINOSAUR.*

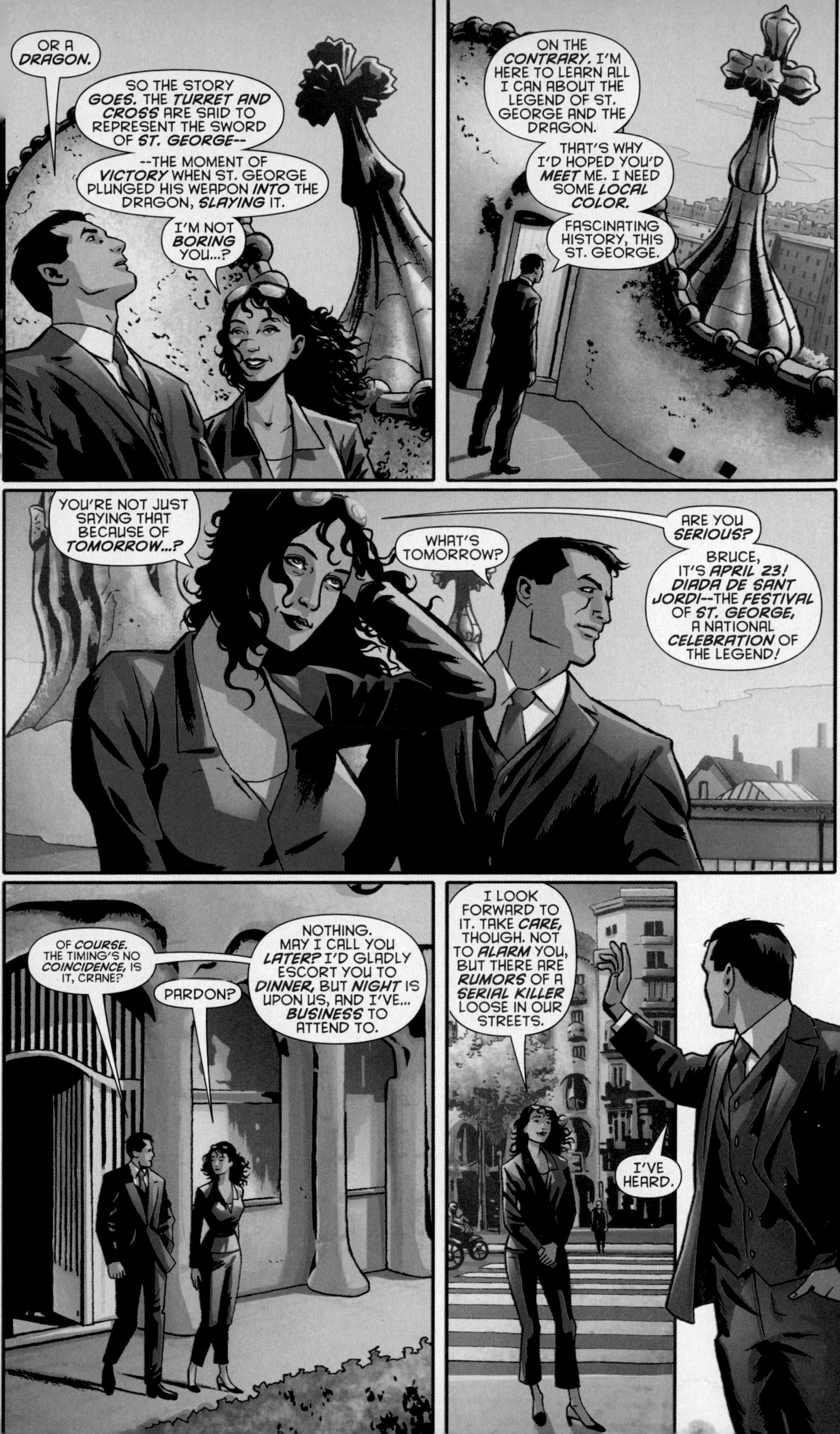
OR A DRAGON.
SO THE STORY GOES. THE TURRET AND CROSS ARE SAID TO REPRESENT THE SWORD OF ST. GEORGE--
--THE MOMENT OF VICTORY WHEN ST. GEORGE PLUNGED HIS WEAPON INTO THE DRAGON, SLAYING IT.
I'M NOT BORING YOU...?
ON THE CONTRARY. I'M HERE TO LEARN ALL I CAN ABOUT THE LEGEND OF ST. GEORGE AND THE DRAGON.
THAT'S WHY I'D HOPED YOU'D MEET ME. I NEED SOME LOCAL COLOR.
FASCINATING HISTORY, THIS ST. GEORGE.
YOU'RE NOT JUST SAYING THAT BECAUSE OF TOMORROW...?
WHAT'S TOMORROW?
ARE YOU SERIOUS?
BRUCE, IT'S APRIL 23! DIADA DE SANT JORDI--THE FESTIVAL OF ST. GEORGE, A NATIONAL CELEBRATION OF THE LEGEND!
OF COURSE. THE TIMING'S NO COINCIDENCE, IS IT, CRANE?
PARDON?
NOTHING. MAY I CALL YOU LATER? I'D GLADLY ESCORT YOU TO DINNER, BUT NIGHT IS UPON US, AND I'VE... BUSINESS TO ATTEND TO.
I LOOK FORWARD TO IT. TAKE CARE, THOUGH. NOT TO ALARM YOU, BUT THERE ARE RUMORS OF A SERIAL KILLER LOOSE IN OUR STREETS.
I'VE HEARD.

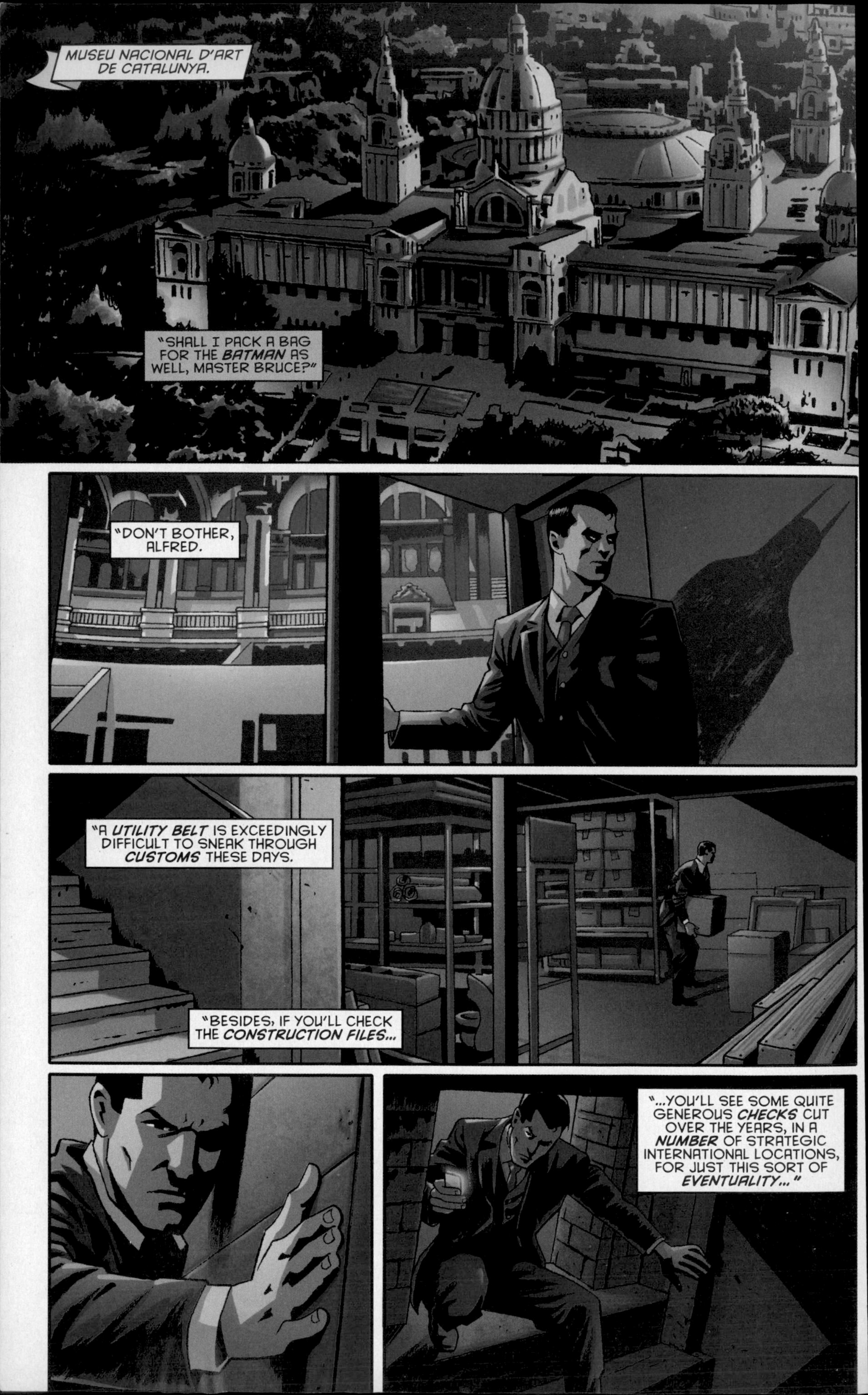
MUSEU NACIONAL D'ART DE CATALUNYA.
"SHALL I PACK A BAG FOR THE BATMAN AS WELL, MASTER BRUCE?"
"DON'T BOTHER, ALFRED.
"A UTILITY BELT IS EXCEEDINGLY DIFFICULT TO SNEAK THROUGH CUSTOMS THESE DAYS.
"BESIDES, IF YOU'LL CHECK THE CONSTRUCTION FILES...
"...YOU'LL SEE SOME QUITE GENEROUS CHECKS CUT OVER THE YEARS, IN A NUMBER OF STRATEGIC INTERNATIONAL LOCATIONS, FOR JUST THIS SORT OF EVENTUALITY..."

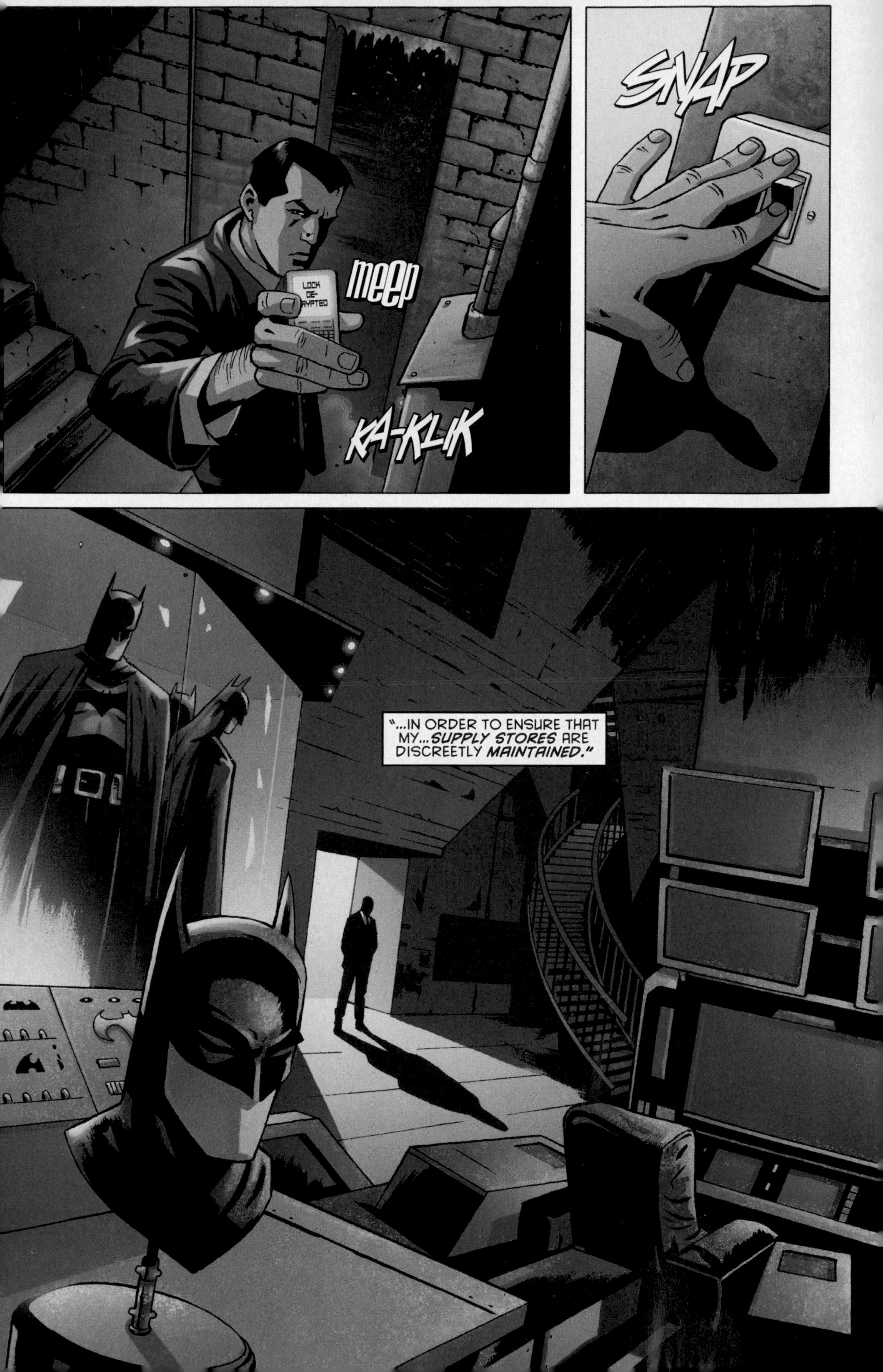
LOCK DE- RYPTED
meep
KA-KLIK
SNAP
"...IN ORDER TO ENSURE THAT MY...SUPPLY STORES ARE DISCREETLY MAINTAINED."

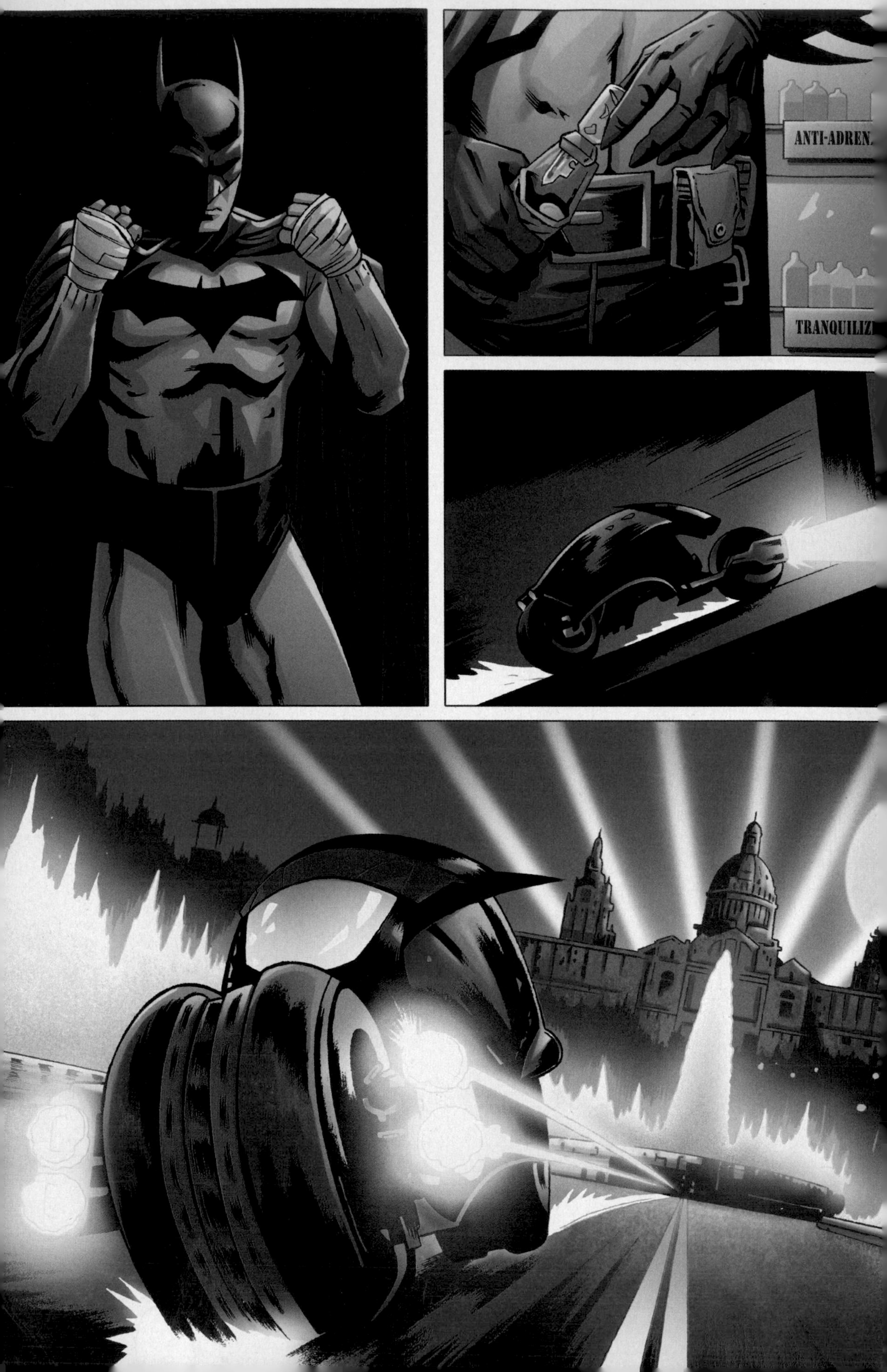
ANTI-ADREN
TRANQUILIZ

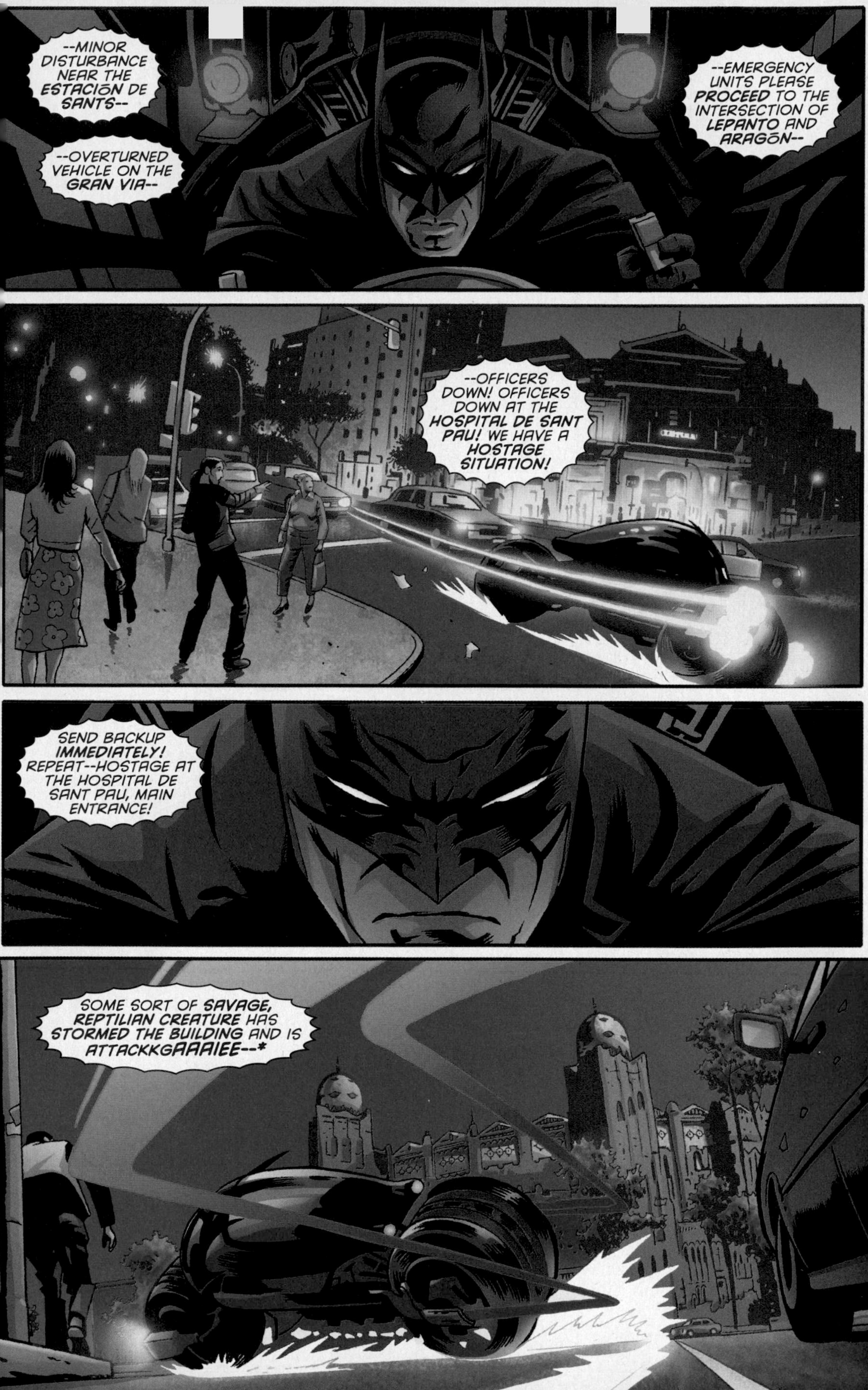
--MINOR DISTURBANCE NEAR THE ESTACIÓN DE SANTS--
--OVERTURNED VEHICLE ON THE GRAN VIA--
--EMERGENCY UNITS PLEASE PROCEED TO THE INTERSECTION OF LEPANTO AND ARAGÓN--
--OFFICERS DOWN! OFFICERS DOWN AT THE HOSPITAL DE SANT PAU! WE HAVE A HOSTAGE SITUATION!
SEND BACKUP IMMEDIATELY! REPEAT--HOSTAGE AT THE HOSPITAL DE SANT PAU, MAIN ENTRANCE!
SOME SORT OF SAVAGE, REPTILIAN CREATURE HAS STORMED THE BUILDING AND IS ATTACKKGAAAIEE--*

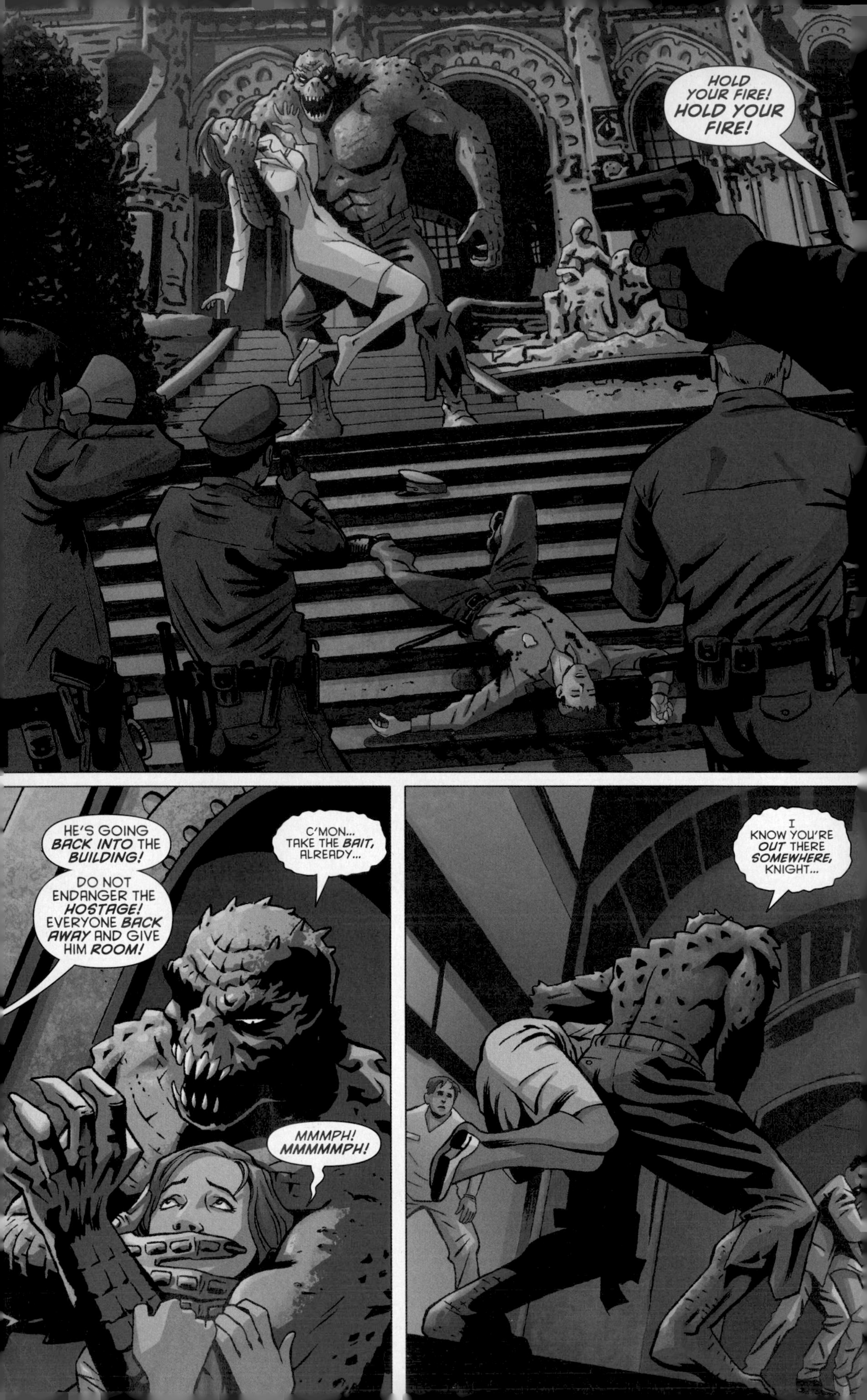
HOLD YOUR FIRE! HOLD YOUR FIRE!
HE'S GOING BACK INTO THE BUILDING!
DO NOT ENDANGER THE HOSTAGE! EVERYONE BACK AWAY AND GIVE HIM ROOM!
C'MON... TAKE THE BAIT, ALREADY...
MMMPH! MMMMMPH!
I KNOW YOU'RE OUT THERE SOMEWHERE, KNIGHT...

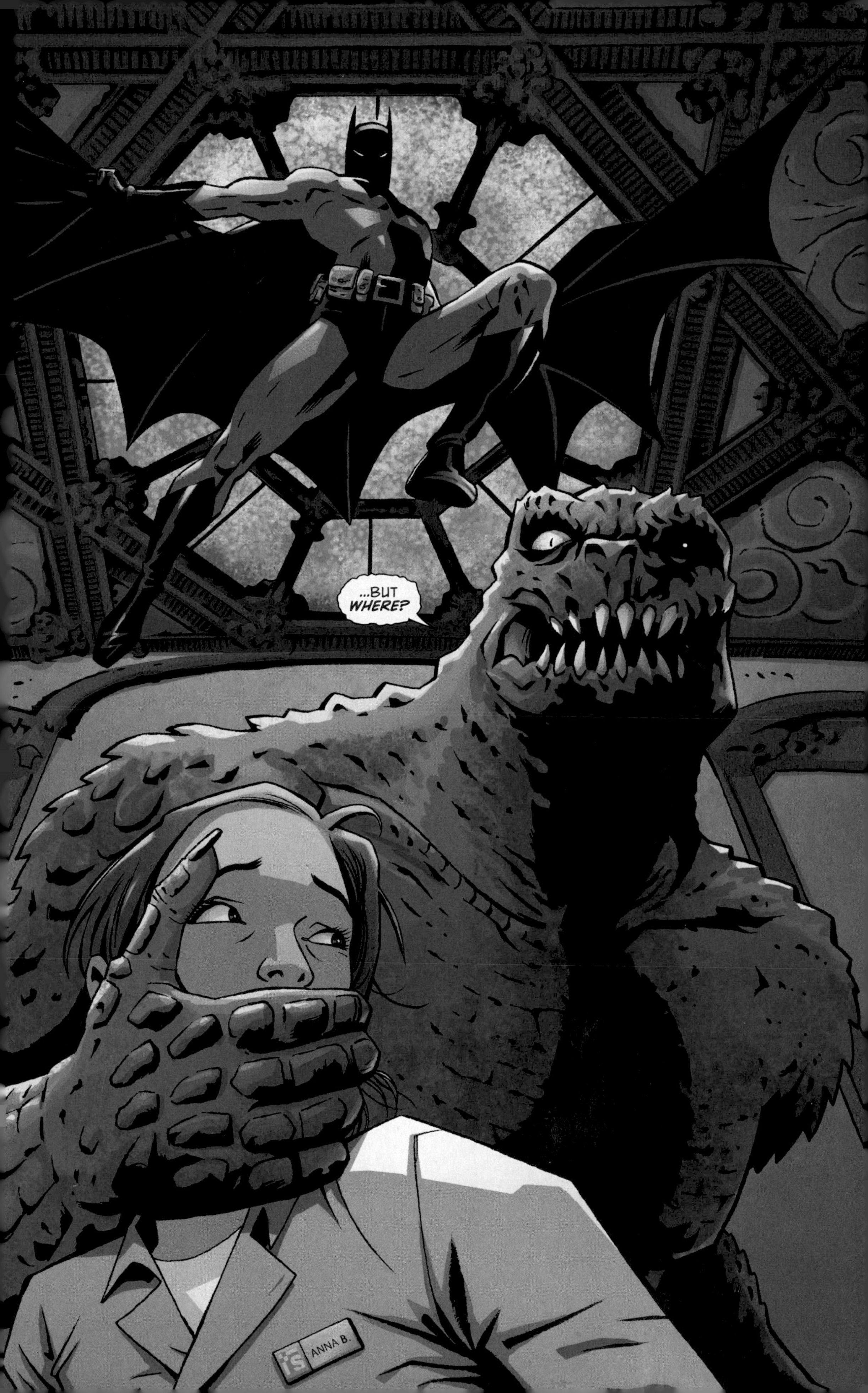
...BUT WHERE?
ANNA B.

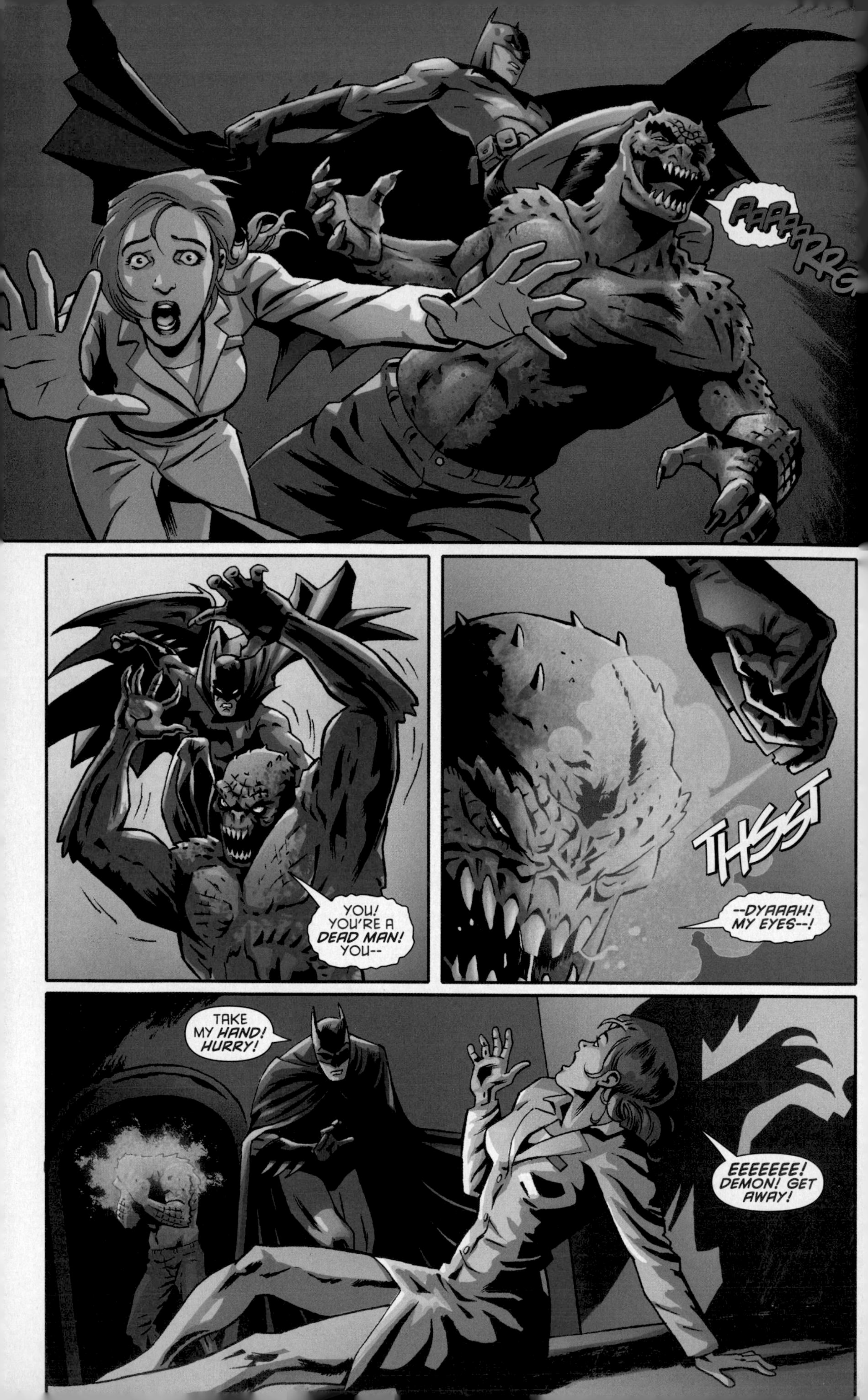
AAAARRRG
YOU! YOU'RE A DEAD MAN! YOU--
THSST
--DYAAAH! MY EYES--!
TAKE MY HAND! HURRY!
EEEEEEE! DEMON! GET AWAY!

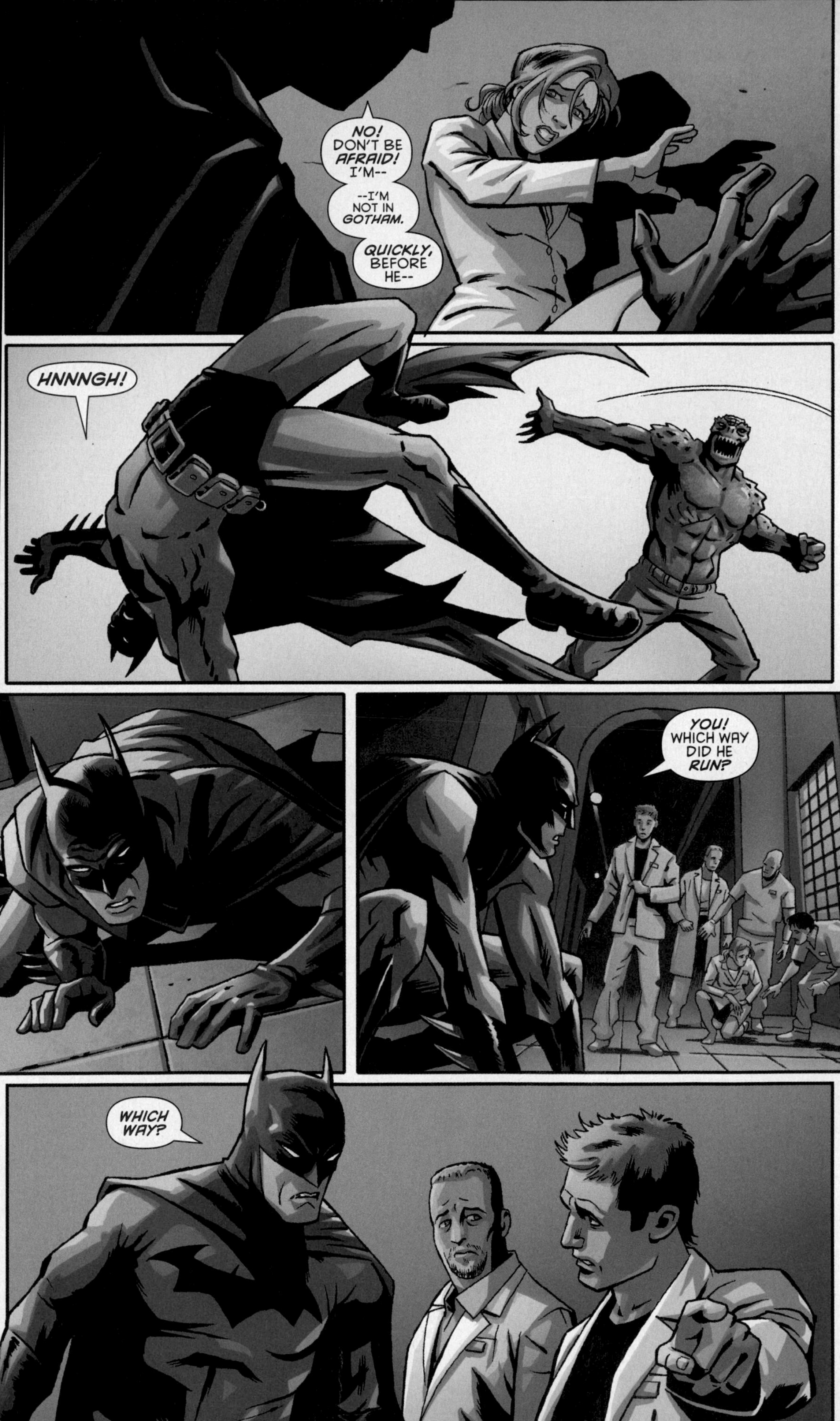
NO! DON'T BE AFRAID! I'M--
--I'M NOT IN GOTHAM.
QUICKLY, BEFORE HE--
HNNNGH!
YOU! WHICH WAY DID HE RUN?
WHICH WAY?

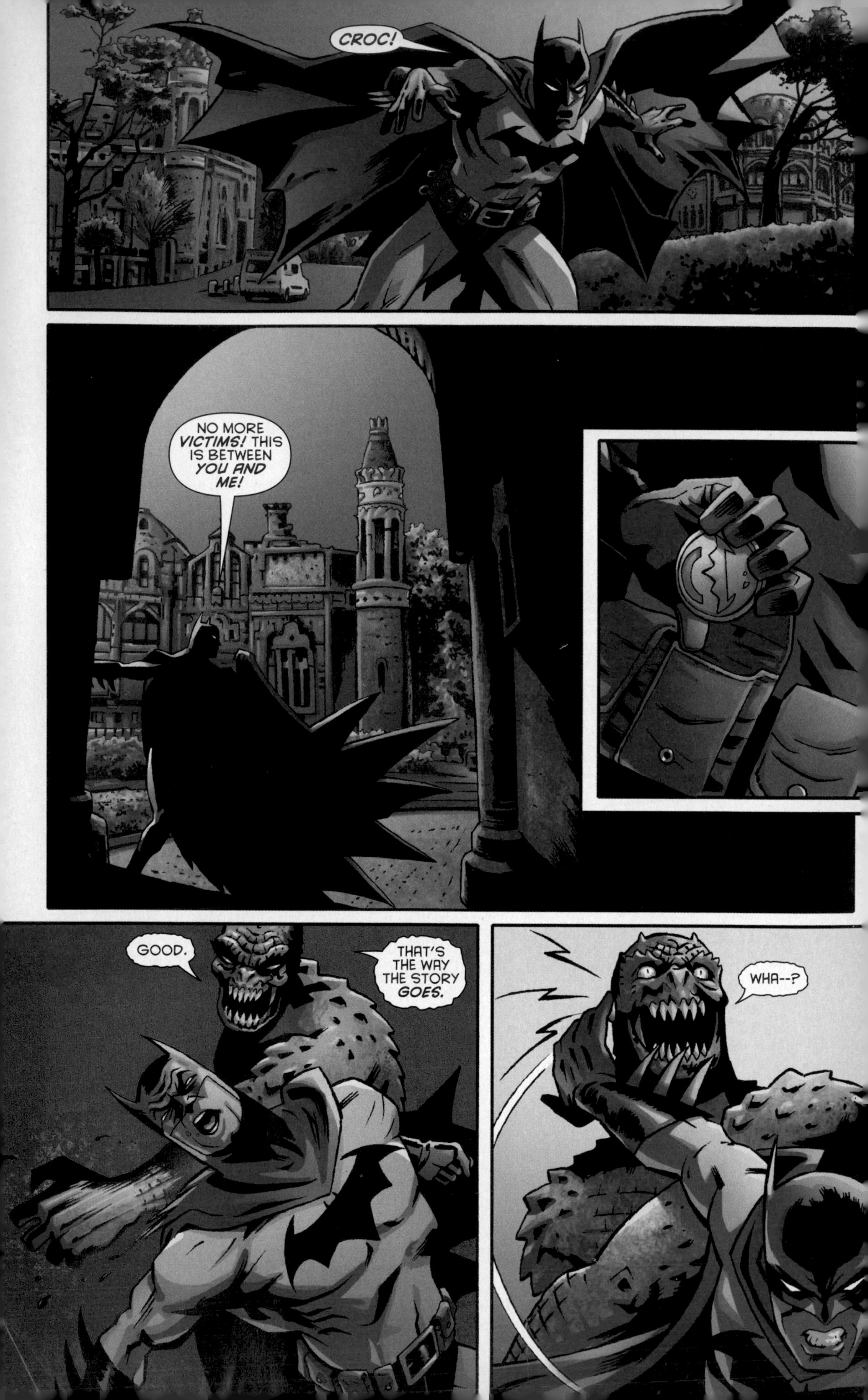
CROC!
NO MORE VICTIMS! THIS IS BETWEEN YOU AND ME!
GOOD.
THAT'S THE WAY THE STORY GOES.
WHA--?

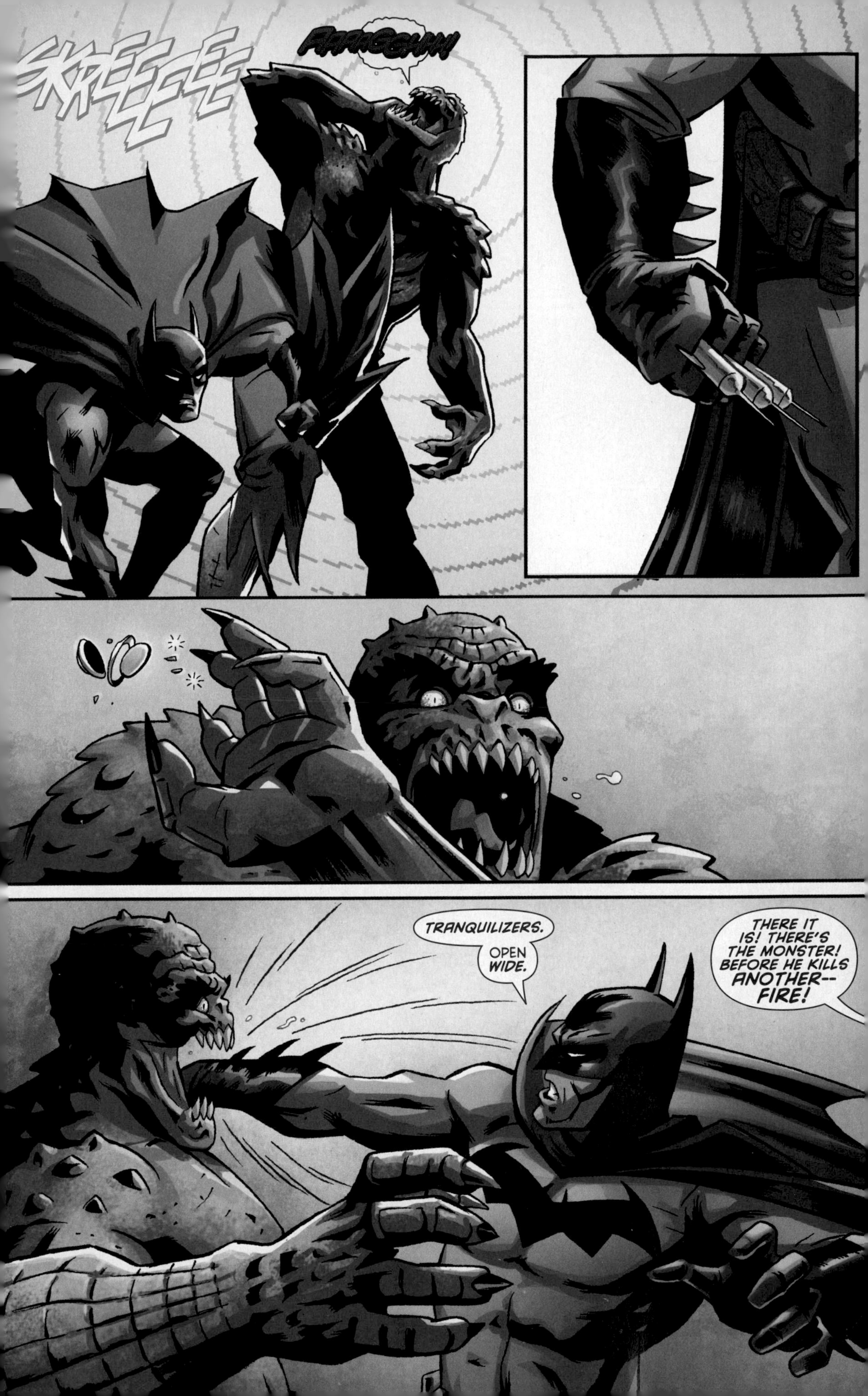

SKREEEEEE
AAAAGGHHH!
TRANQUILIZERS.
OPEN WIDE.
THERE IT IS! THERE'S THE MONSTER! BEFORE HE KILLS ANOTHER-- FIRE!

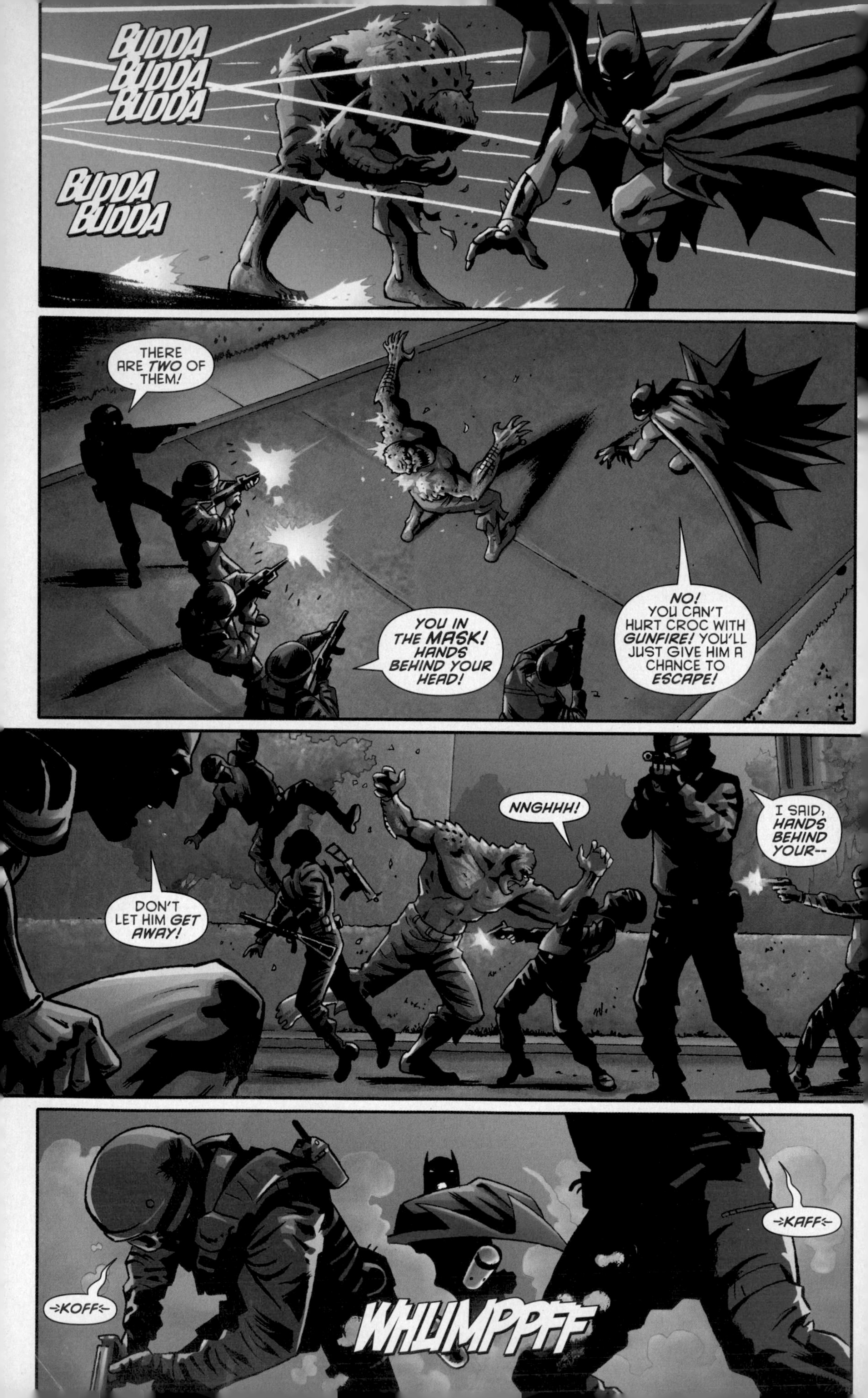
BUDDA BUDDA BUDDA
BUDDA BUDDA
THERE ARE TWO OF THEM!
YOU IN THE MASK! HANDS BEHIND YOUR HEAD!
NO! YOU CAN'T HURT CROC WITH GUNFIRE! YOU'LL JUST GIVE HIM A CHANCE TO ESCAPE!
DON'T LET HIM GET AWAY!
NNGHHH!
I SAID, HANDS BEHIND YOUR--
KAFF
KOFF
WHUMPPFF

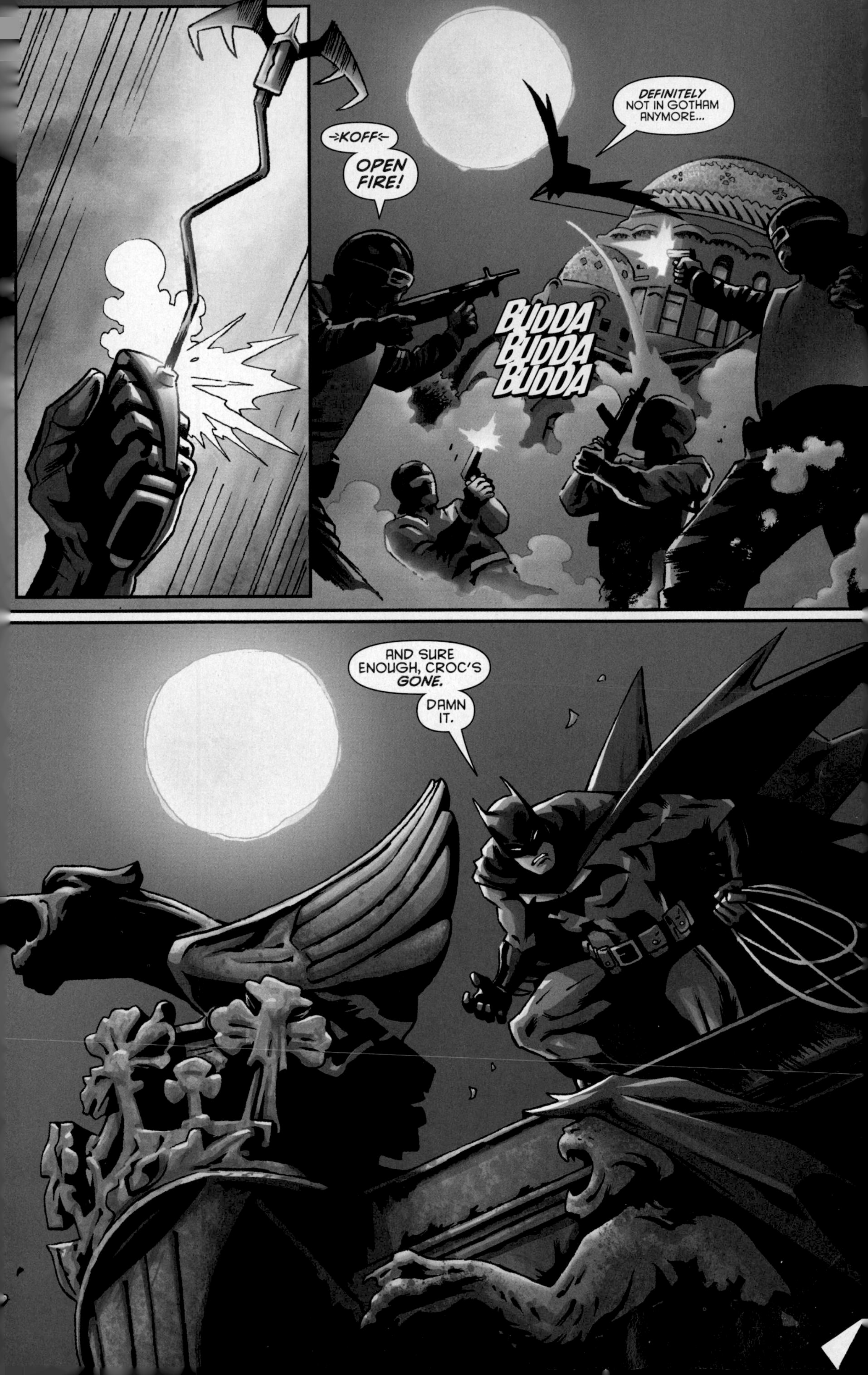

-KOFF-
OPEN FIRE!
DEFINITELY NOT IN GOTHAM ANYMORE...
BUDDA BUDDA BUDDA
AND SURE ENOUGH, CROC'S GONE.
DAMN IT.

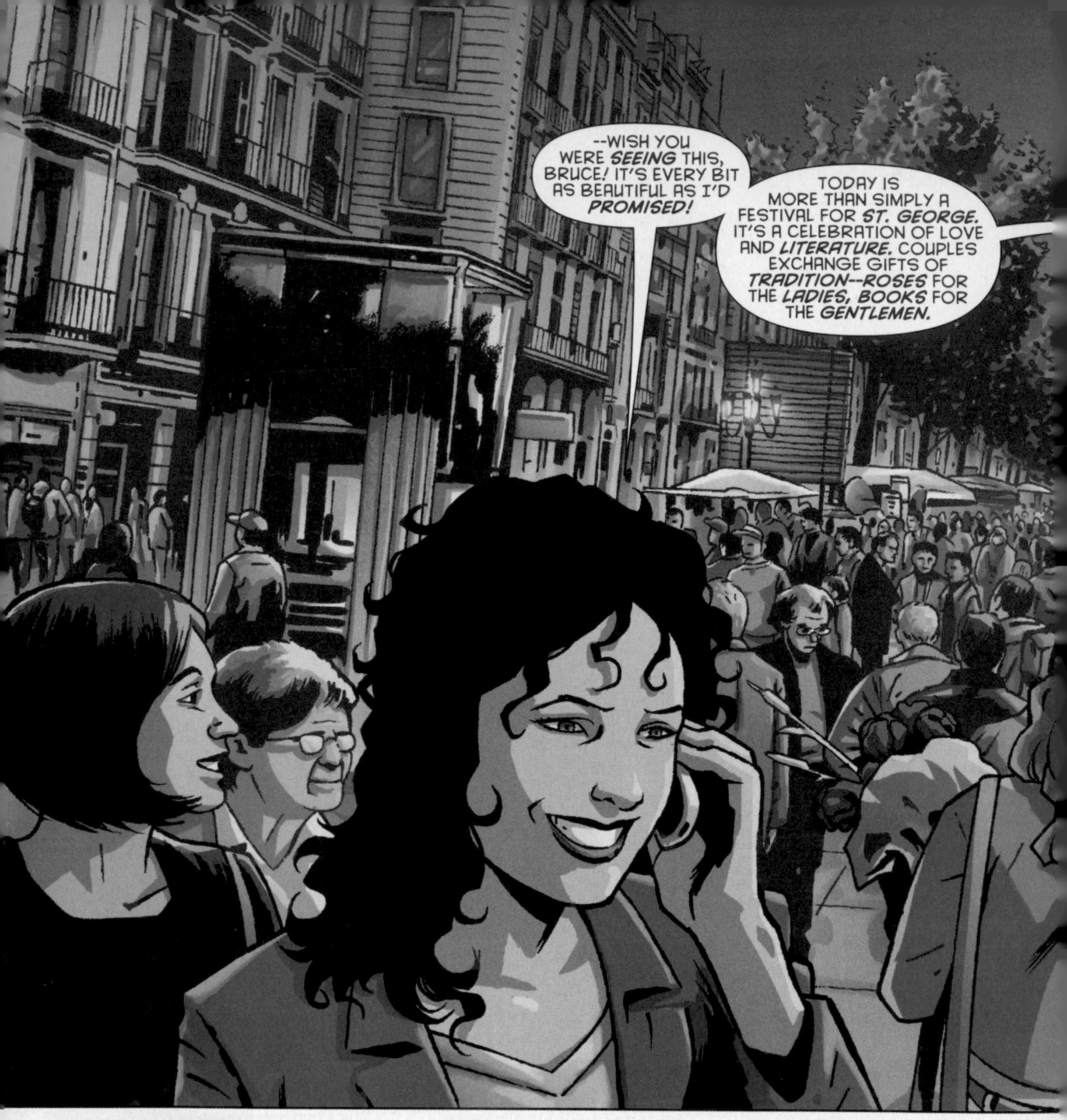
--WISH YOU WERE SEEING THIS, BRUCE! IT'S EVERY BIT AS BEAUTIFUL AS I'D PROMISED!
TODAY IS MORE THAN SIMPLY A FESTIVAL FOR ST. GEORGE. IT'S A CELEBRATION OF LOVE AND LITERATURE. COUPLES EXCHANGE GIFTS OF TRADITION--ROSES FOR THE LADIES, BOOKS FOR THE GENTLEMEN.

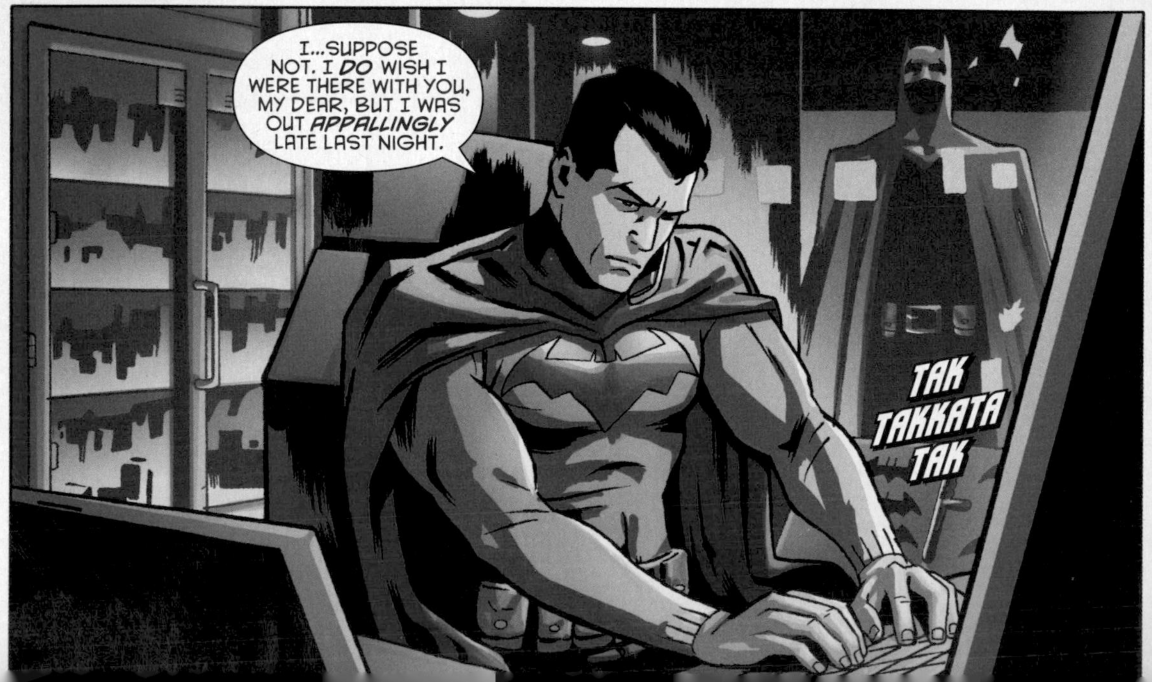
I...SUPPOSE NOT. I DO WISH I WERE THERE WITH YOU, MY DEAR, BUT I WAS OUT APPALLINGLY LATE LAST NIGHT.
TAK TAKKATA TAK

THE RAMBLA *ALONE* IS *TEEMING* WITH ROMANCE! LOVERS EVERYWHERE, POETRY AND *FLOWERS...*YOU SHOULDN'T BE *MISSING* THIS!

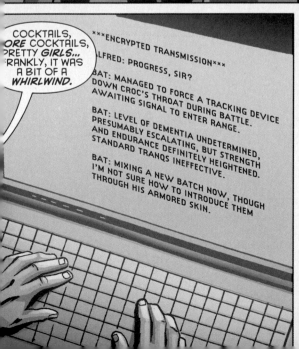

COCKTAILS, *MORE* COCKTAILS, *PRETTY GIRLS...* *FRANKLY,* IT WAS A BIT OF A *WHIRLWIND.*

×××ENCRYPTED TRANSMISSION×××

ALFRED: PROGRESS, SIR?

BAT: MANAGED TO FORCE A TRACKING DEVICE DOWN CROC'S THROAT DURING BATTLE. AWAITING SIGNAL TO ENTER RANGE.

BAT: LEVEL OF DEMENTIA UNDETERMINED, PRESUMABLY ESCALATING, BUT STRENGTH AND ENDURANCE DEFINITELY HEIGHTENED. STANDARD TRANQS INEFFECTIVE.

BAT: MIXING A NEW BATCH NOW, THOUGH I'M NOT SURE HOW TO INTRODUCE THEM THROUGH HIS ARMORED SKIN.

CRIS? CRIS, DID I *LOSE* YOU?

...

I'M *HERE,* BRUCE. I JUST...

...YOU *DISAPPOINT* ME.

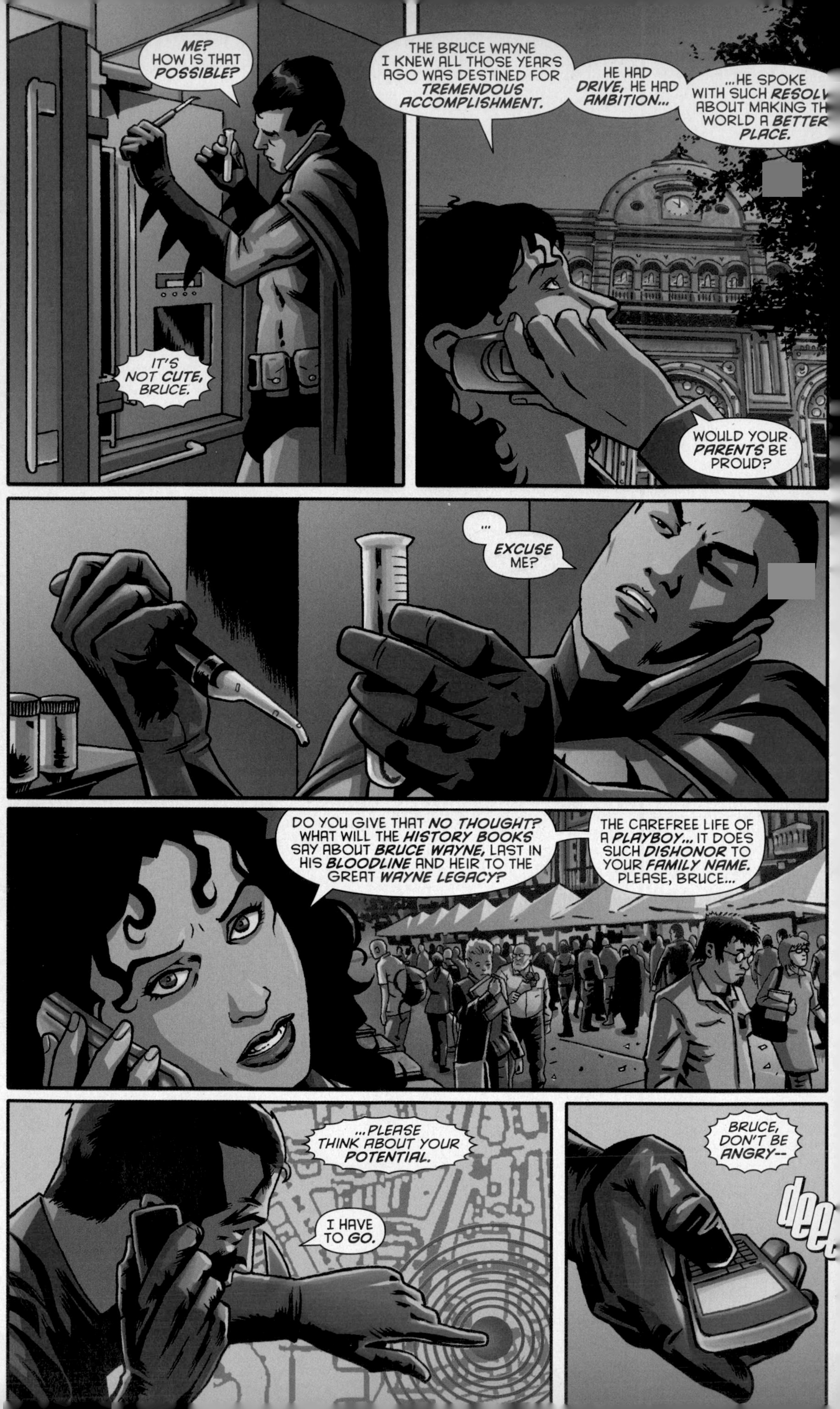
ME? HOW IS THAT POSSIBLE?
IT'S NOT CUTE, BRUCE.
THE BRUCE WAYNE I KNEW ALL THOSE YEARS AGO WAS DESTINED FOR TREMENDOUS ACCOMPLISHMENT.
HE HAD DRIVE, HE HAD AMBITION...
...HE SPOKE WITH SUCH RESOLV ABOUT MAKING TH WORLD A BETTER PLACE.
WOULD YOUR PARENTS BE PROUD?
... EXCUSE ME?
DO YOU GIVE THAT NO THOUGHT? WHAT WILL THE HISTORY BOOKS SAY ABOUT BRUCE WAYNE, LAST IN HIS BLOODLINE AND HEIR TO THE GREAT WAYNE LEGACY?
THE CAREFREE LIFE OF A PLAYBOY... IT DOES SUCH DISHONOR TO YOUR FAMILY NAME. PLEASE, BRUCE...
...PLEASE THINK ABOUT YOUR POTENTIAL.
I HAVE TO GO.
BRUCE, DON'T BE ANGRY--

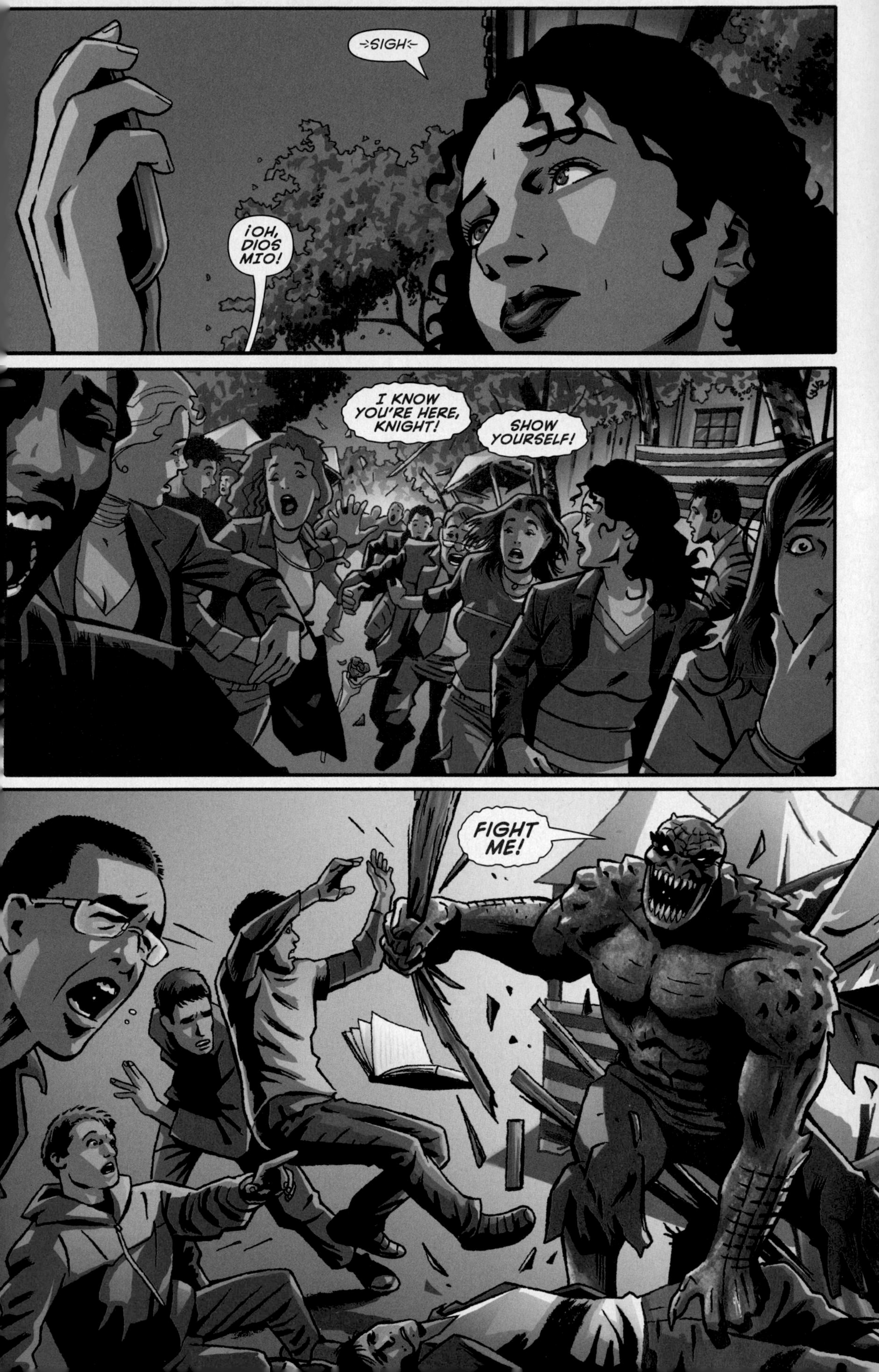
-SIGH-
¡OH, DIOS MIO!
I KNOW YOU'RE HERE, KNIGHT!
SHOW YOURSELF!
FIGHT ME!

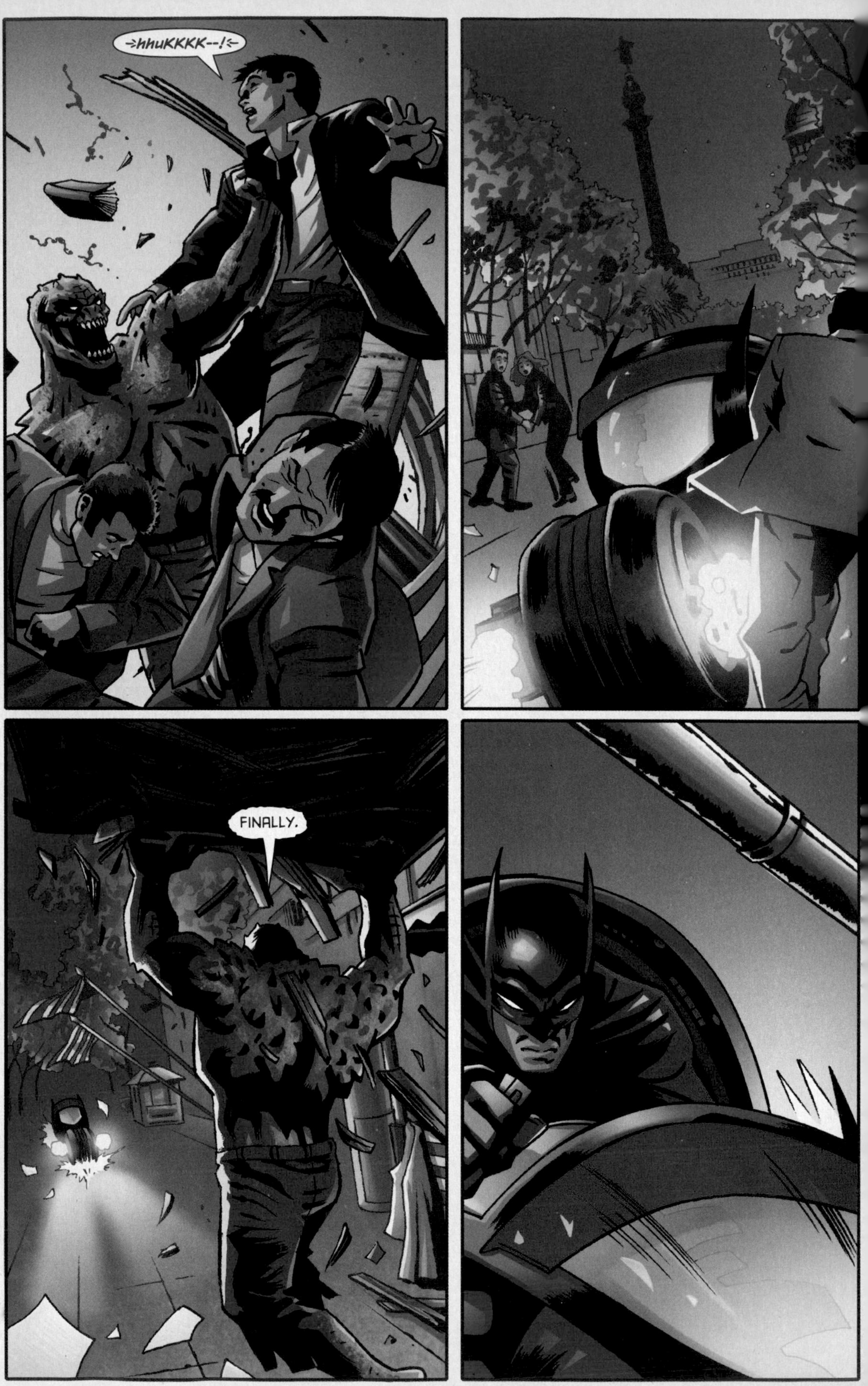
-hhuKKKK--!-
FINALLY.

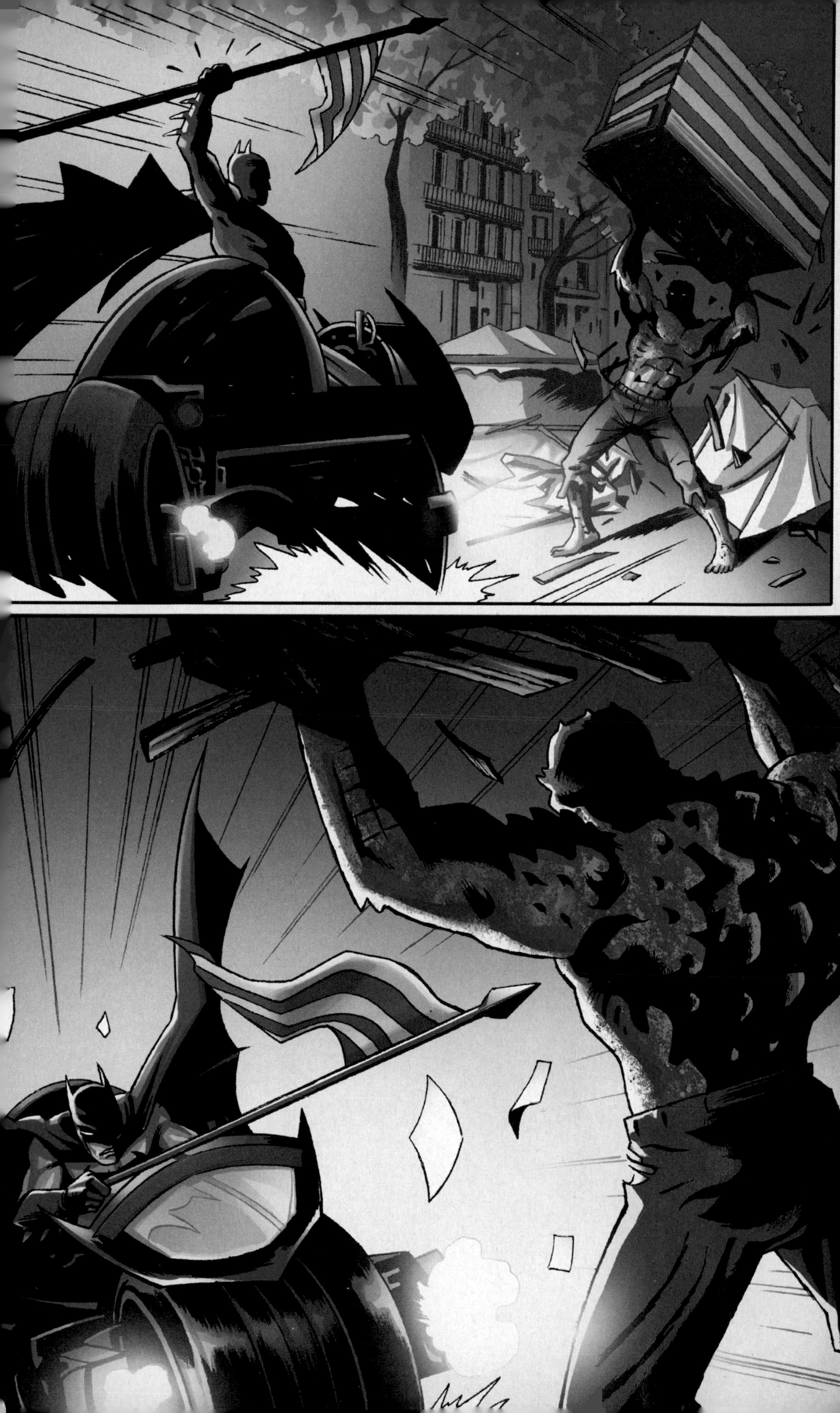

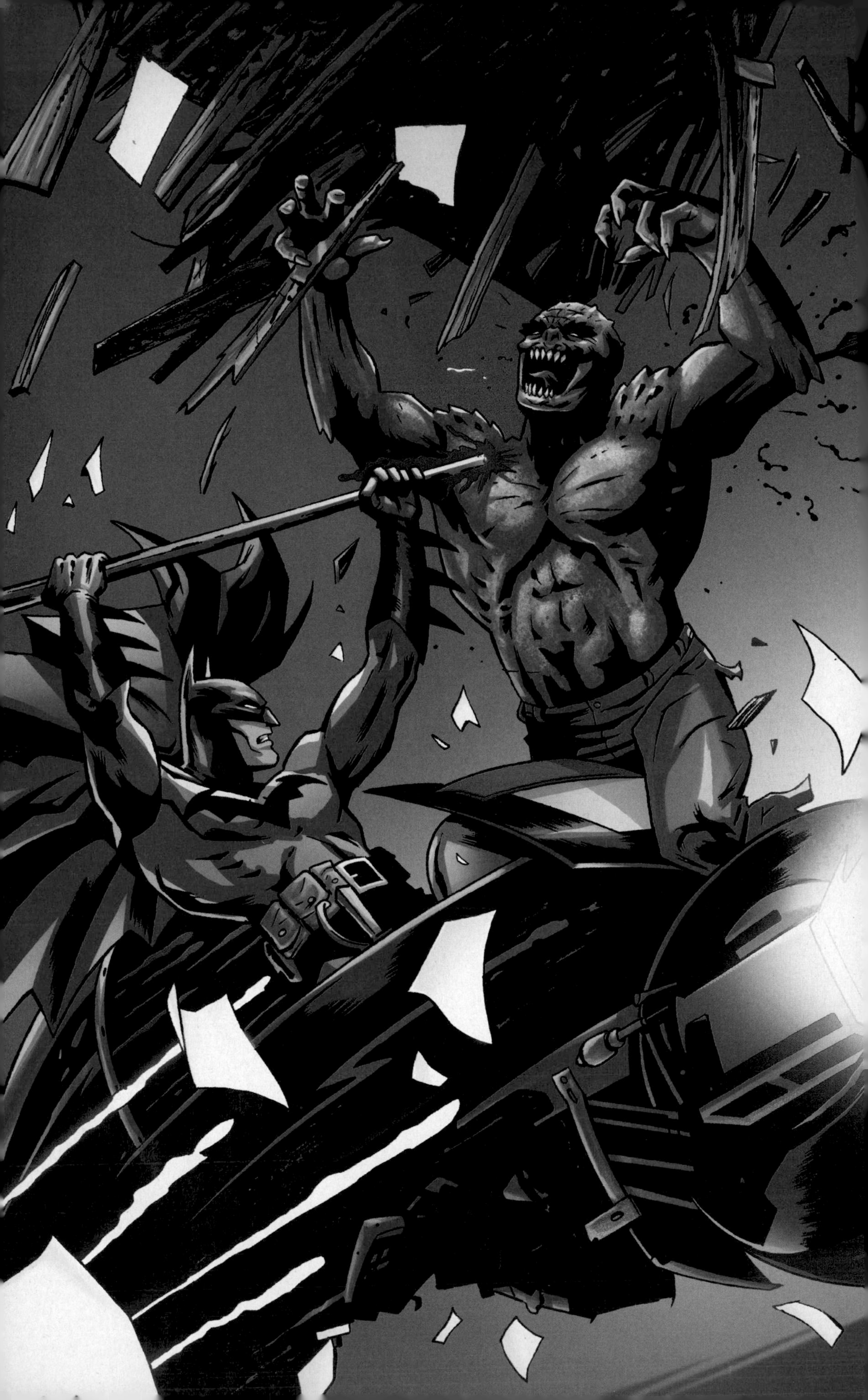

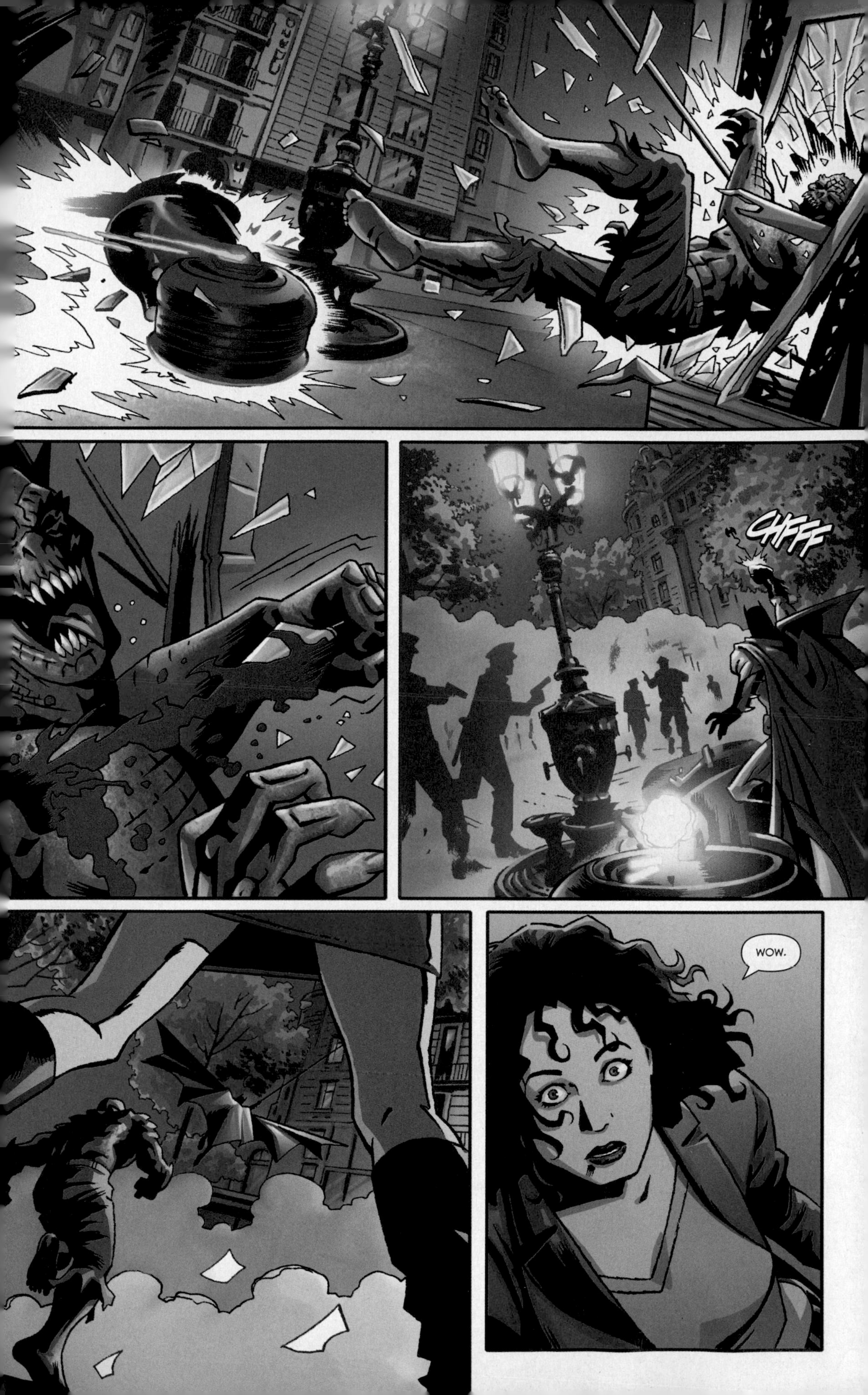
CHFFF
WOW.

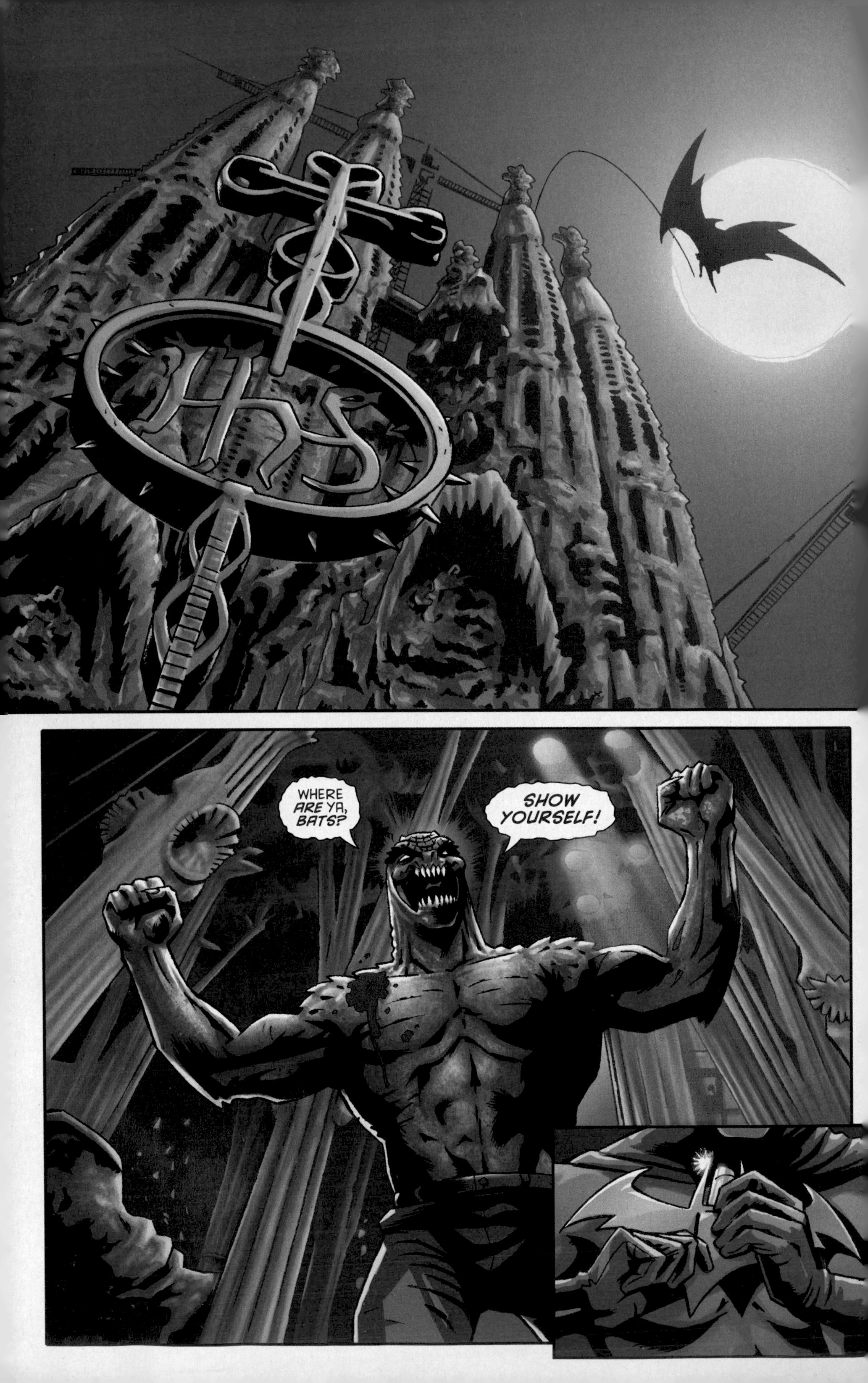
WHERE ARE YA, BATS?
SHOW YOURSELF!

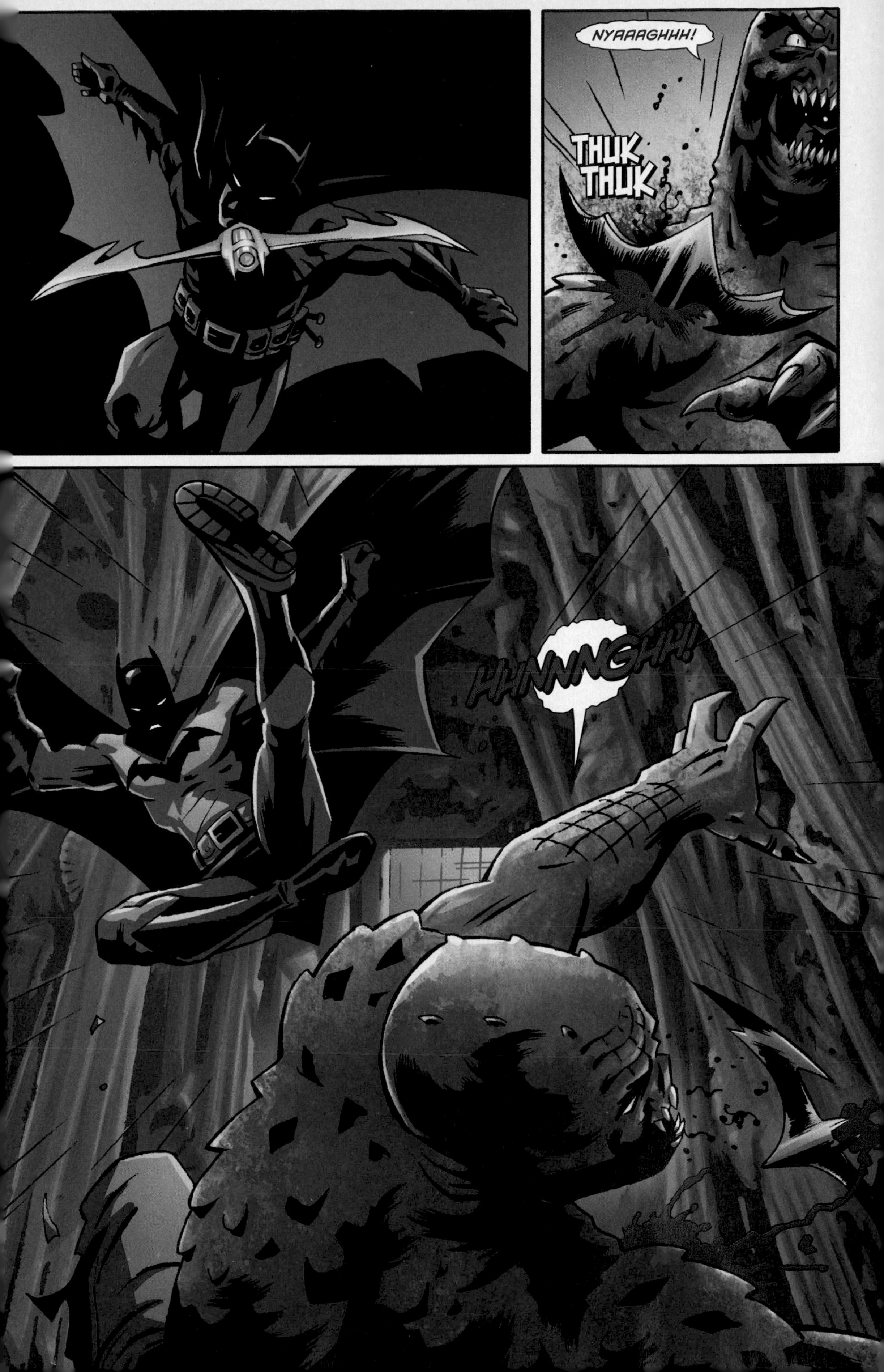
NYAAAGHHH!
THUK THUK
HHNNNGHH!

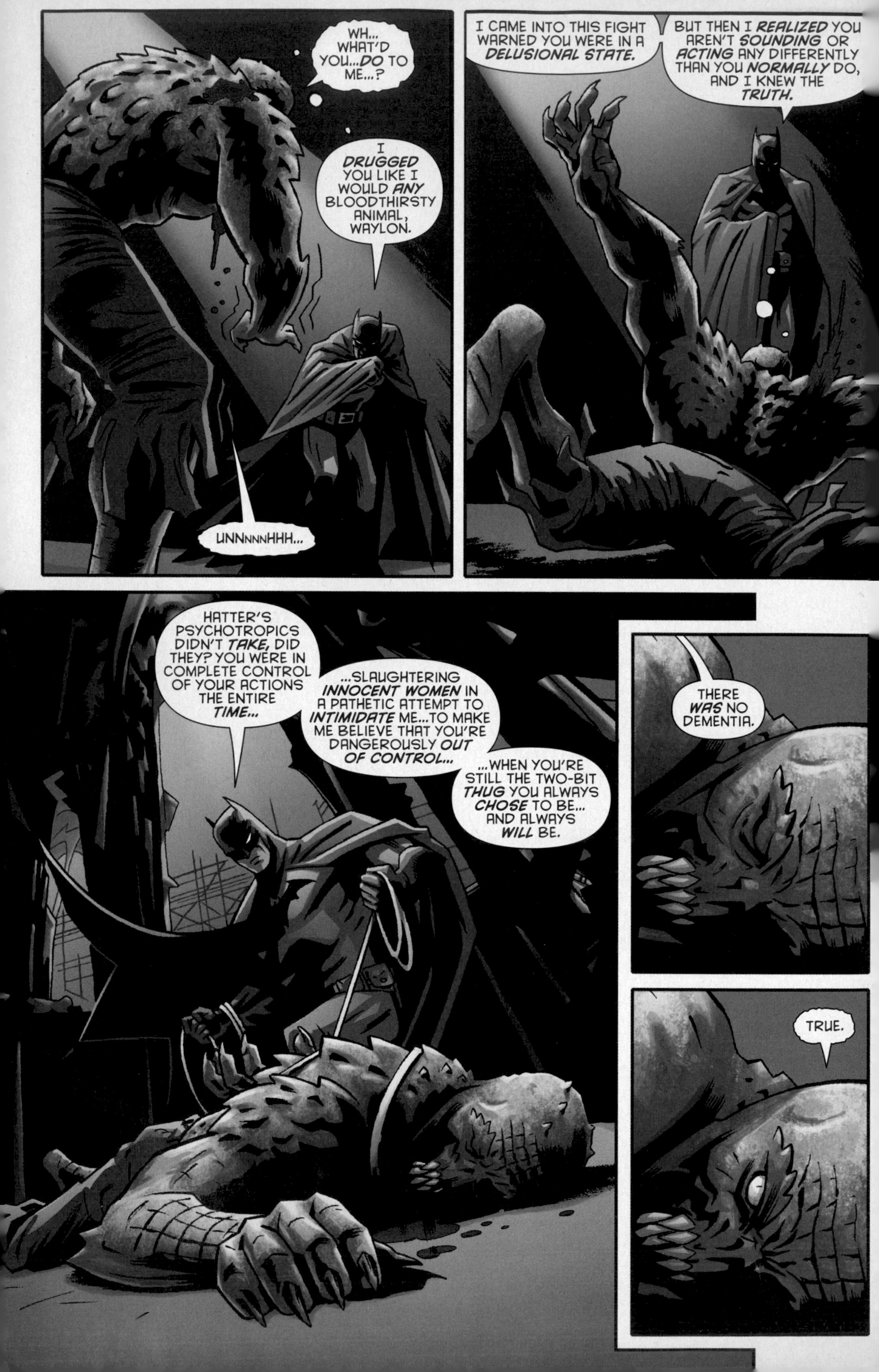
WH... WHAT'D YOU...DO TO ME...?
I DRUGGED YOU LIKE I WOULD ANY BLOODTHIRSTY ANIMAL, WAYLON.
UNNNNNHHH...
I CAME INTO THIS FIGHT WARNED YOU WERE IN A DELUSIONAL STATE.
BUT THEN I REALIZED YOU AREN'T SOUNDING OR ACTING ANY DIFFERENTLY THAN YOU NORMALLY DO, AND I KNEW THE TRUTH.
HATTER'S PSYCHOTROPICS DIDN'T TAKE, DID THEY? YOU WERE IN COMPLETE CONTROL OF YOUR ACTIONS THE ENTIRE TIME...
...SLAUGHTERING INNOCENT WOMEN IN A PATHETIC ATTEMPT TO INTIMIDATE ME...TO MAKE ME BELIEVE THAT YOU'RE DANGEROUSLY OUT OF CONTROL...
...WHEN YOU'RE STILL THE TWO-BIT THUG YOU ALWAYS CHOSE TO BE... AND ALWAYS WILL BE.
THERE WAS NO DEMENTIA.
TRUE.

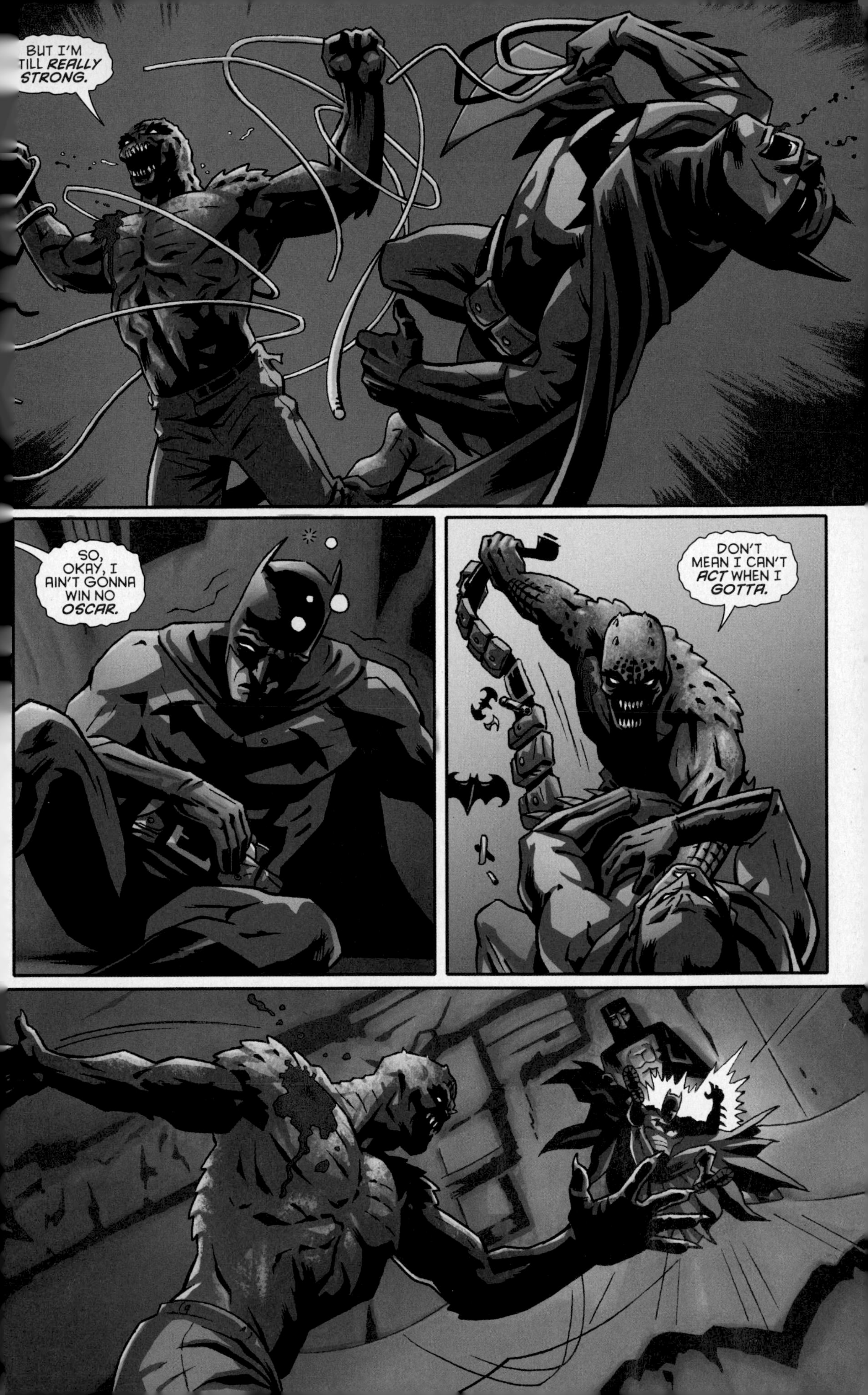
BUT I'M
TILL REALLY
STRONG.
SO, OKAY, I AIN'T GONNA WIN NO OSCAR.
DON'T MEAN I CAN'T ACT WHEN I GOTTA.

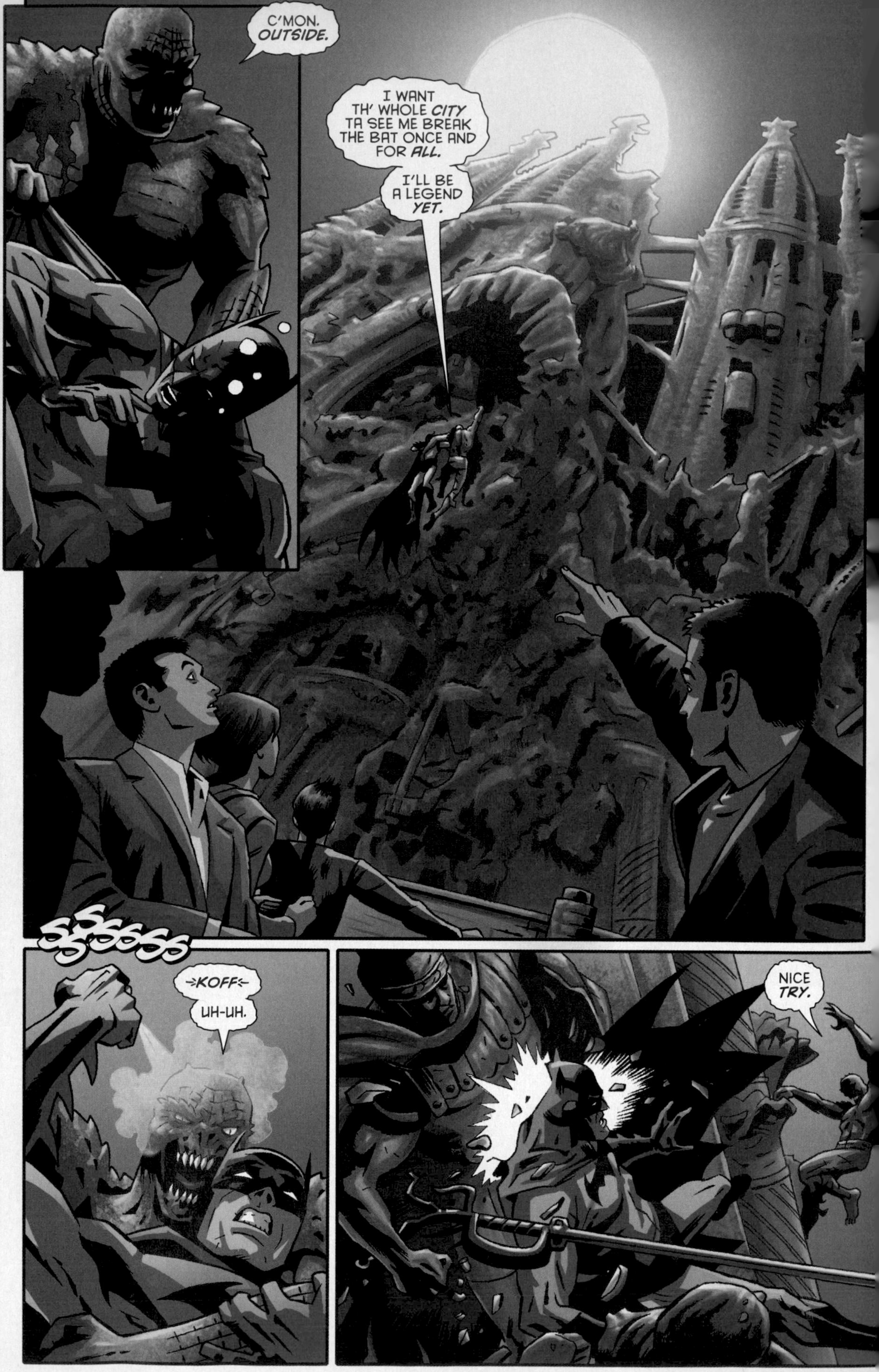
C'MON. OUTSIDE.
I WANT TH' WHOLE CITY TA SEE ME BREAK THE BAT ONCE AND FOR ALL.
I'LL BE A LEGEND YET.
SSSSSSSSSS
-KOFF-
UH-UH.
NICE TRY.

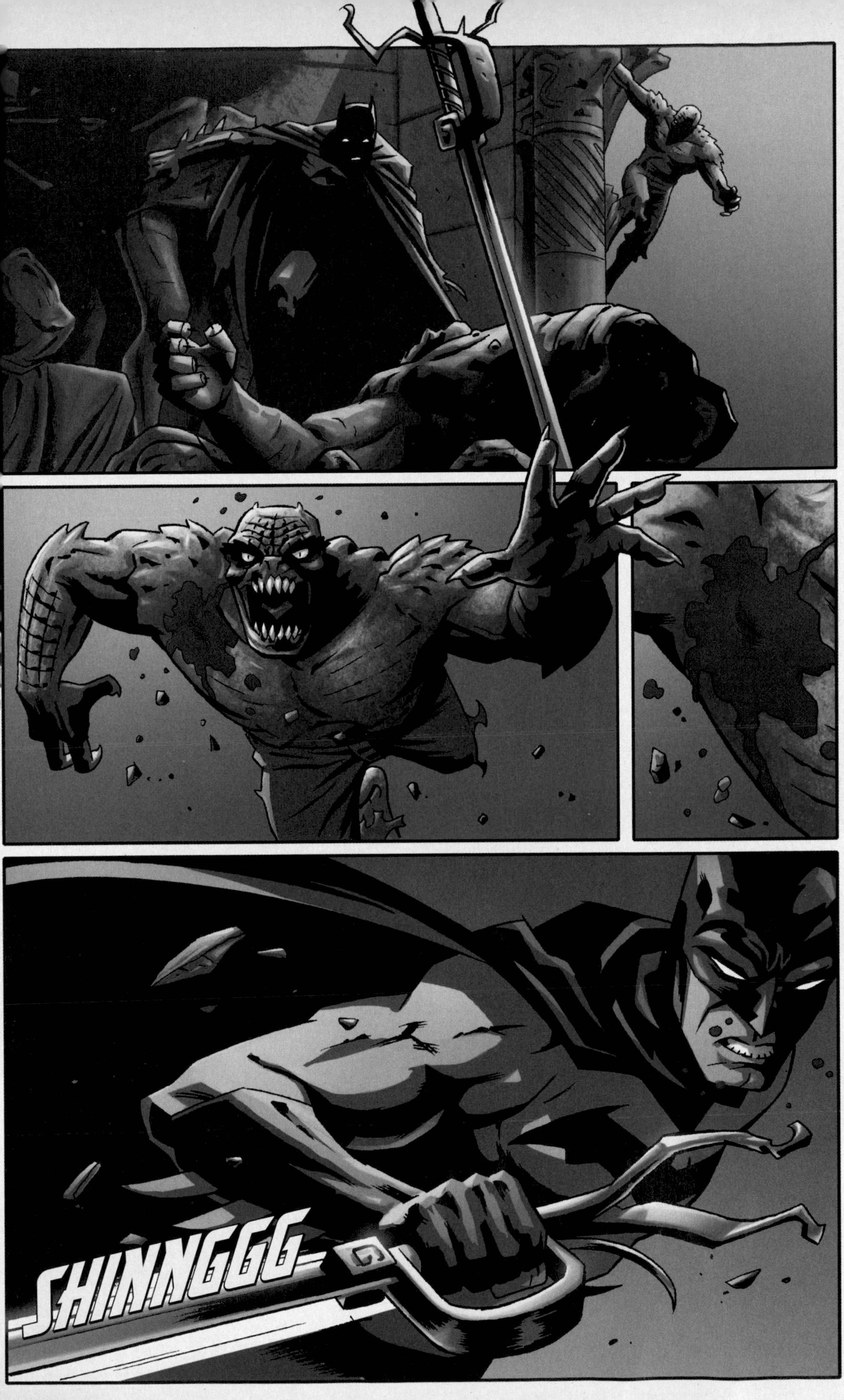
SHINNGGG

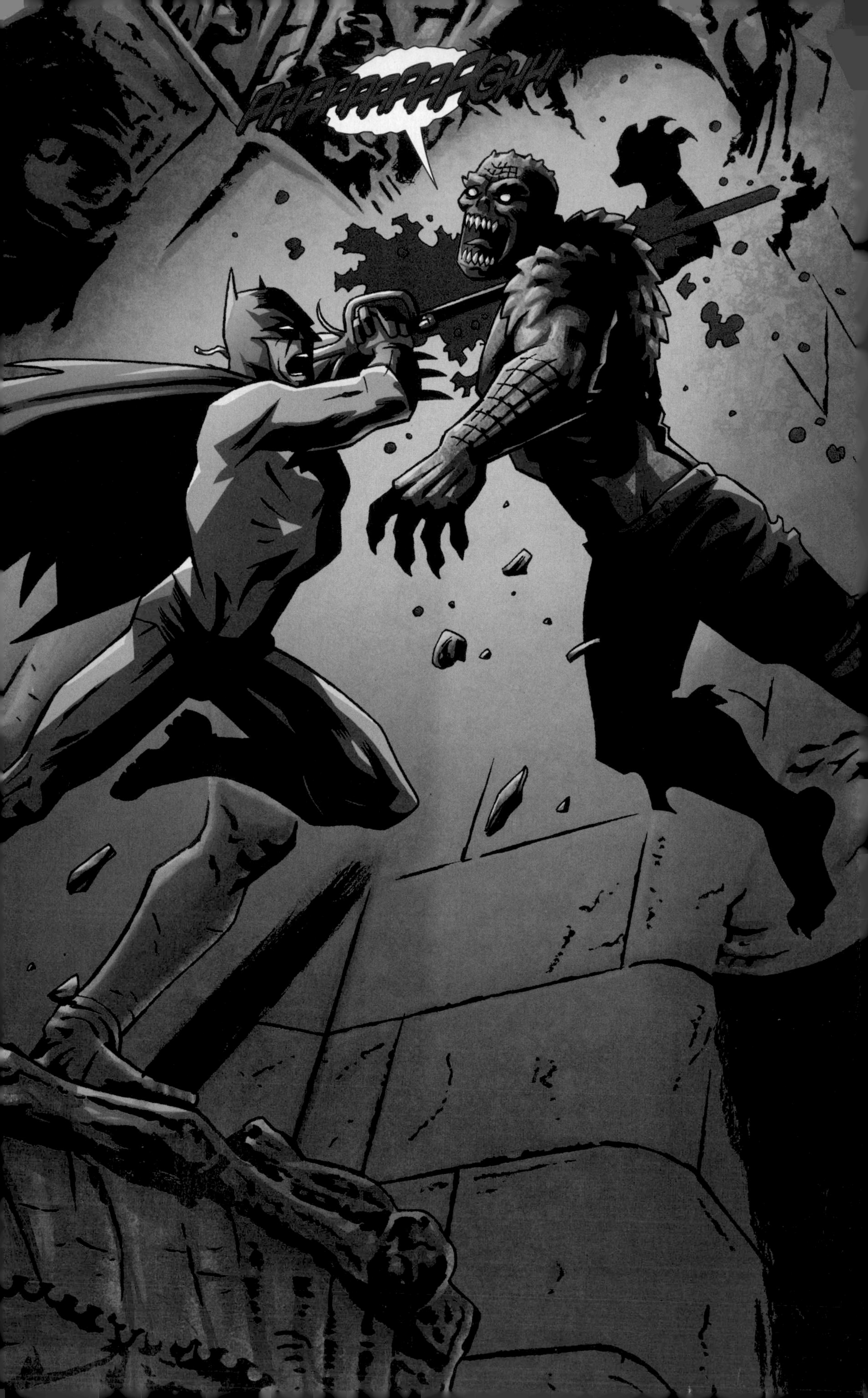
AAAAAAAAARGHH!

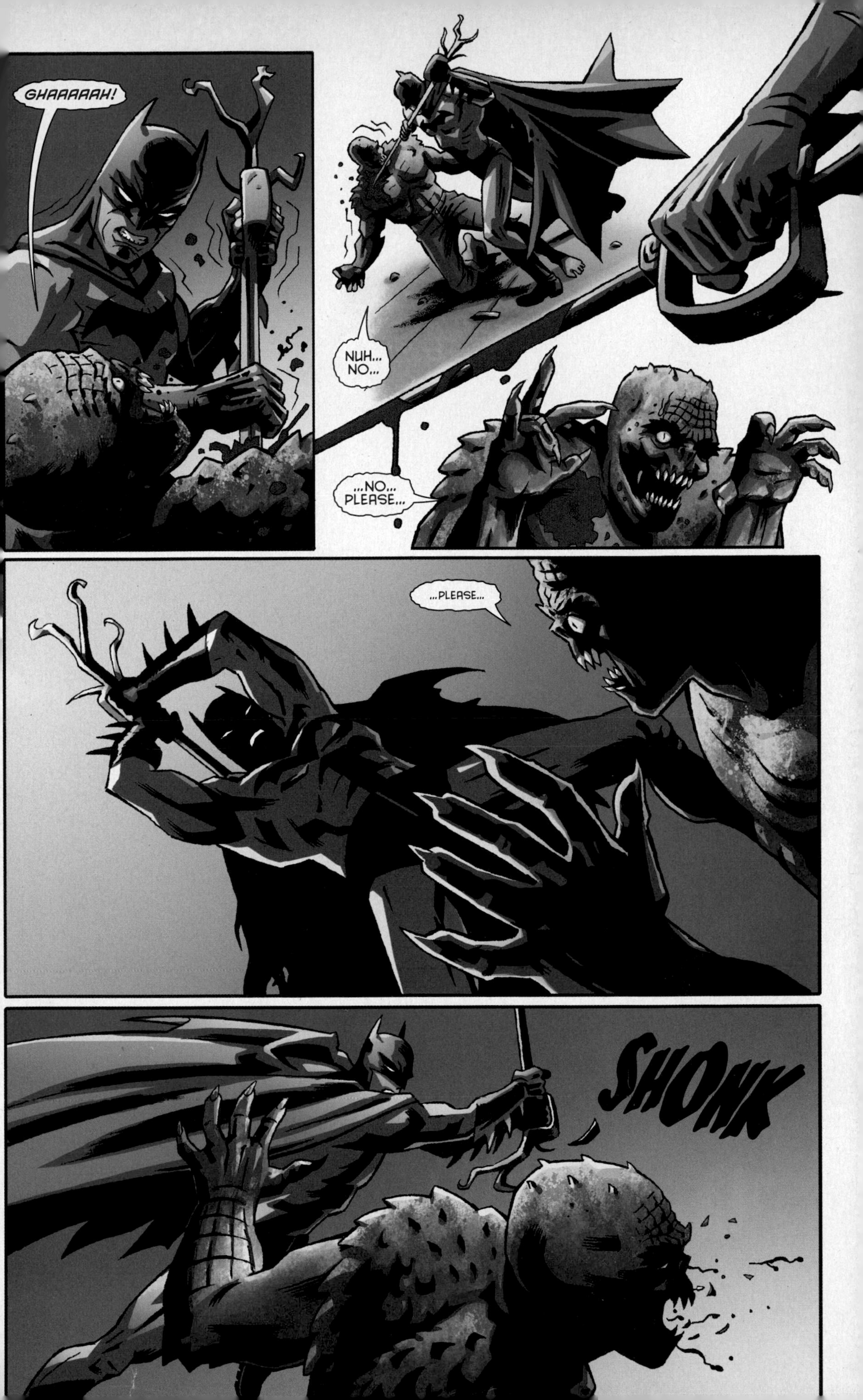

GHAAAAAH!
NUH... NO...
...NO... PLEASE...
...PLEASE...
SHONK

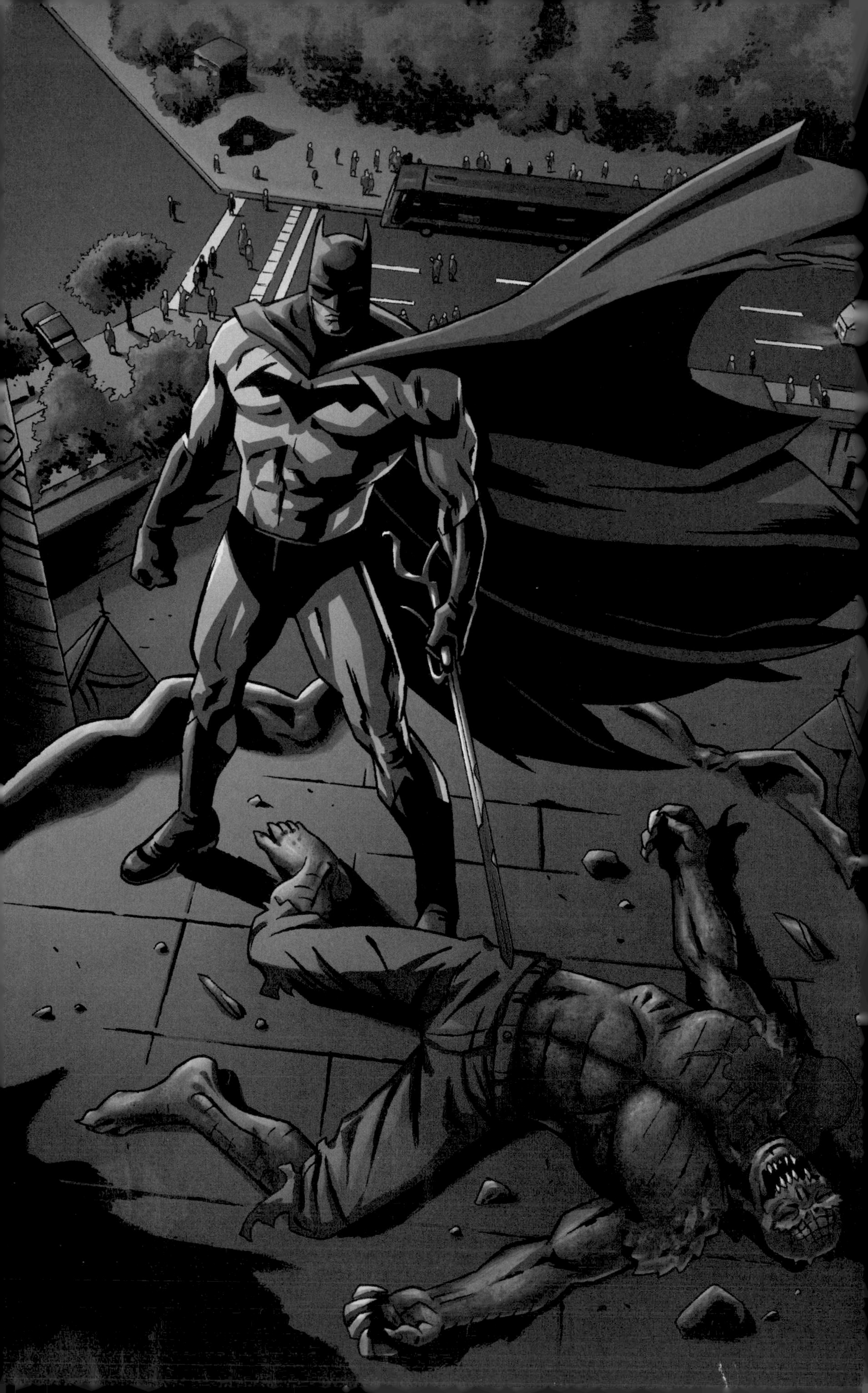

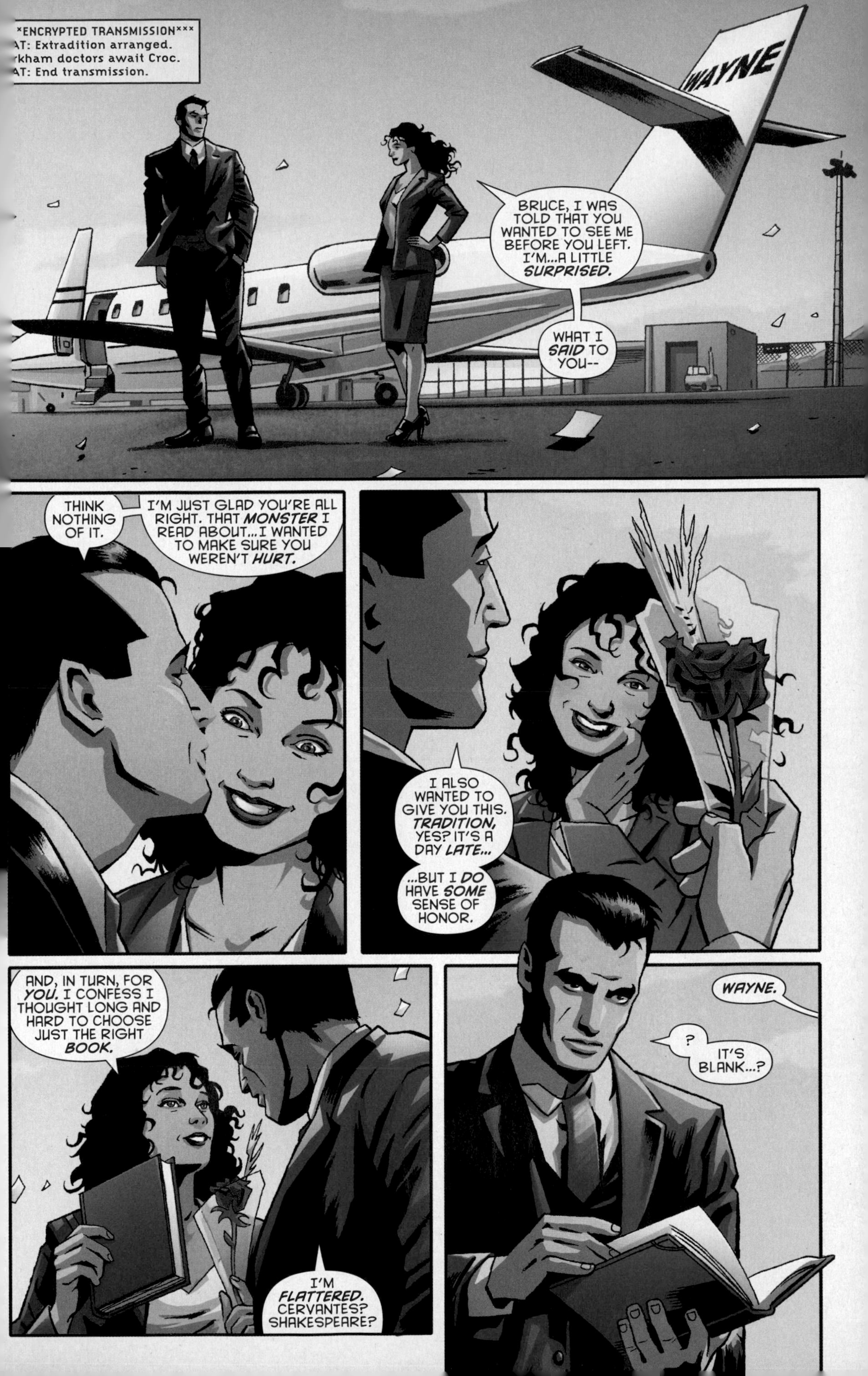
*ENCRYPTED TRANSMISSION***
AT: Extradition arranged.
rkham doctors await Croc.
AT: End transmission.
WAYNE
BRUCE, I WAS TOLD THAT YOU WANTED TO SEE ME BEFORE YOU LEFT. I'M...A LITTLE SURPRISED.
WHAT I SAID TO YOU--
THINK NOTHING OF IT.
I'M JUST GLAD YOU'RE ALL RIGHT. THAT MONSTER I READ ABOUT...I WANTED TO MAKE SURE YOU WEREN'T HURT.
I ALSO WANTED TO GIVE YOU THIS. TRADITION, YES? IT'S A DAY LATE...
...BUT I DO HAVE SOME SENSE OF HONOR.
AND, IN TURN, FOR YOU. I CONFESS I THOUGHT LONG AND HARD TO CHOOSE JUST THE RIGHT BOOK.
I'M FLATTERED. CERVANTES? SHAKESPEARE?
WAYNE.
?
IT'S BLANK...?

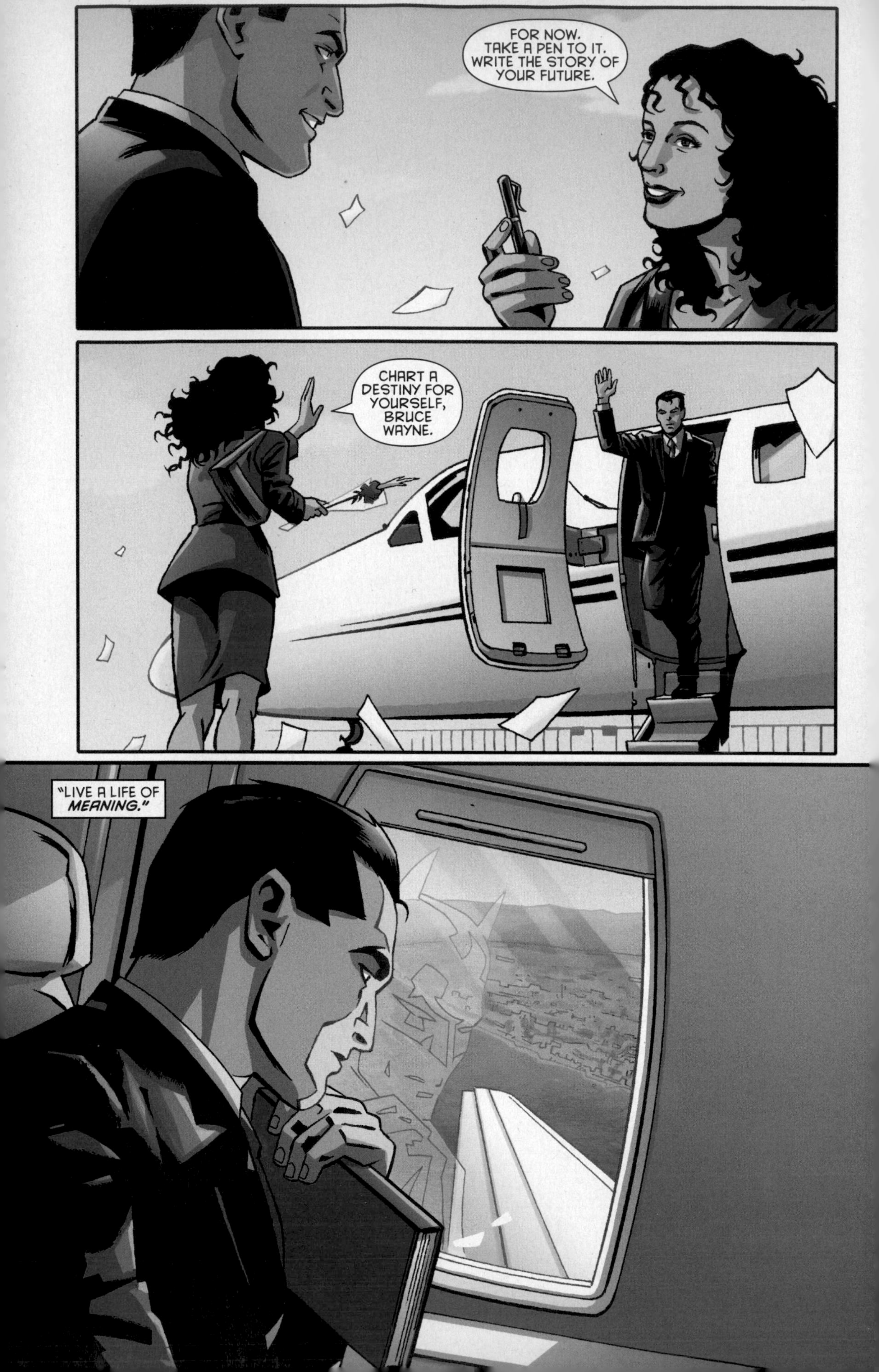
FOR NOW. TAKE A PEN TO IT. WRITE THE STORY OF YOUR FUTURE.
CHART A DESTINY FOR YOURSELF, BRUCE WAYNE.
"LIVE A LIFE OF MEANING."

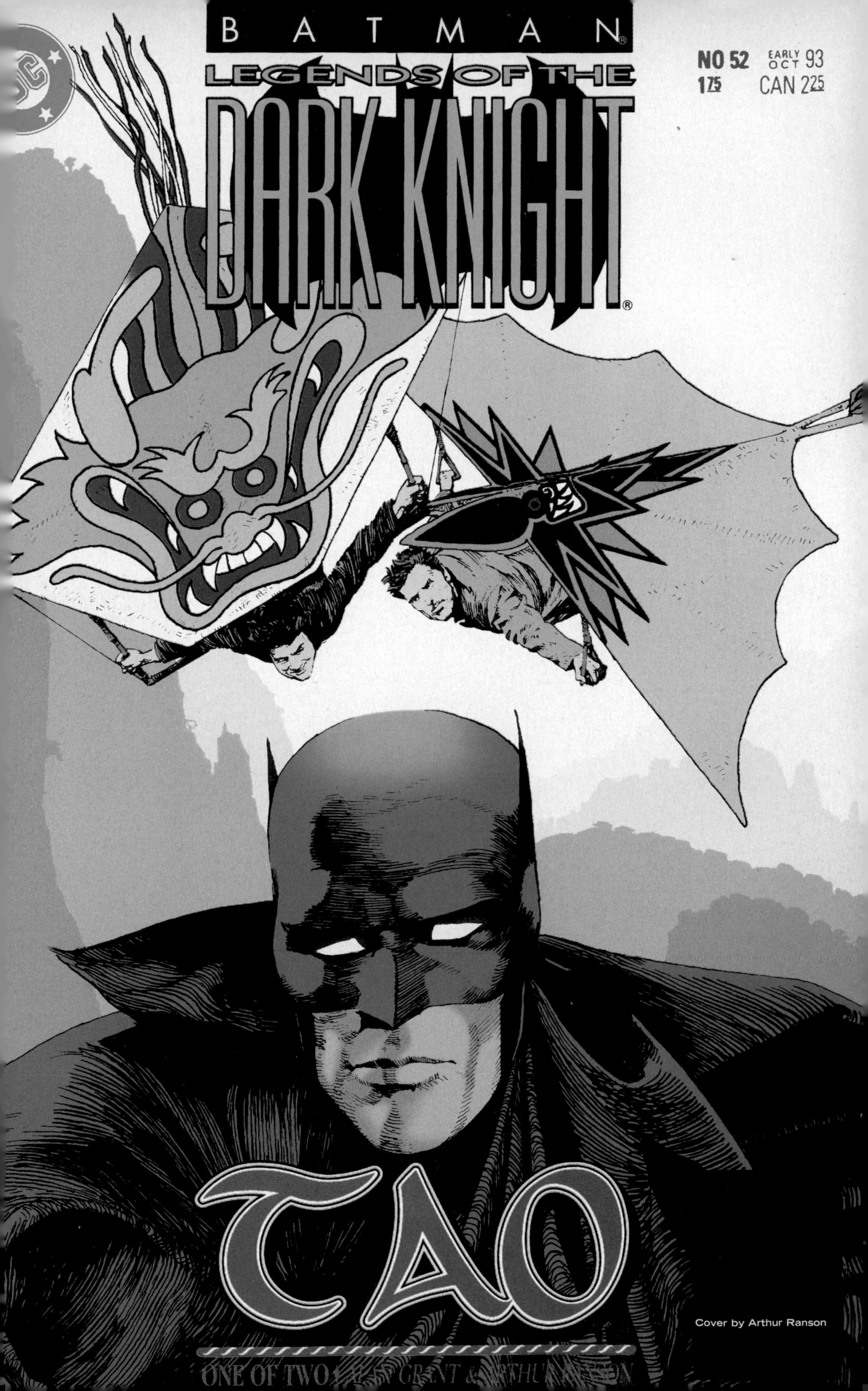
BATMAN
LEGENDS OF THE
DARK KNIGHT
NO 52
EARLY OCT 93
1.75
CAN 2.25
TAO
ONE OF TWO
Cover by Arthur Ranson

TAO
PART ONE

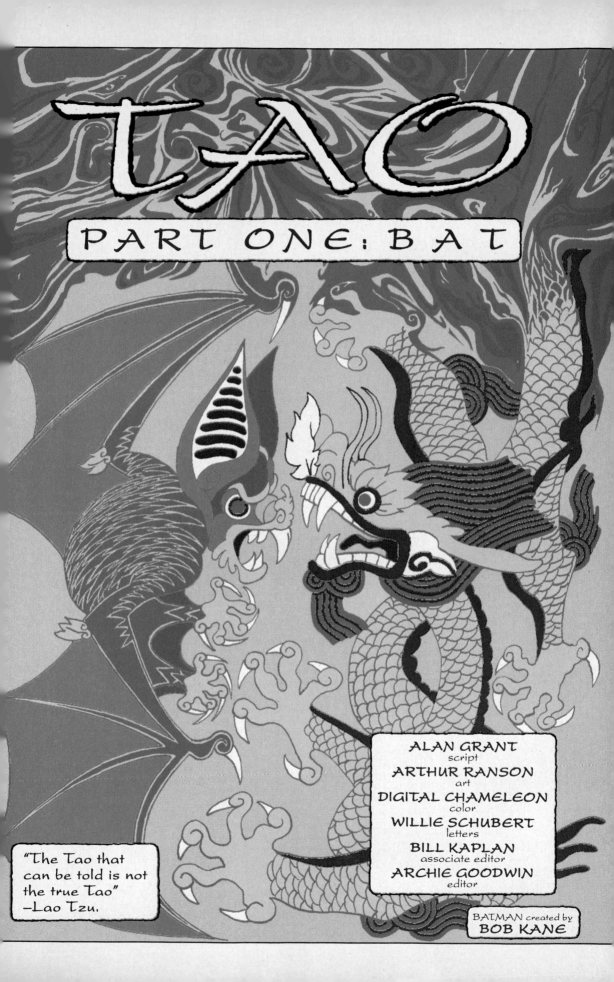

TAO

PART ONE: BAT

ALAN GRANT
script

ARTHUR RANSON
art

DIGITAL CHAMELEON
color

WILLIE SCHUBERT
letters

BILL KAPLAN
associate editor

ARCHIE GOODWIN
editor

"The Tao that can be told is not the true Tao"
—Lao Tzu.

BATMAN created by
BOB KANE

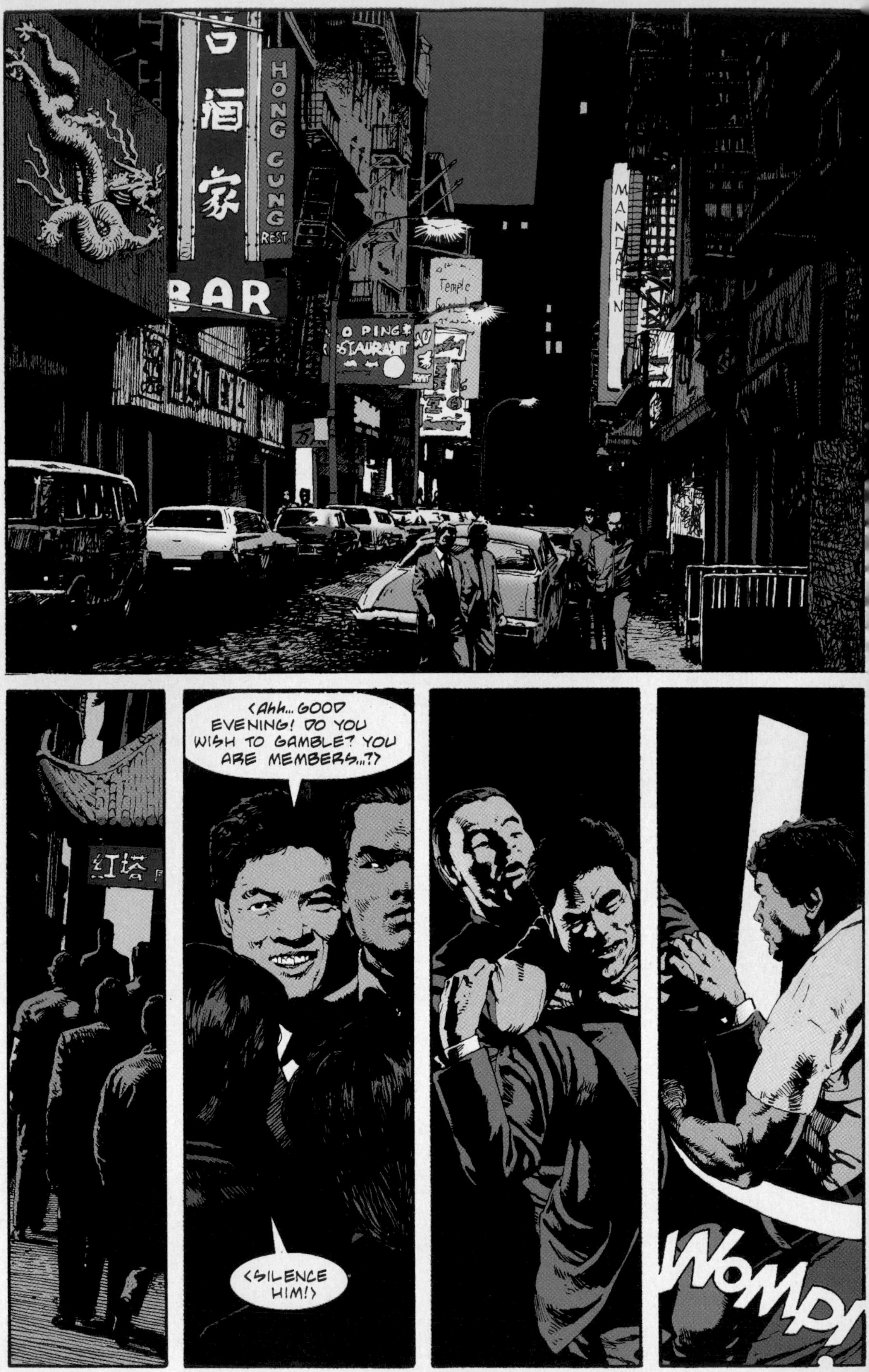
HONG GUNG REST.
BAR
O PING RESTAURANT
Temple
MANDARIN
<AHH... GOOD EVENING! DO YOU WISH TO GAMBLE? YOU ARE MEMBERS...?>
<SILENCE HIM!>
WOMP!

<WHAT IN THE NAME--?>

<LO WEN SHO!>

<WE HAVE COME TO COLLECT YOUR GAMBLING TAX.>

<NO! I HAVE A LICENSE-- I PAY THE CITY!>

<GO BACK TO YOUR MASTER. TELL HIM LO WEN SHO DOES NOT BOW BEFORE THUGS AND GANGSTERS!>

<THEN YOUR HEAD ROLLS, FOOL--!>

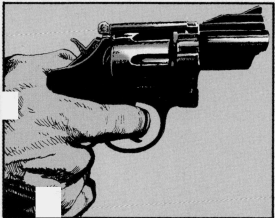

THWIP!

THWIT!

<WHAT--?>

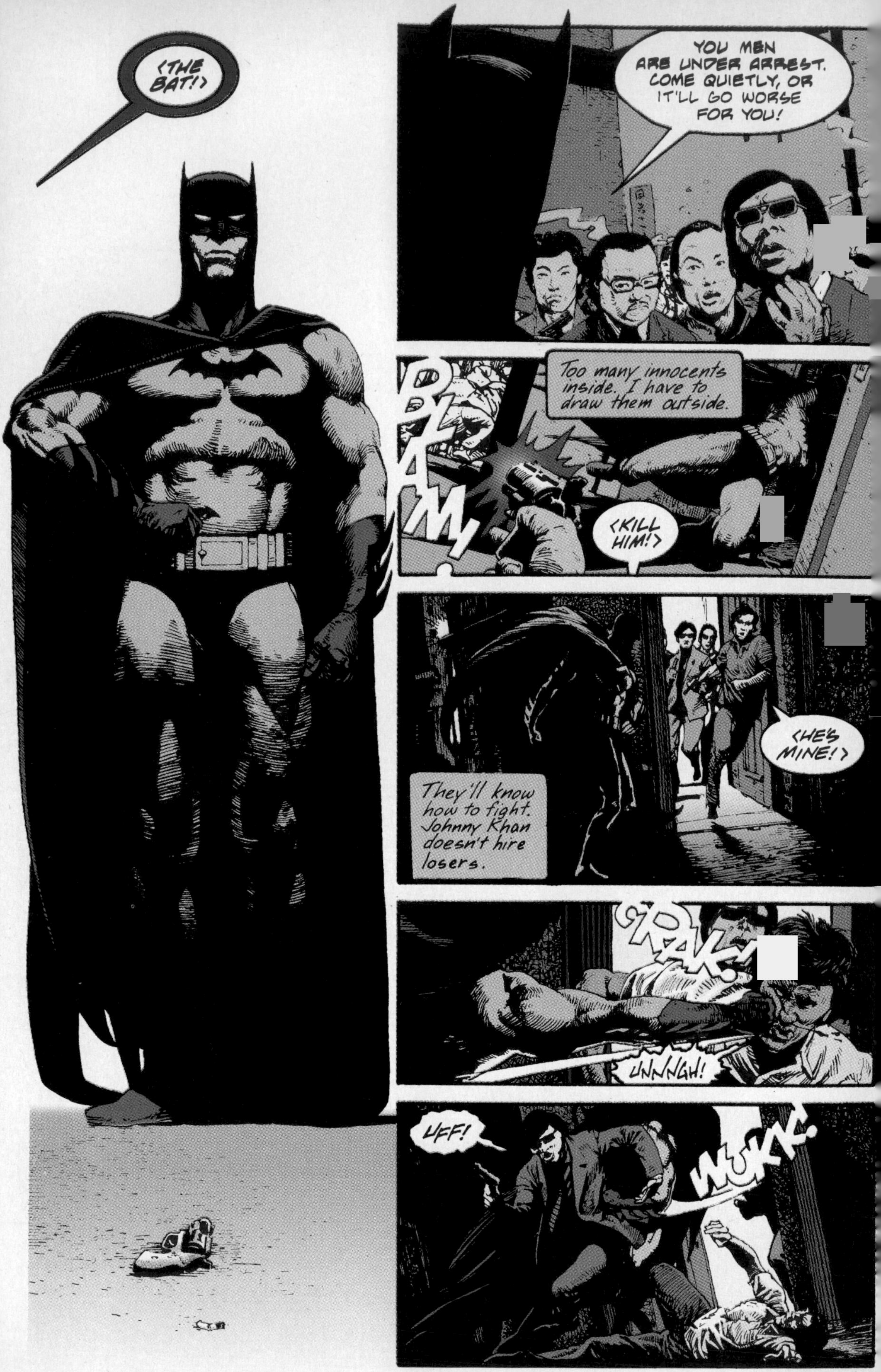

<THE BAT!>
YOU MEN ARE UNDER ARREST. COME QUIETLY, OR IT'LL GO WORSE FOR YOU!
Too many innocents inside. I have to draw them outside.
BLAM!
<KILL HIM!>
They'll know how to fight. Johnny Khan doesn't hire losers.
<HE'S MINE!>
KRAK!
UNNNGH!
UFF!
WUKK!

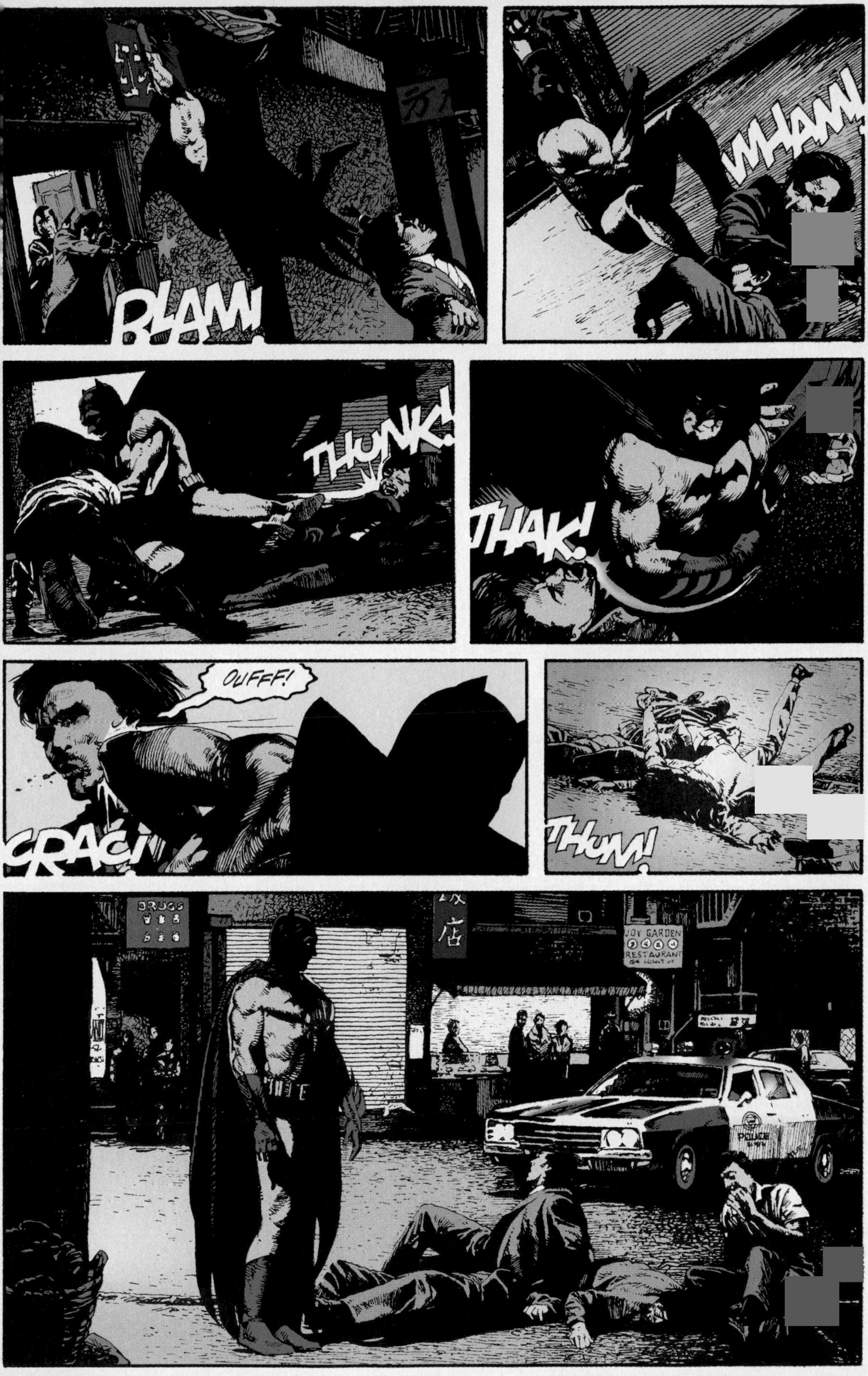
BLAM!
WHAM!
THUNK!
THAK!
OUFFF!
CRACK!
THUMP!
DRUGS
JOY GARDEN
RESTAURANT
POLICE

‹--YOUR FORTUNE TOLD, YOUNG SIR?›

‹ENTER! GOOD LUCK OR MISFORTUNE--A LOVELY WIFE OR A SHREW.... THE TORTOISE SHELL WILL SHOW ALL YOUR TOMORROWS!›

‹SIT, SIT!›

‹MAY THE STAR-GODS BLESS THIS AUGURY. MAY YOU FIND THE FORTUNE YOU SEEK.›

KRAAAK!

‹D-DEATH!›

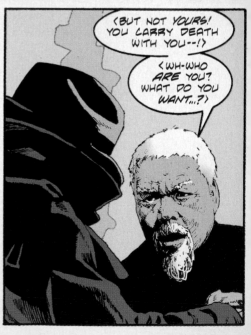

‹BUT NOT YOURS! YOU CARRY DEATH WITH YOU--!›

‹WH-WHO ARE YOU? WHAT DO YOU WANT...?›

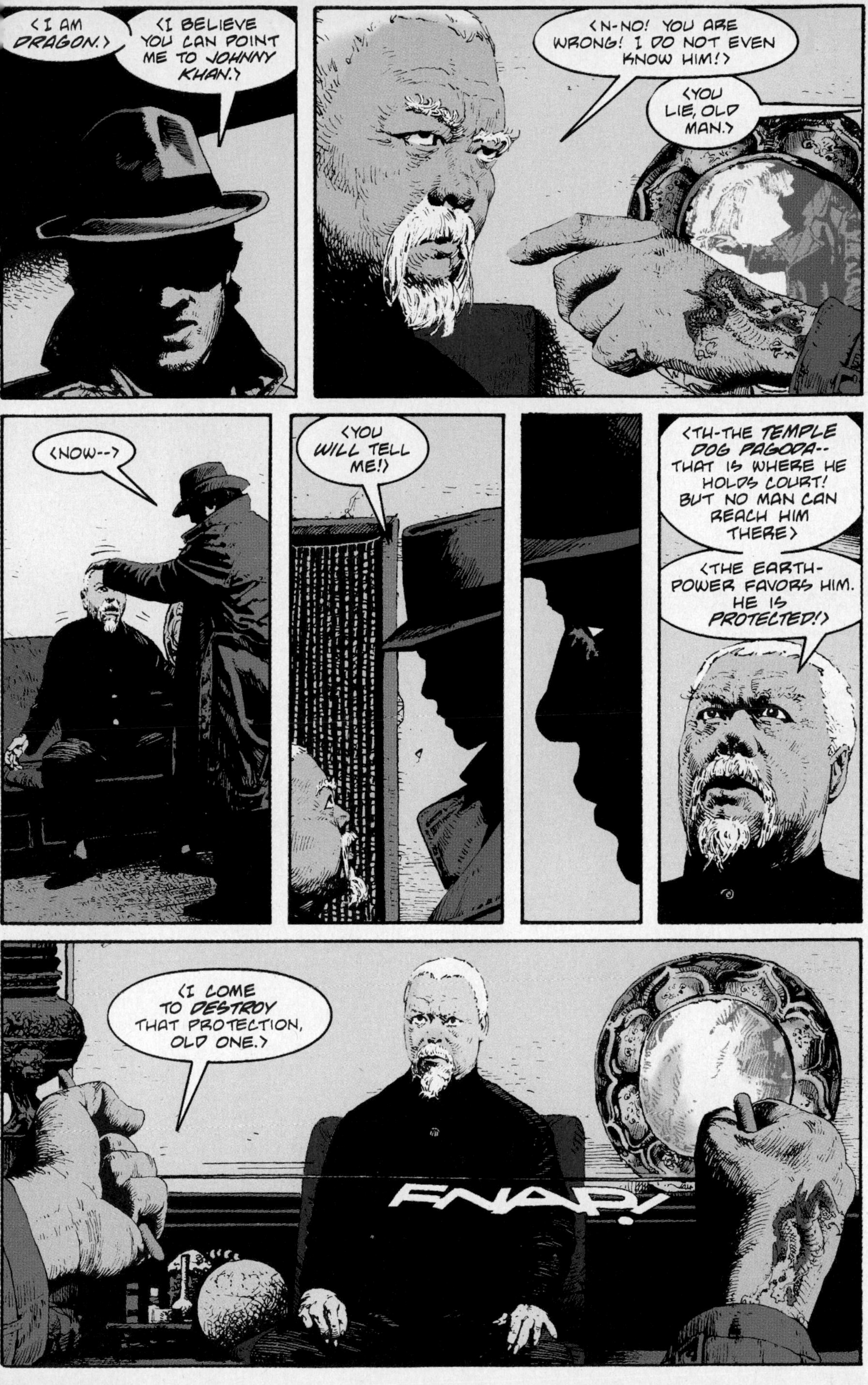

<I AM DRAGON.>
<I BELIEVE YOU CAN POINT ME TO JOHNNY KHAN.>
<N-NO! YOU ARE WRONG! I DO NOT EVEN KNOW HIM!>
<YOU LIE, OLD MAN.>
<NOW-->
<YOU WILL TELL ME!>
<TH-THE TEMPLE DOG PAGODA-- THAT IS WHERE HE HOLDS COURT! BUT NO MAN CAN REACH HIM THERE>
<THE EARTH-POWER FAVORS HIM. HE IS PROTECTED!>
<I COME TO DESTROY THAT PROTECTION, OLD ONE.>
FNAP!

<YOU WILL HELP ME.>

LET THE MIRROR ANCHOR YOU--

BIND YOUR GHOST--

TIE IT FOREVER TO THIS SPOT!

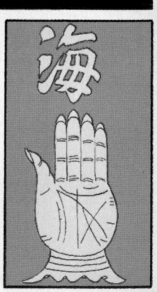

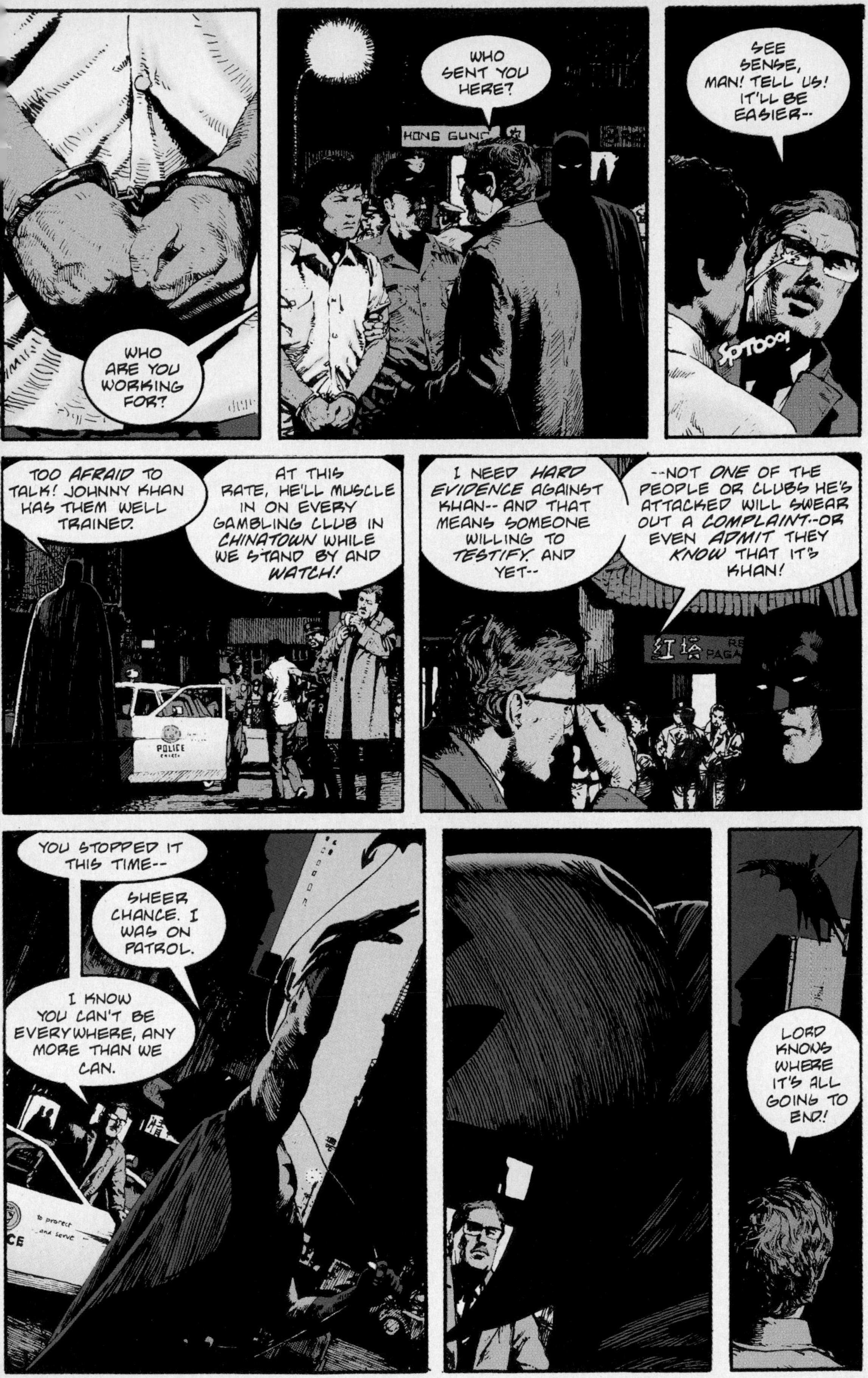
WHO ARE YOU WORKING FOR?
WHO SENT YOU HERE?
HONG GUNG
SEE SENSE, MAN! TELL US! IT'LL BE EASIER--
SPTOOO!
TOO AFRAID TO TALK! JOHNNY KHAN HAS THEM WELL TRAINED.
AT THIS RATE, HE'LL MUSCLE IN ON EVERY GAMBLING CLUB IN CHINATOWN WHILE WE STAND BY AND WATCH!
POLICE
I NEED HARD EVIDENCE AGAINST KHAN-- AND THAT MEANS SOMEONE WILLING TO TESTIFY. AND YET--
--NOT ONE OF THE PEOPLE OR CLUBS HE'S ATTACKED WILL SWEAR OUT A COMPLAINT--OR EVEN ADMIT THEY KNOW THAT IT'S KHAN!
YOU STOPPED IT THIS TIME--
SHEER CHANCE. I WAS ON PATROL.
I KNOW YOU CAN'T BE EVERYWHERE, ANY MORE THAN WE CAN.
to protect and serve
LORD KNOWS WHERE IT'S ALL GOING TO END!

<HIM?>

<CAN IT BE?>

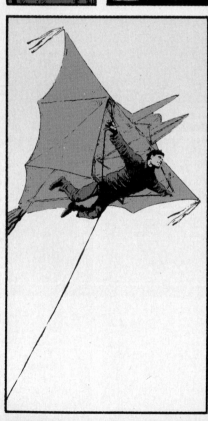

<HERE?>

<TRULY THE STAR-GODS SMILE!>

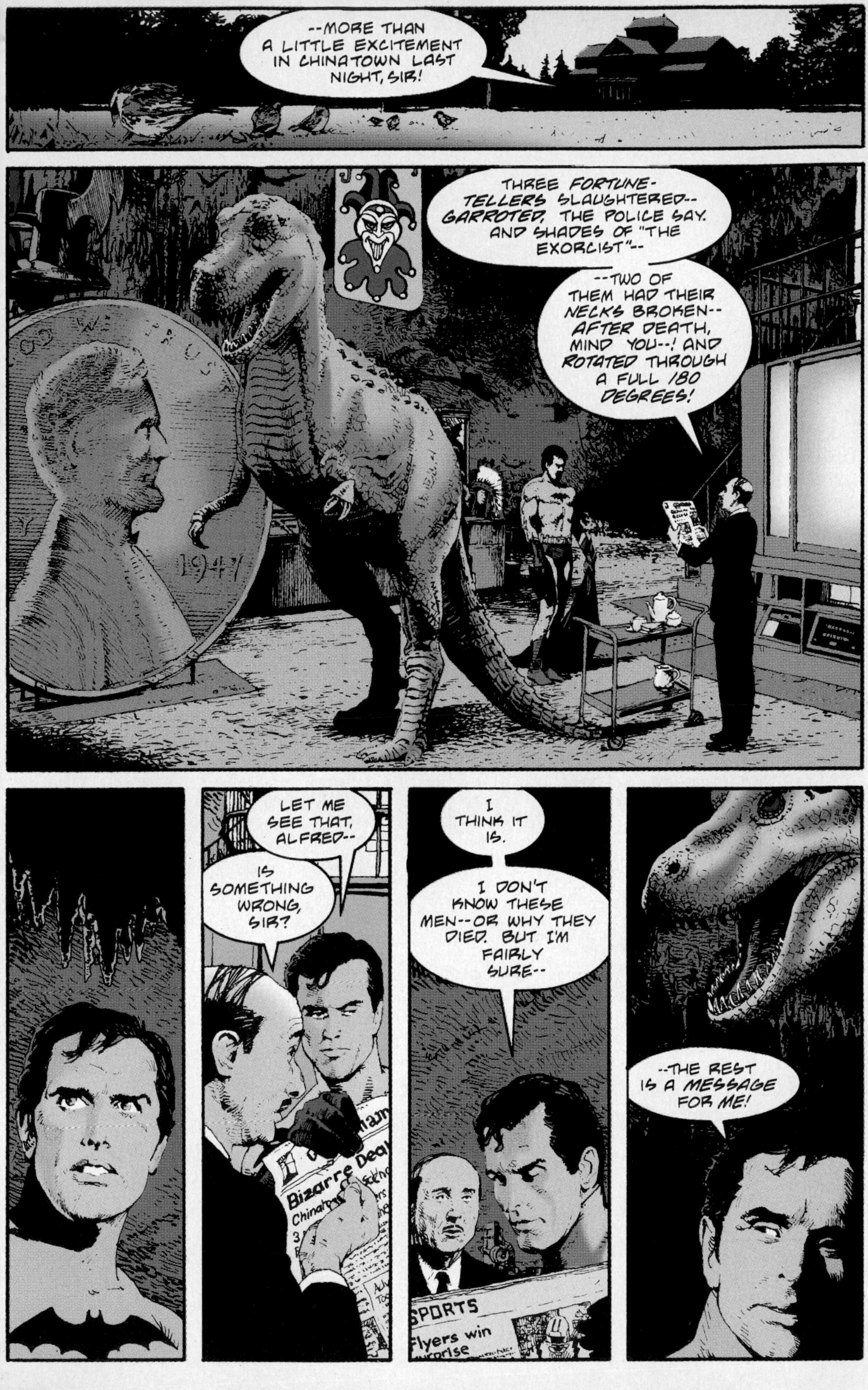
--MORE THAN A LITTLE EXCITEMENT IN CHINATOWN LAST NIGHT, SIR!
THREE FORTUNE-TELLERS SLAUGHTERED--GARROTED, THE POLICE SAY. AND SHADES OF "THE EXORCIST"--
--TWO OF THEM HAD THEIR NECKS BROKEN--AFTER DEATH, MIND YOU--! AND ROTATED THROUGH A FULL 180 DEGREES!
LET ME SEE THAT, ALFRED--
IS SOMETHING WRONG, SIR?
Bizarre Deal
Chinatown
I THINK IT IS.
I DON'T KNOW THESE MEN--OR WHY THEY DIED. BUT I'M FAIRLY SURE--
SPORTS
Flyers win
--THE REST IS A MESSAGE FOR ME!

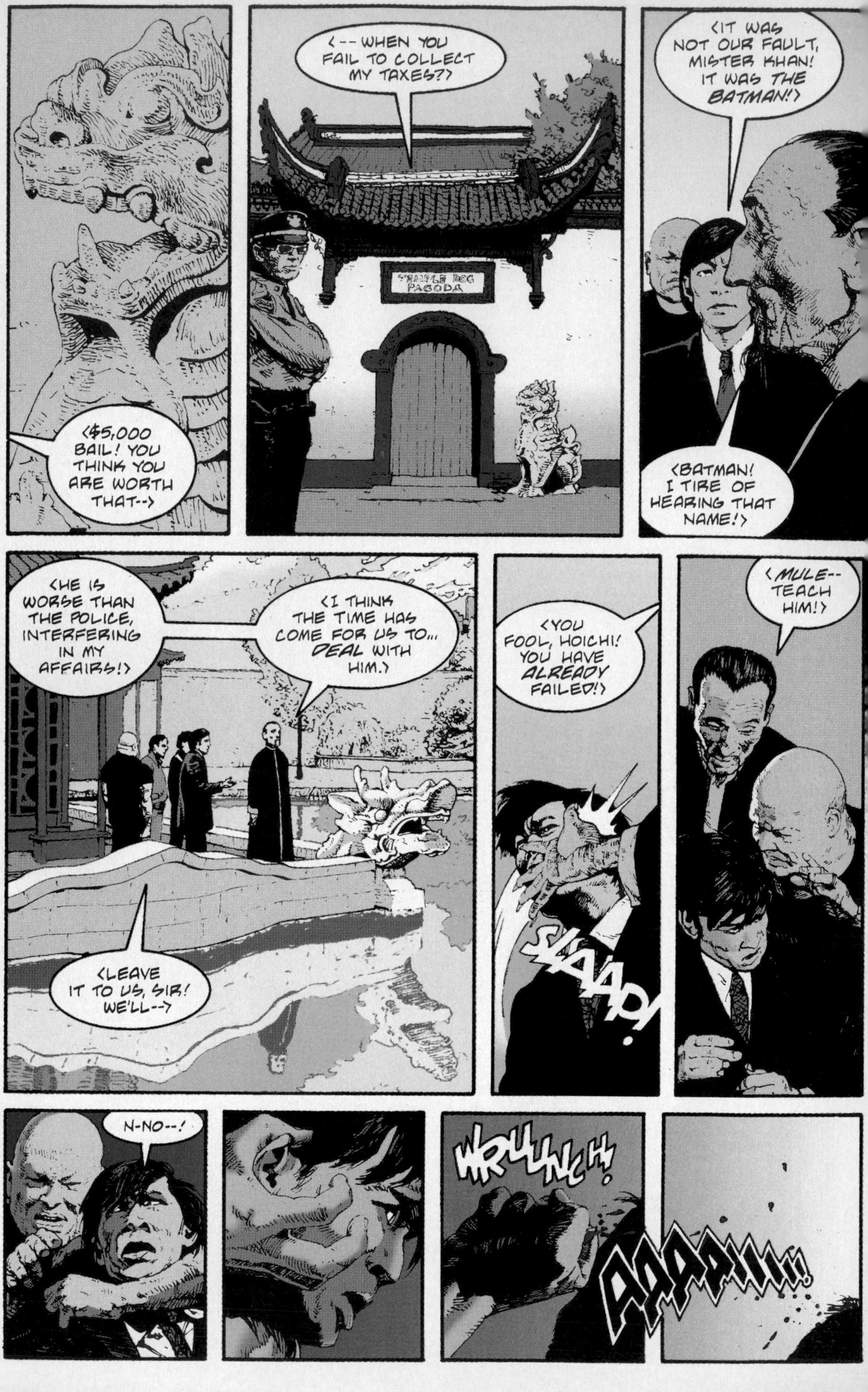
<$5,000 BAIL! YOU THINK YOU ARE WORTH THAT-->
<--WHEN YOU FAIL TO COLLECT MY TAXES?>
TEMPLE DOG PAGODA
<IT WAS NOT OUR FAULT, MISTER KHAN! IT WAS THE BATMAN!>
<BATMAN! I TIRE OF HEARING THAT NAME!>
<HE IS WORSE THAN THE POLICE, INTERFERING IN MY AFFAIRS!>
<I THINK THE TIME HAS COME FOR US TO... DEAL WITH HIM.>
<LEAVE IT TO US, SIR! WE'LL-->
<YOU FOOL, HOICHI! YOU HAVE ALREADY FAILED!>
SLAAAP!
<MULE--TEACH HIM!>
N-NO--!
WRUUNCH!
AAAAIIII!

<LET THIS BE A REMINDER TO ALL OF YOU. FAIL ME AGAIN, AND-->

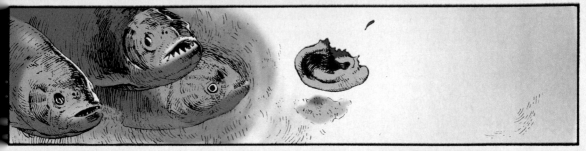

<--THAT WILL BE YOUR FATE!>

I DO NOT LIKE THIS. SOMETHING... FEELS WRONG.

BUT HOW, SIR? WE ARE PROTECTED--!

NEVERTHELESS... A WISE MAN RELIES ON NOTHING. DOUBLE THE GUARD. PUT ALL THE MEN ON ALERT.

SOMETHING IS GOING TO HAPPEN!

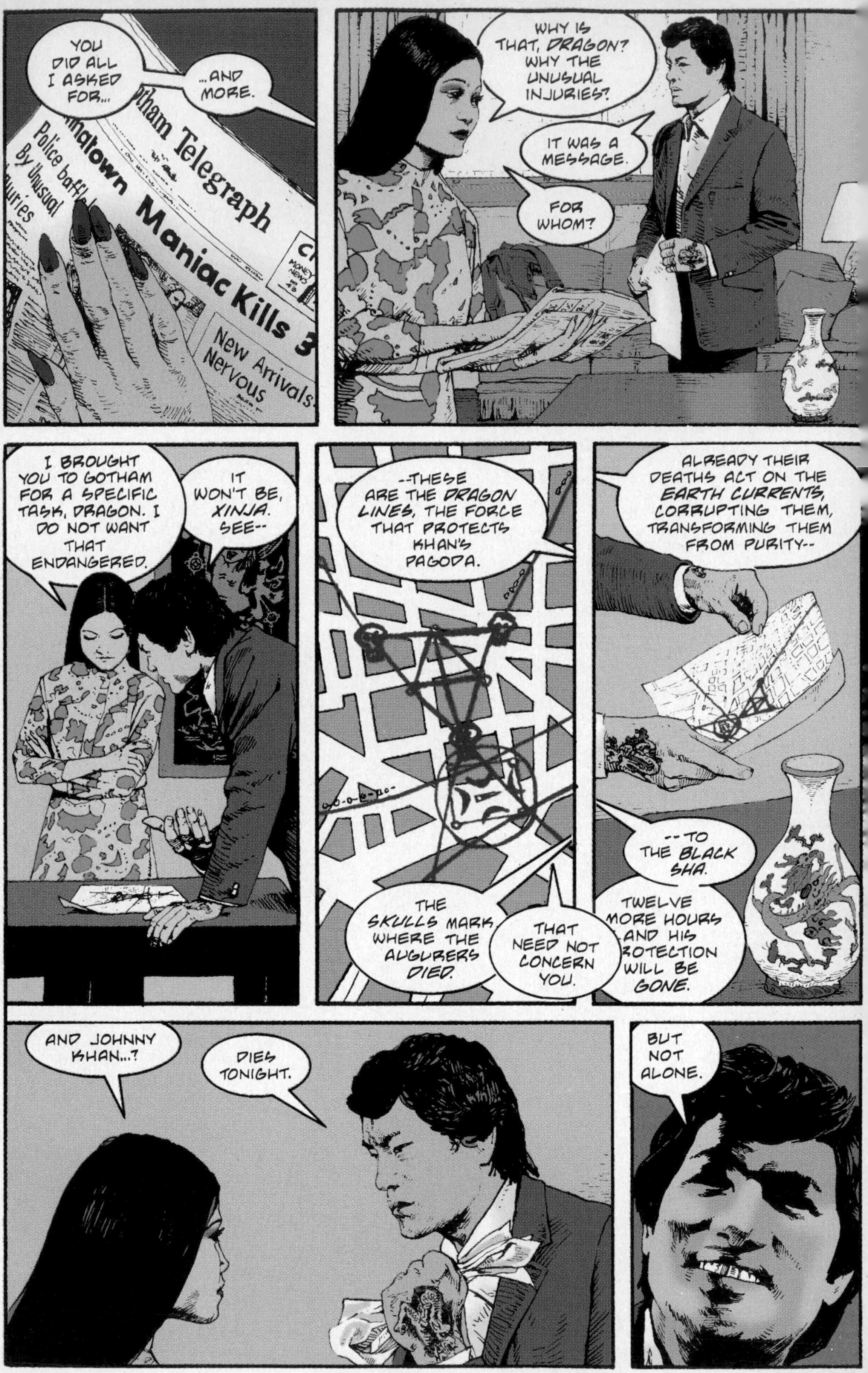
YOU DID ALL I ASKED FOR...
...AND MORE.
Gotham Telegraph
Chinatown Maniac Kills 3
Police baffled By Unusual Injuries
New Arrivals Nervous
WHY IS THAT, DRAGON? WHY THE UNUSUAL INJURIES?
IT WAS A MESSAGE.
FOR WHOM?
I BROUGHT YOU TO GOTHAM FOR A SPECIFIC TASK, DRAGON. I DO NOT WANT THAT ENDANGERED.
IT WON'T BE, XINJA. SEE--
--THESE ARE THE DRAGON LINES, THE FORCE THAT PROTECTS KHAN'S PAGODA.
THE SKULLS MARK WHERE THE AUGURERS DIED.
THAT NEED NOT CONCERN YOU.
ALREADY THEIR DEATHS ACT ON THE EARTH CURRENTS, CORRUPTING THEM, TRANSFORMING THEM FROM PURITY--
--TO THE BLACK SHA.
TWELVE MORE HOURS AND HIS PROTECTION WILL BE GONE.
AND JOHNNY KHAN...?
DIES TONIGHT.
BUT NOT ALONE.

IT'S CALLED FENG SHUI—THE ART OF GEOMANCY.

THE CHINESE BELIEVE THAT LINES OF FORCE—OR ENERGY CURRENTS—CRISS-CROSS THE SURFACE OF THE EARTH.

LIKE THE ENGLISH LEY LINES...?

MORE OR LESS. THEY'RE GENERALLY HELD TO BE BENEVOLENT—AND CONTROLLABLE.

STORY IS THAT JOHNNY KHAN USED GEOMANCERS TO SITE HIS PAGODA—HENCE ITS "PROTECTED" STATUS.

BUT SOMEONE WHO KNOWS WHAT HE'S DOING CAN CHANGE THE ENERGIES—CORRUPT THEM—AND WARP THEIR INFLUENCE TO EVIL.

THAT'S WHY THOSE FORTUNE TELLERS DIED!

YOU SAID IT WAS A MESSAGE FOR YOU, SIR?

IN MEDIEVAL TIMES IT WAS BELIEVED THAT WHEN A FORTUNE TELLER DIED, HE WENT STRAIGHT TO HELL. THERE, HIS HEAD WAS TWISTED SO HE COULD ONLY EVER LOOK BEHIND HIM—

—PUNISHMENT FOR TRYING TO PLAY AT GOD.

SURELY THAT WAS A CHRISTIAN BELIEF...?

YES. THAT'S HOW I KNOW THE KILLER'S TALKING TO ME.

I DON'T UNDERSTAND...?

HE'S REMINDING ME OF OUR PREVIOUS ENCOUNTERS...

During my studies in the East I'd heard a lot about Taoism. They said its practitioners were magicians-- alchemists--men of power who could read the future.

Those were secrets I wanted to know.

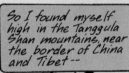

So I found myself high in the Tanggula Shan mountains, near the border of China and Tibet--

<MASTER SHAO-LA!>

<MASTER SHAO-LA...?>

<MASTER SHAO-LA!>

<SIR...?>

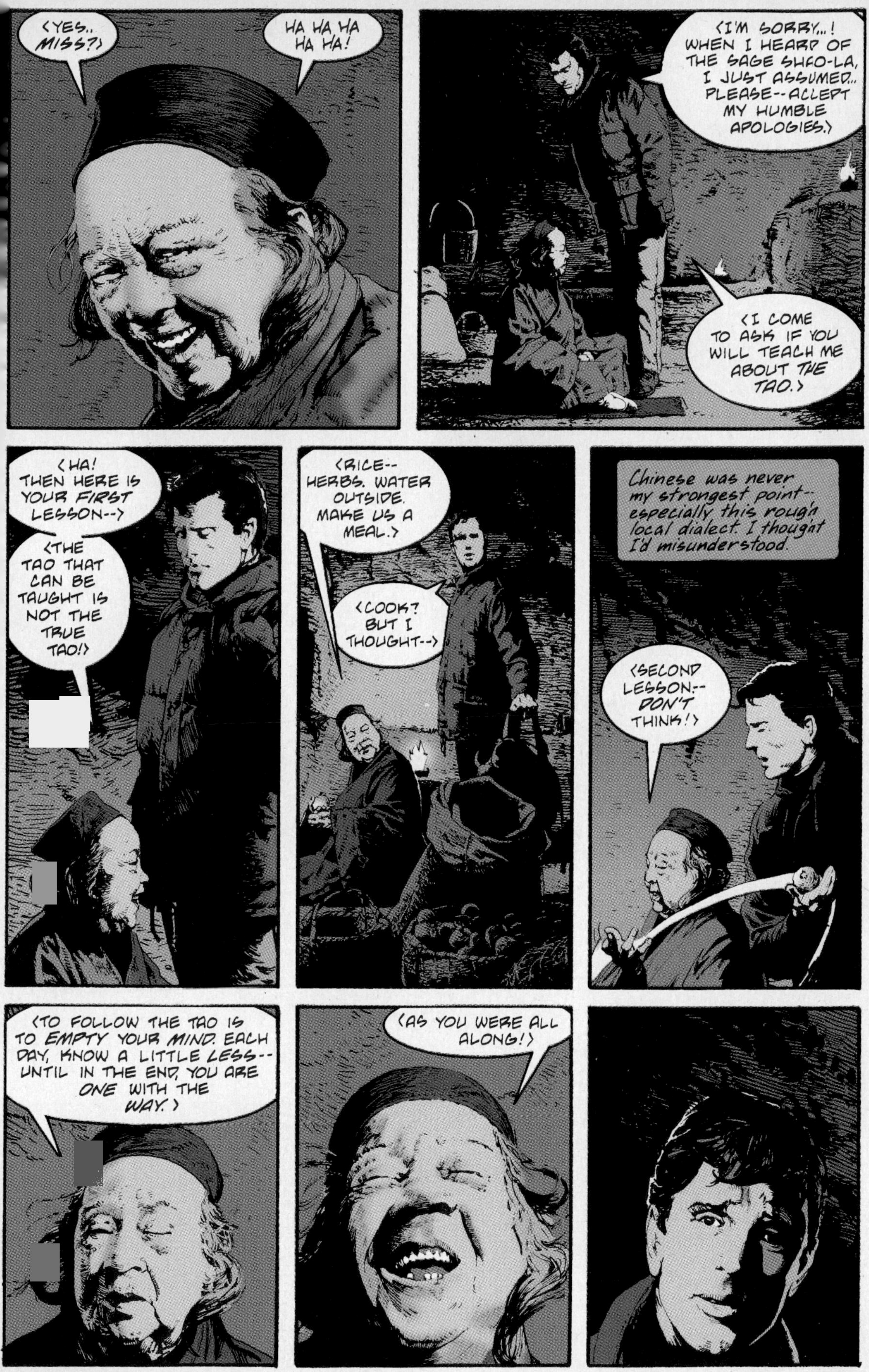
<YES.. MISS?>
HA HA HA HA HA!
<I'M SORRY...! WHEN I HEARD OF THE SAGE SHAO-LA, I JUST ASSUMED.. PLEASE--ACCEPT MY HUMBLE APOLOGIES.>
<I COME TO ASK IF YOU WILL TEACH ME ABOUT THE TAO.>
<HA! THEN HERE IS YOUR FIRST LESSON-->
<THE TAO THAT CAN BE TAUGHT IS NOT THE TRUE TAO!>
<RICE--HERBS. WATER OUTSIDE. MAKE US A MEAL.>
<COOK? BUT I THOUGHT-->
Chinese was never my strongest point--especially this rough local dialect. I thought I'd misunderstood.
<SECOND LESSON:--DON'T THINK!>
<TO FOLLOW THE TAO IS TO EMPTY YOUR MIND. EACH DAY, KNOW A LITTLE LESS--UNTIL IN THE END, YOU ARE ONE WITH THE WAY.>
<AS YOU WERE ALL ALONG!>

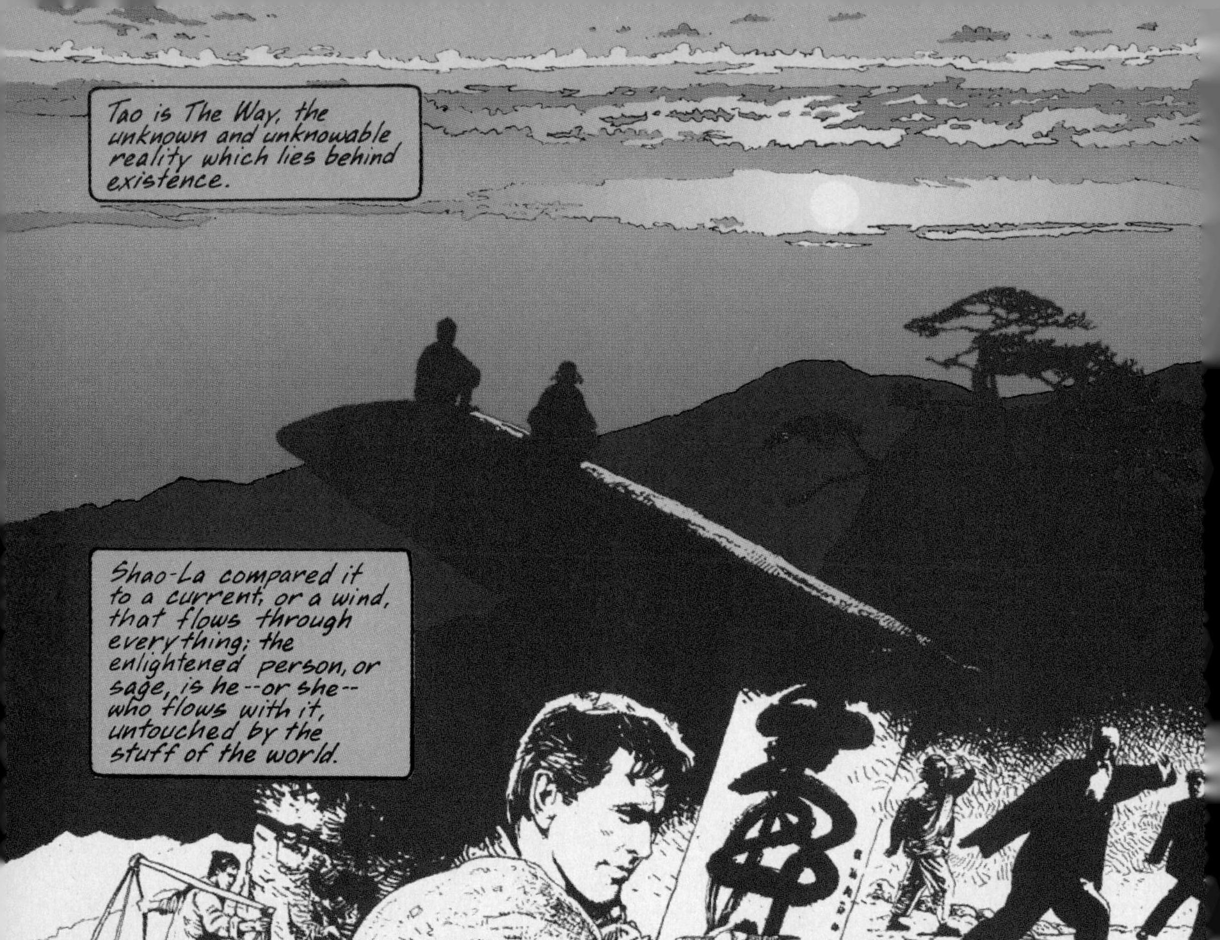

Tao is The Way, the unknown and unknowable reality which lies behind existence.
Shao-La compared it to a current, or a wind, that flows through everything; the enlightened person, or sage, is he--or she--who flows with it, untouched by the stuff of the world.

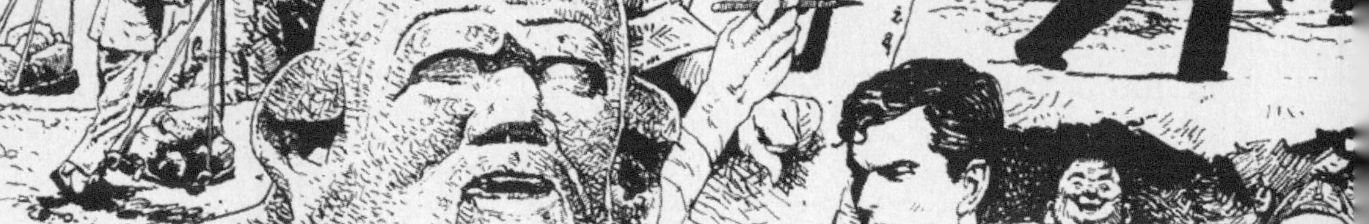

It's intuitive, anti-intellectual--and Shao-La had an interesting initiation--
‹YOU WANT ME TO WHAT?›

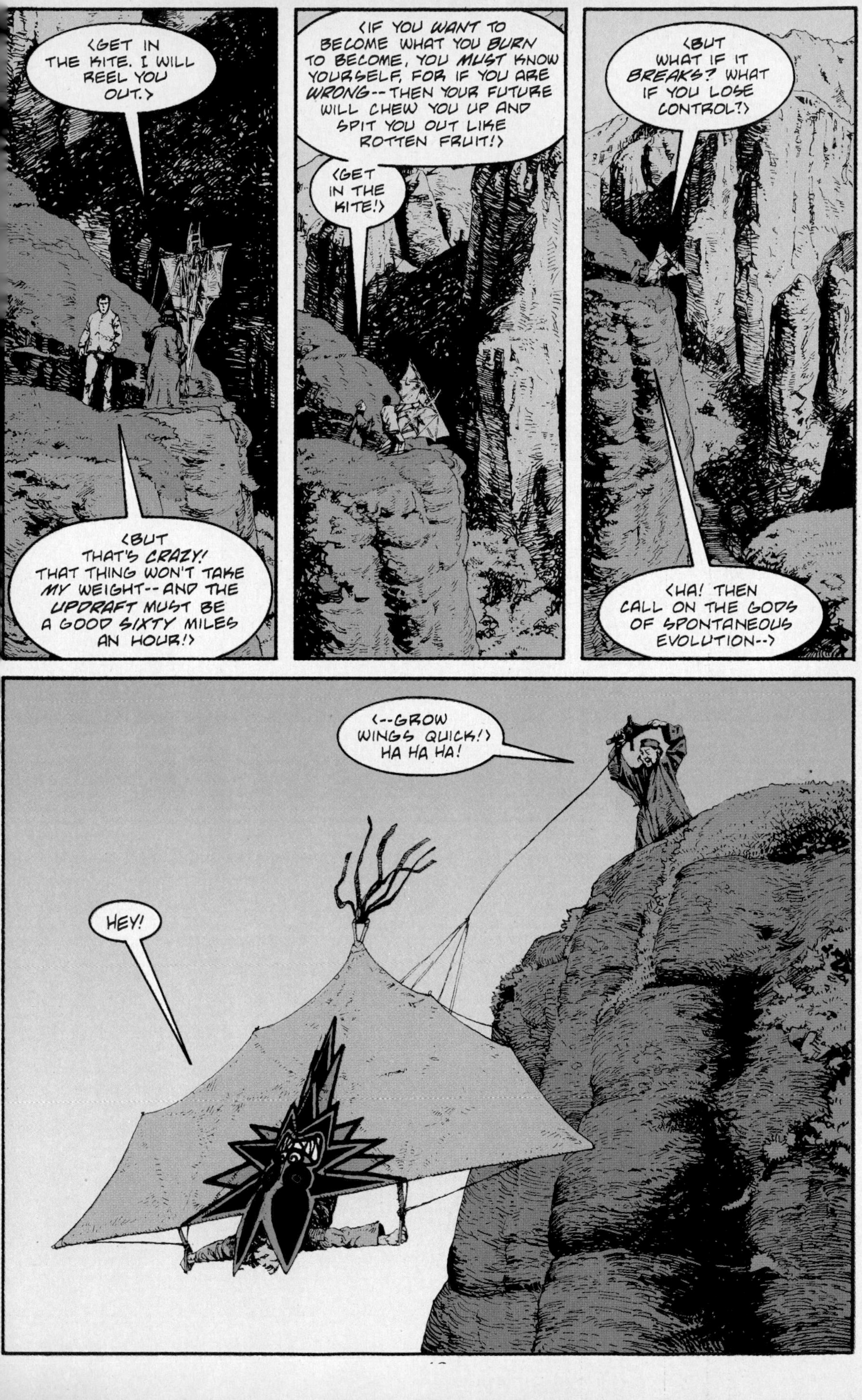
<GET IN THE KITE. I WILL REEL YOU OUT.>
<BUT THAT'S *CRAZY!* THAT THING WON'T TAKE *MY* WEIGHT--AND THE *UPDRAFT* MUST BE A GOOD *SIXTY* MILES AN HOUR!>
<IF YOU *WANT* TO BECOME WHAT YOU *BURN* TO BECOME, YOU *MUST* KNOW YOURSELF, FOR IF YOU ARE *WRONG*--THEN YOUR FUTURE WILL CHEW YOU UP AND SPIT YOU OUT LIKE ROTTEN FRUIT!>
<GET IN THE KITE!>
<BUT WHAT IF IT *BREAKS?* WHAT IF YOU LOSE CONTROL?>
<HA! THEN CALL ON THE GODS OF SPONTANEOUS EVOLUTION-->
<--GROW WINGS QUICK!> HA HA HA!
HEY!

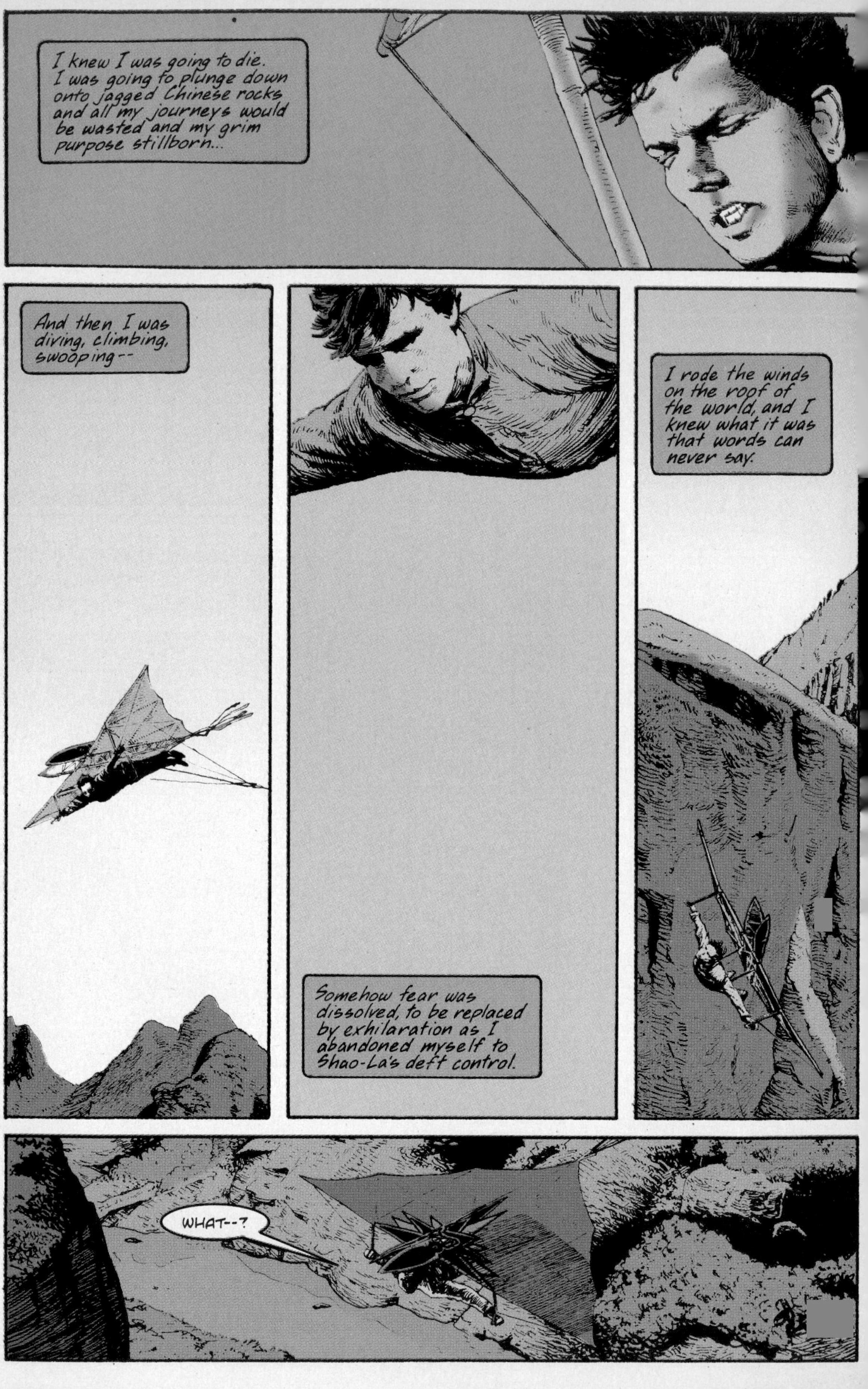
I knew I was going to die. I was going to plunge down onto jagged Chinese rocks and all my journeys would be wasted and my grim purpose stillborn...
And then I was diving, climbing, swooping--
Somehow fear was dissolved, to be replaced by exhilaration as I abandoned myself to Shao-La's deft control.
I rode the winds on the roof of the world, and I knew what it was that words can never say.
WHAT--?

WHAT IN THE NAME--?

HE'S CRAZY! WHERE DID HE GO--?

⟨H'SIEN-TAN... ENOUGH!⟩

⟨HE IS A WESTERNER! HE DOES NOT KNOW THE GAME!⟩

⟨H'SIEN-TAN! DO YOU HEAR?⟩

⟨ENOUGH!⟩

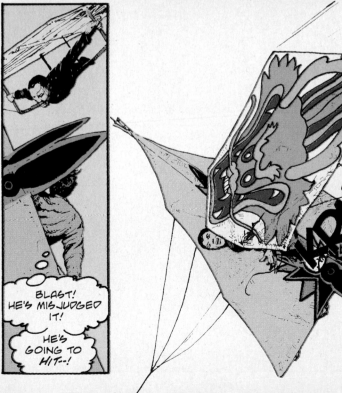

BLAST! HE'S MISJUDGED IT!

HE'S GOING TO HIT--!

KRAAK!

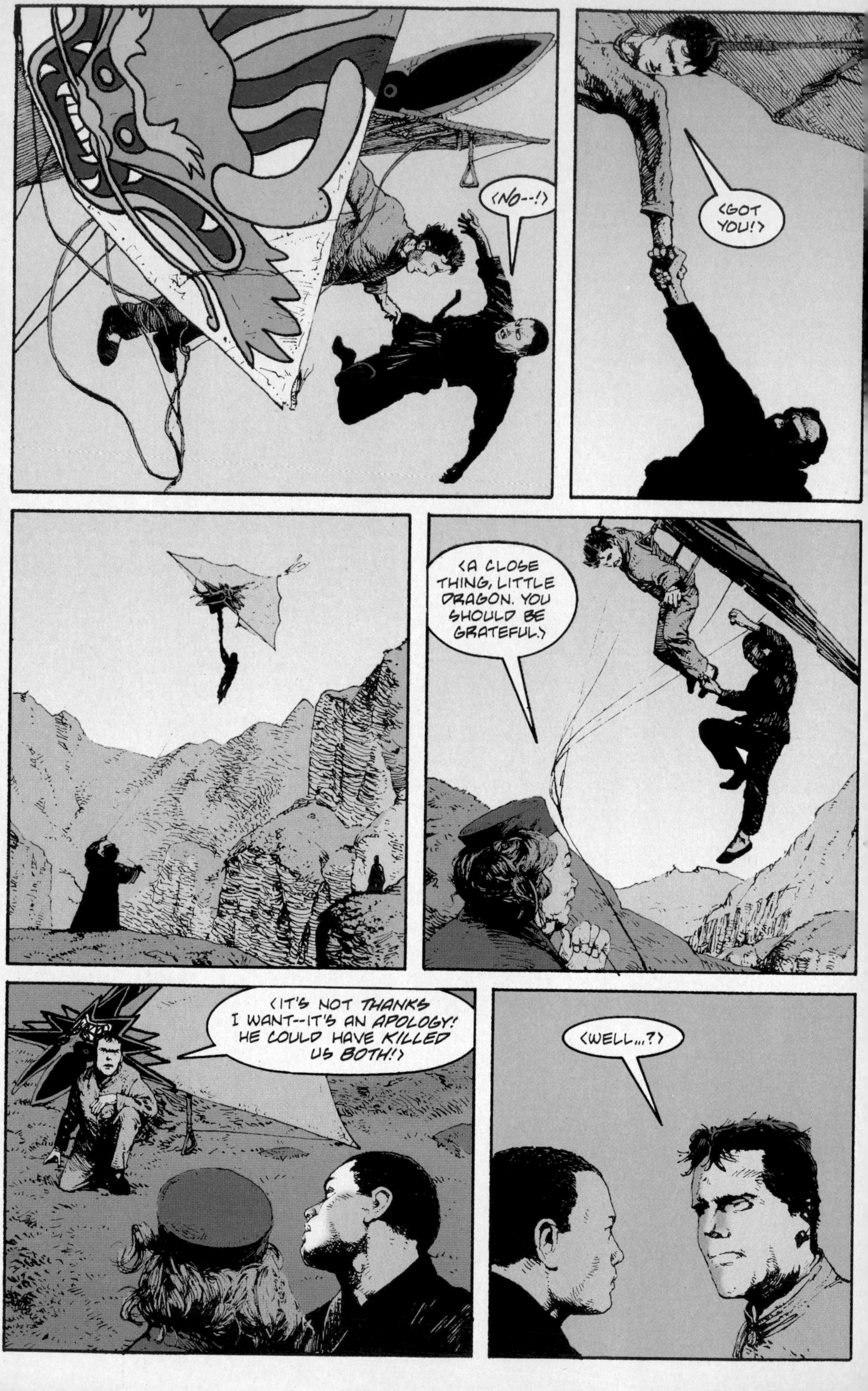
<NO--!>
<GOT YOU!>
<A CLOSE THING, LITTLE DRAGON. YOU SHOULD BE GRATEFUL.>
<IT'S NOT THANKS I WANT--IT'S AN APOLOGY! HE COULD HAVE KILLED US BOTH!>
<WELL...?>

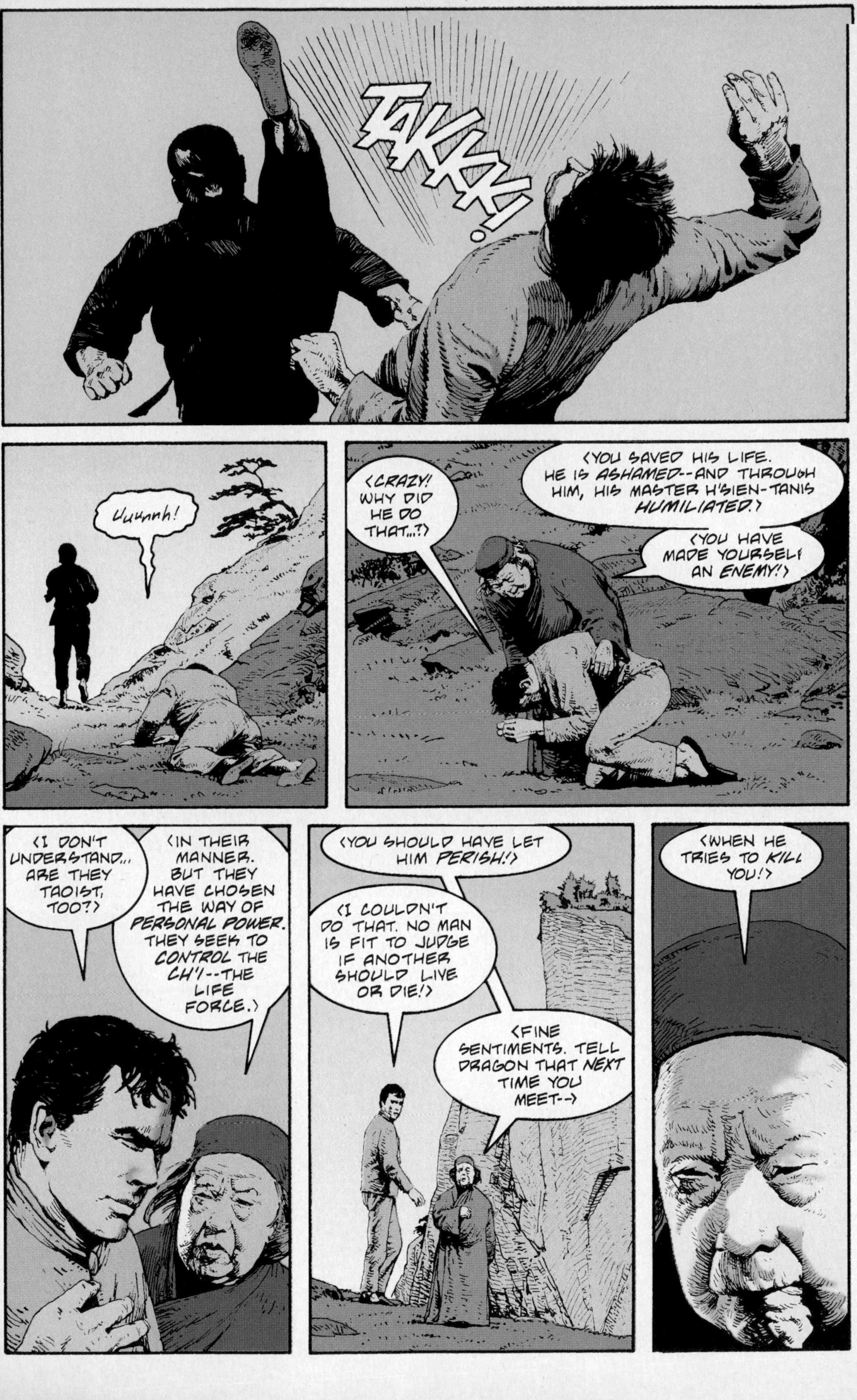
TAKKK!
Uuunnh!
<CRAZY! WHY DID HE DO THAT...?>
<YOU SAVED HIS LIFE. HE IS ASHAMED--AND THROUGH HIM, HIS MASTER H'SIEN-TANIS HUMILIATED.>
<YOU HAVE MADE YOURSELF AN ENEMY!>
<I DON'T UNDERSTAND... ARE THEY TAOIST, TOO?>
<IN THEIR MANNER. BUT THEY HAVE CHOSEN THE WAY OF PERSONAL POWER. THEY SEEK TO CONTROL THE CH'I--THE LIFE FORCE.>
<YOU SHOULD HAVE LET HIM PERISH!>
<I COULDN'T DO THAT. NO MAN IS FIT TO JUDGE IF ANOTHER SHOULD LIVE OR DIE!>
<FINE SENTIMENTS. TELL DRAGON THAT NEXT TIME YOU MEET-->
<WHEN HE TRIES TO KILL YOU!>

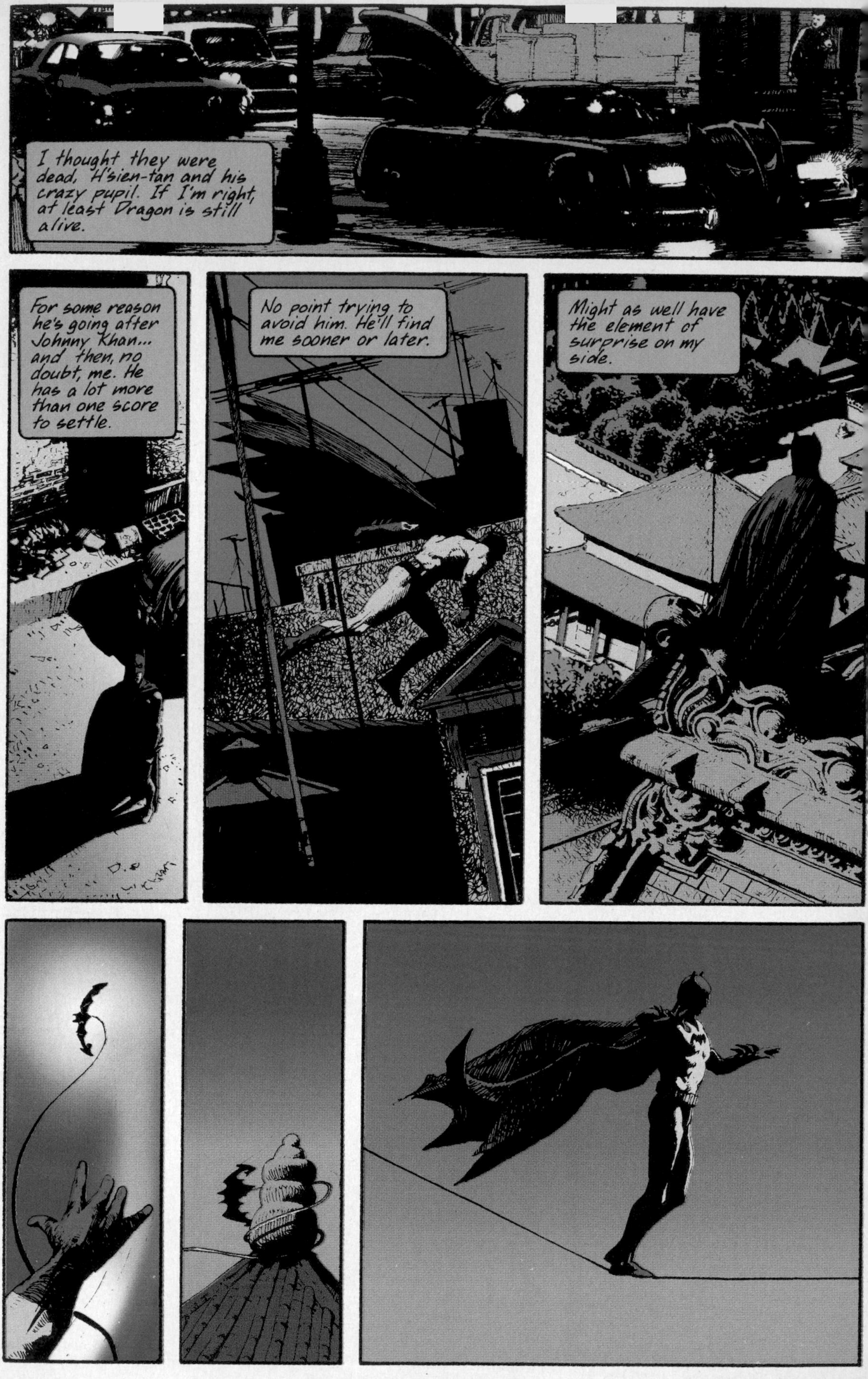
I thought they were dead, H'sien-tan and his crazy pupil. If I'm right, at least Dragon is still alive.
For some reason he's going after Johnny Khan... and then, no doubt, me. He has a lot more than one score to settle.
No point trying to avoid him. He'll find me sooner or later.
Might as well have the element of surprise on my side.

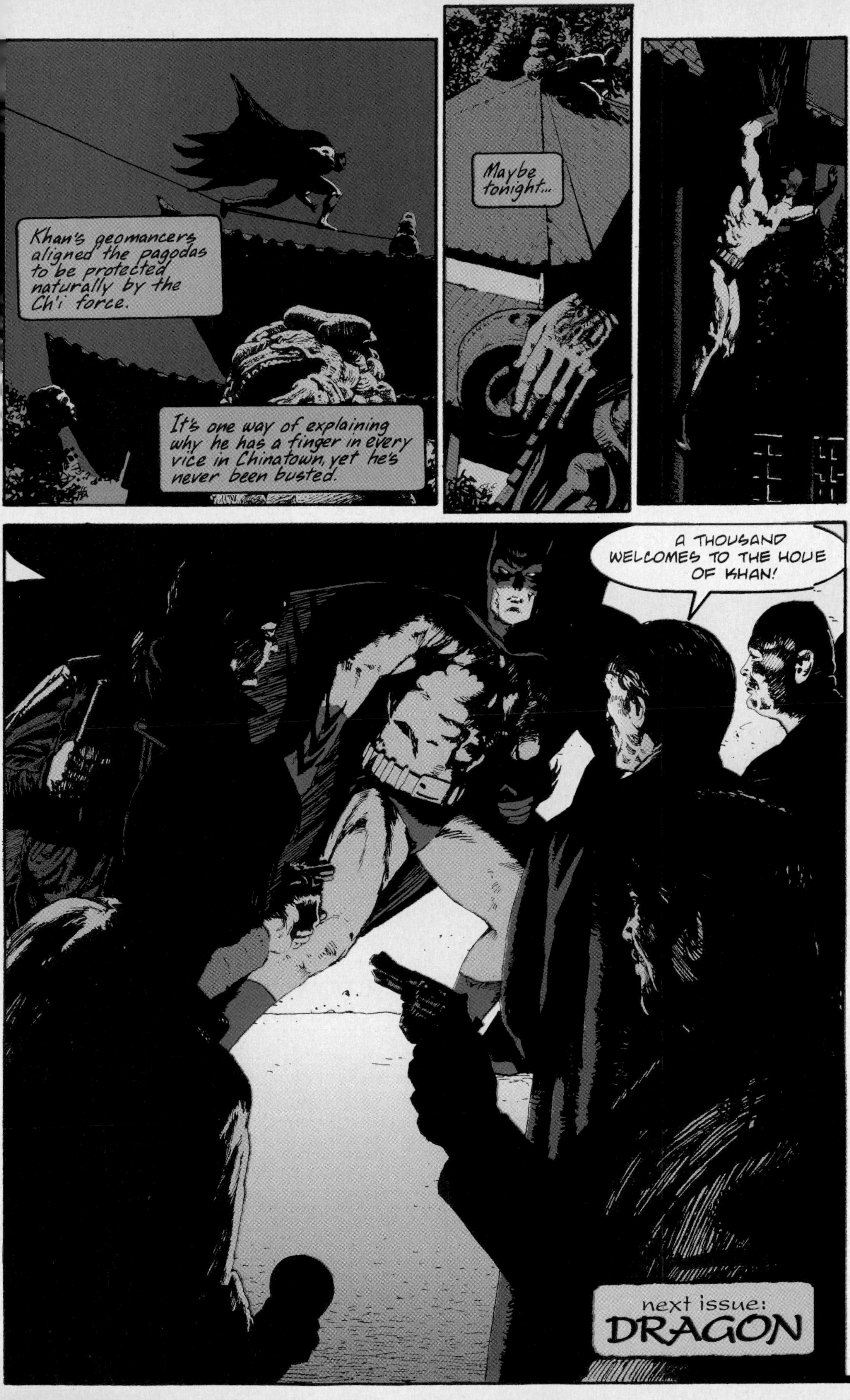
Khan's geomancers aligned the pagodas to be protected naturally by the Ch'i force.
It's one way of explaining why he has a finger in every vice in Chinatown, yet he's never been busted.
Maybe tonight...
A THOUSAND WELCOMES TO THE HOUE OF KHAN!
next issue: DRAGON

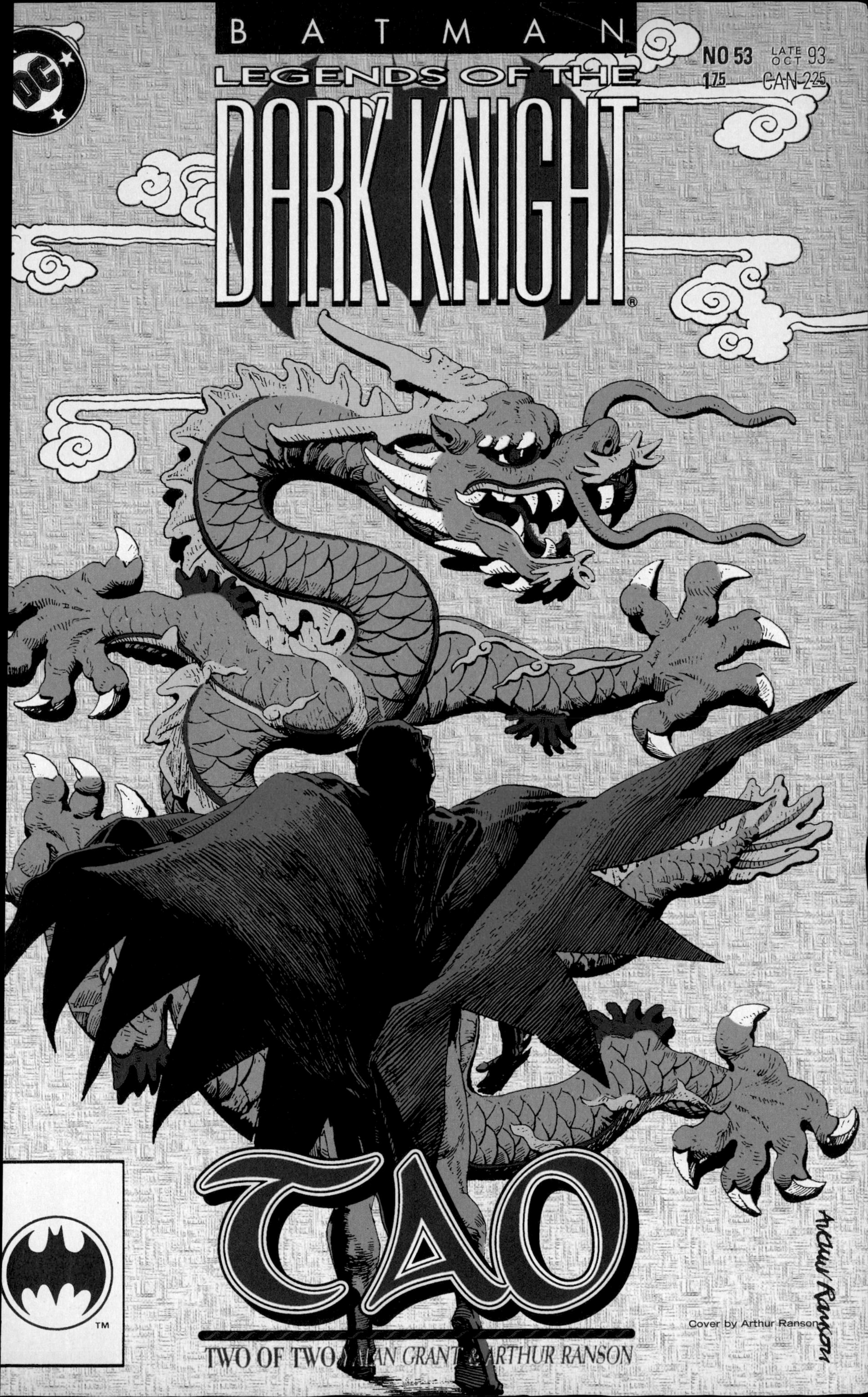
BATMAN
LEGENDS OF THE
DARK KNIGHT
NO 53
LATE OCT 93
1.75
CAN 2.25
TAO
TWO OF TWO · ALAN GRANT · ARTHUR RANSON
Cover by Arthur Ranson

TAO
PART TWO

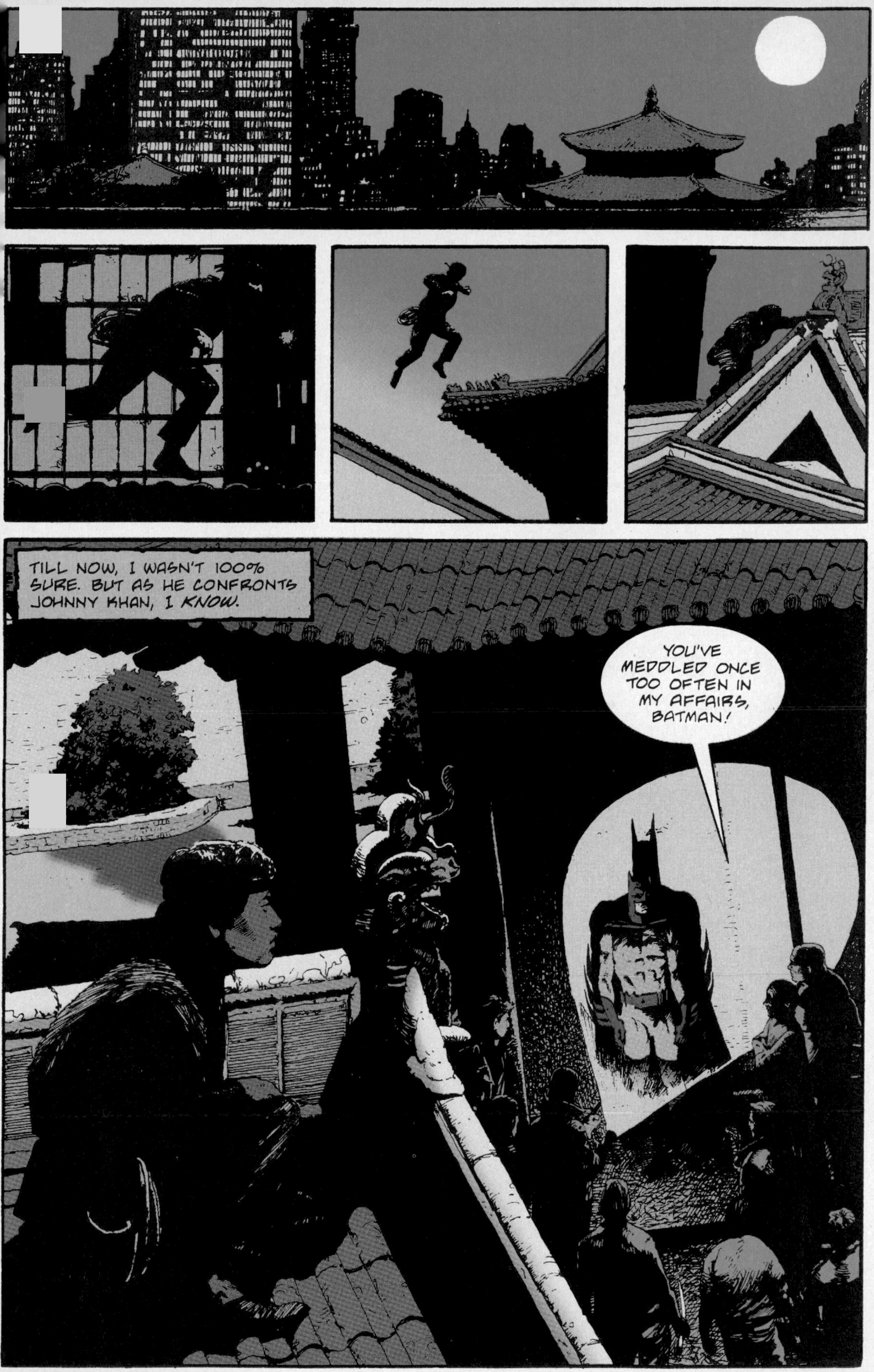
TILL NOW, I WASN'T 100% SURE. BUT AS HE CONFRONTS JOHNNY KHAN, I KNOW.
YOU'VE MEDDLED ONCE TOO OFTEN IN MY AFFAIRS, BATMAN!

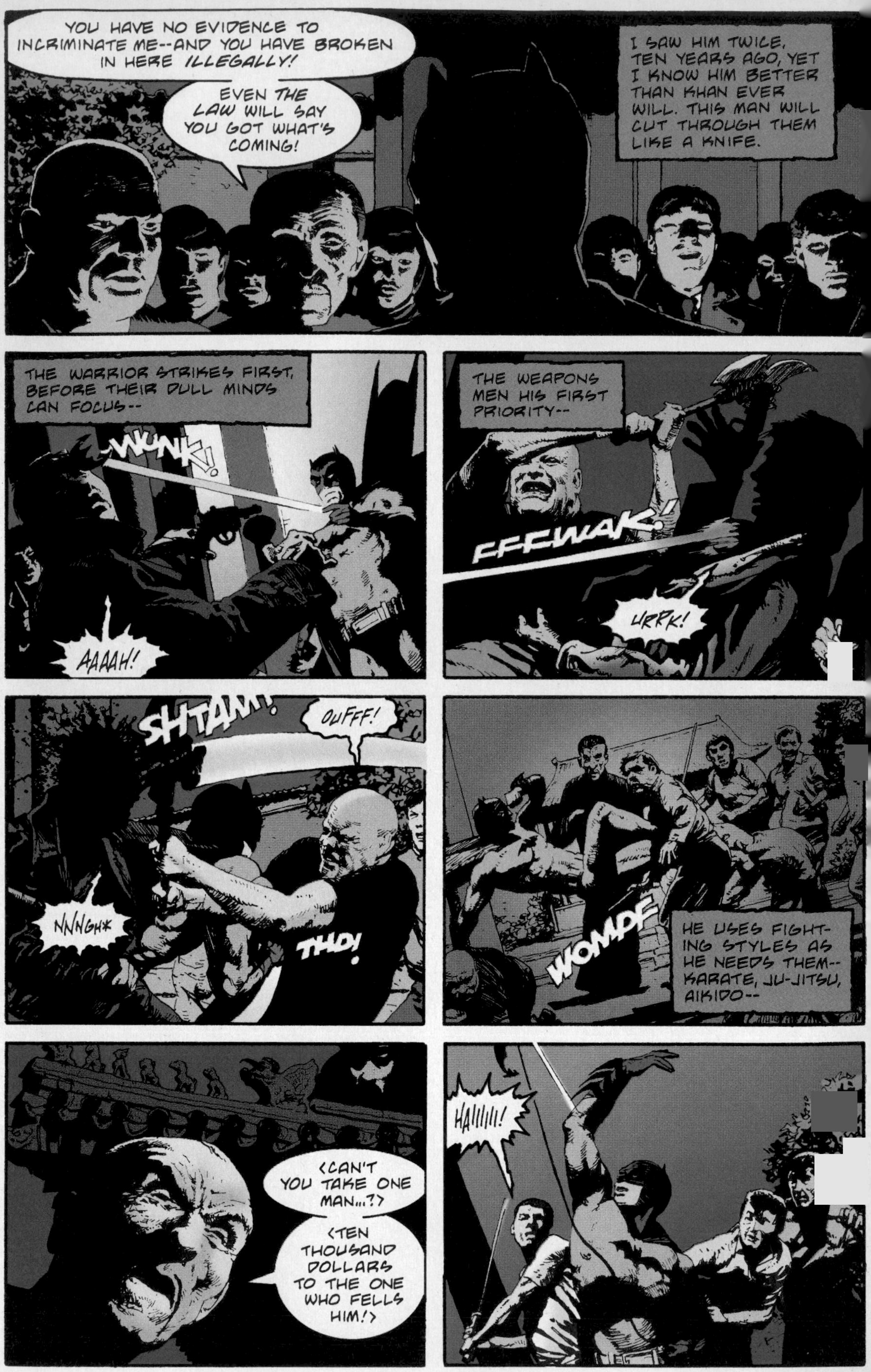
YOU HAVE NO EVIDENCE TO INCRIMINATE ME--AND YOU HAVE BROKEN IN HERE *ILLEGALLY!*
EVEN *THE* LAW WILL SAY YOU GOT WHAT'S COMING!
I SAW HIM TWICE, TEN YEARS AGO, YET I KNOW HIM BETTER THAN KHAN EVER WILL. THIS MAN WILL CUT THROUGH THEM LIKE A KNIFE.
THE WARRIOR STRIKES FIRST, BEFORE THEIR DULL MINDS CAN FOCUS--
WUNK!
AAAAH!
THE WEAPONS MEN HIS FIRST PRIORITY--
FFFWAK!
URRK!
SHTAMM!
OUFFF!
NNNGH*
THD!
WOMPF
HE USES FIGHTING STYLES AS HE NEEDS THEM--KARATE, JU-JITSU, AIKIDO--
<CAN'T YOU TAKE ONE MAN...?>
<TEN THOUSAND DOLLARS TO THE ONE WHO FELLS HIM!>
HAIIIII!

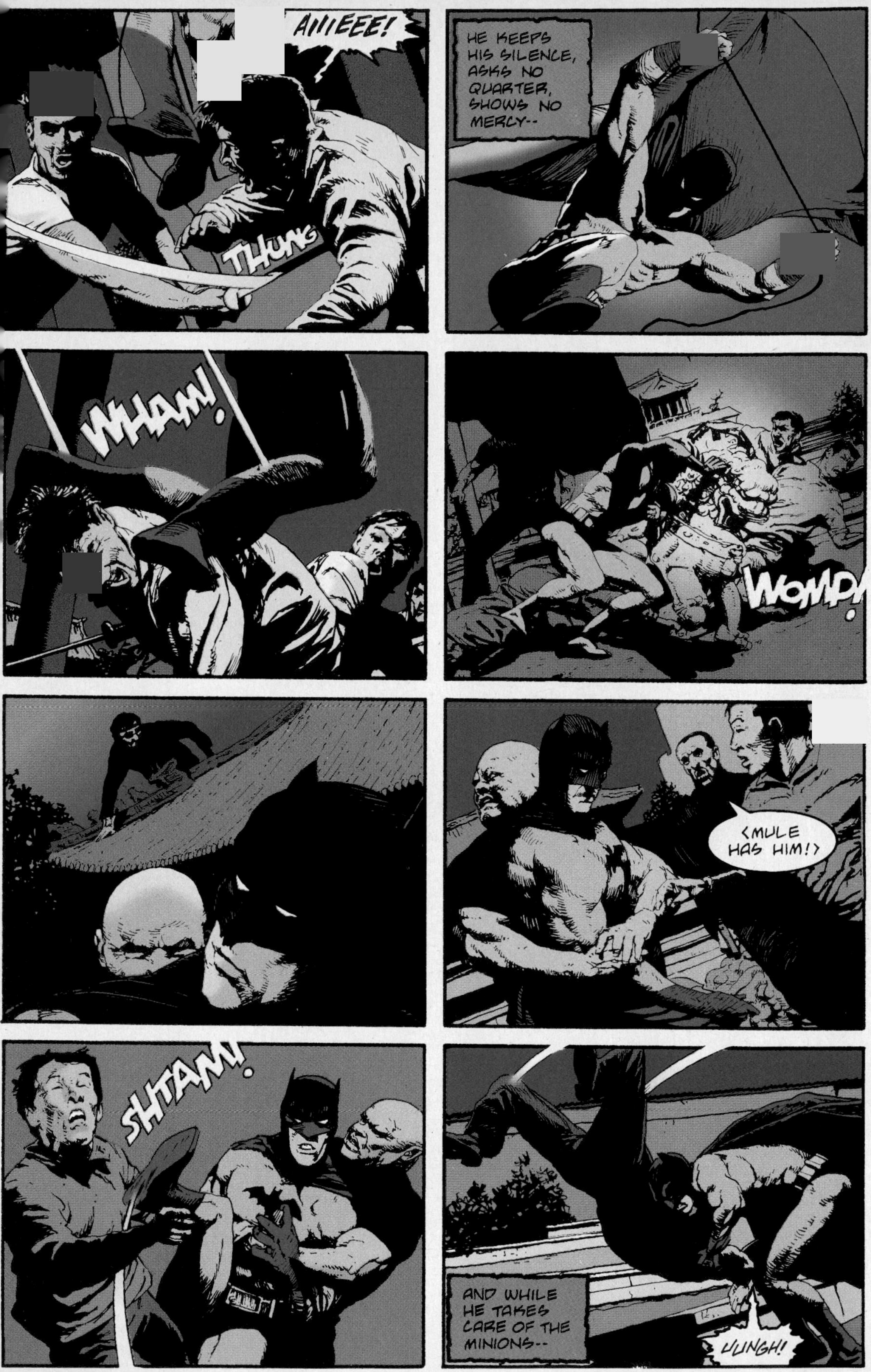
AIIIEEE!
THUNG
HE KEEPS HIS SILENCE, ASKS NO QUARTER, SHOWS NO MERCY--
WHAM!
WOMP!
<MULE HAS HIM!>
SHTAM!
AND WHILE HE TAKES CARE OF THE MINIONS--
UUNGH!

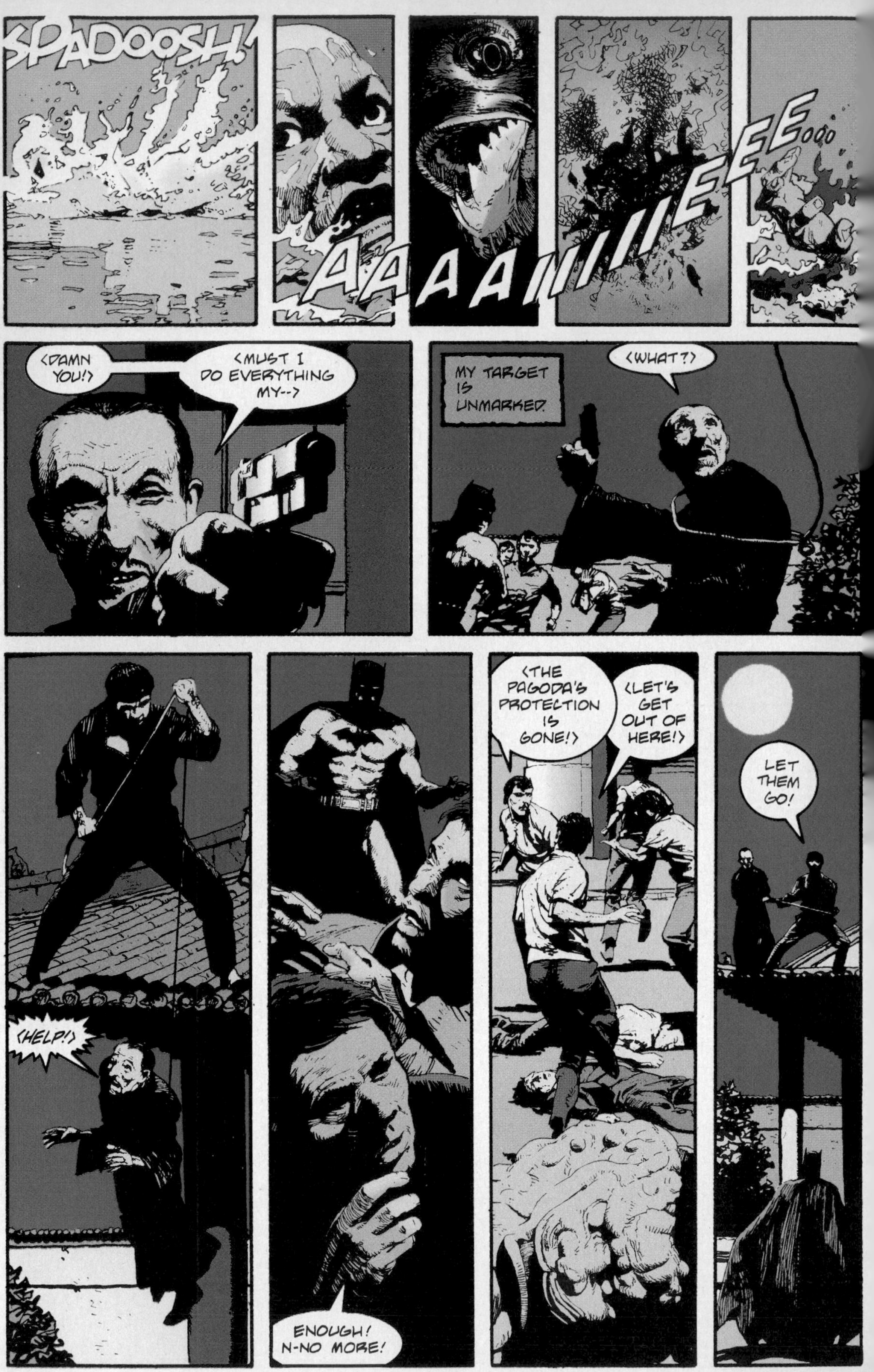
SPADOOSH!
AAAAIIIIIIIEEEEooo
<DAMN YOU!>
<MUST I DO EVERYTHING MY-->
MY TARGET IS UNMARKED.
<WHAT?>
<HELP!>
ENOUGH! N-NO MORE!
<THE PAGODA'S PROTECTION IS GONE!>
<LET'S GET OUT OF HERE!>
LET THEM GO!

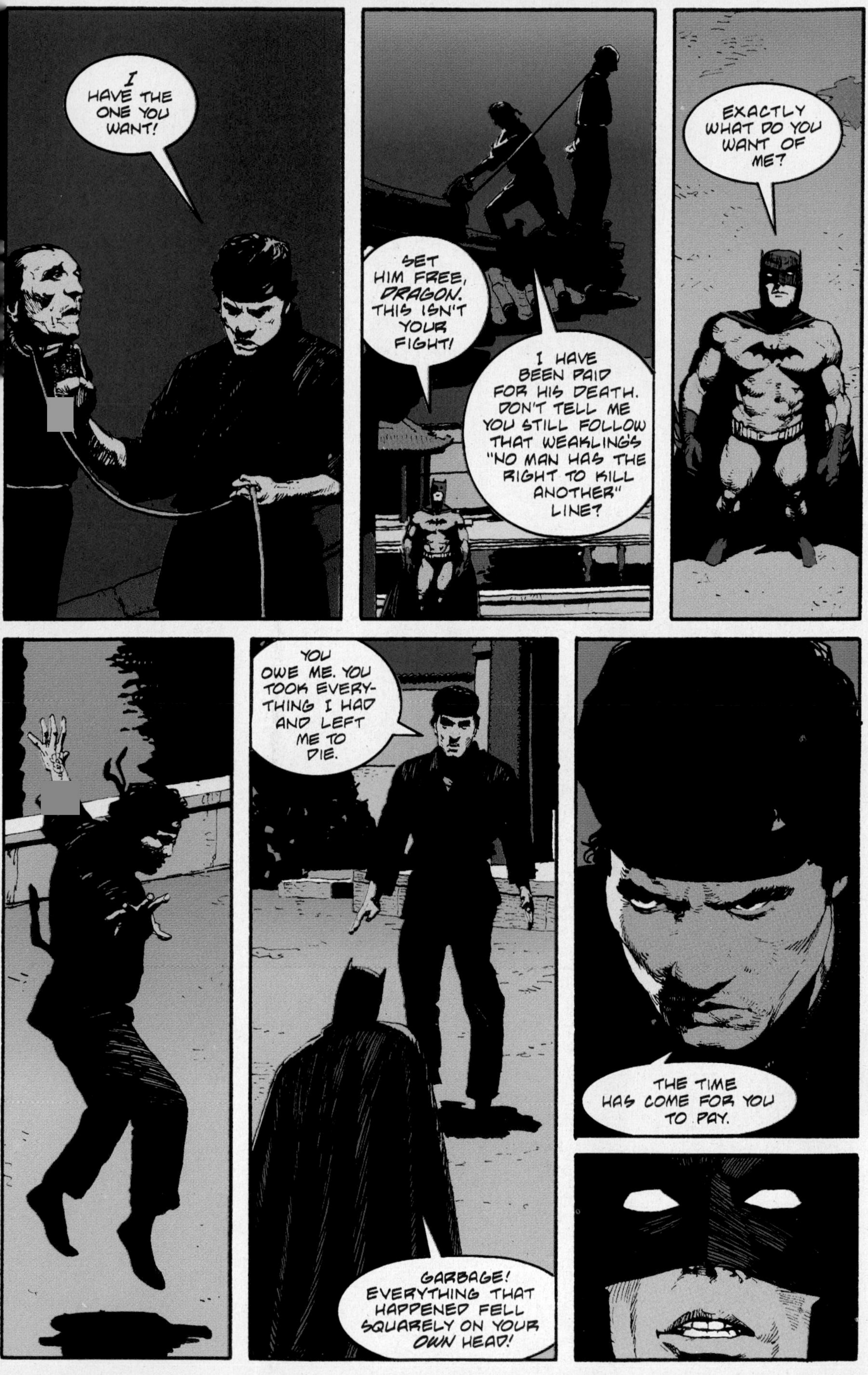
I HAVE THE ONE YOU WANT!
SET HIM FREE, DRAGON. THIS ISN'T YOUR FIGHT!
I HAVE BEEN PAID FOR HIS DEATH. DON'T TELL ME YOU STILL FOLLOW THAT WEAKLING'S "NO MAN HAS THE RIGHT TO KILL ANOTHER" LINE?
EXACTLY WHAT DO YOU WANT OF ME?
YOU OWE ME. YOU TOOK EVERY-THING I HAD AND LEFT ME TO DIE.
GARBAGE! EVERYTHING THAT HAPPENED FELL SQUARELY ON YOUR OWN HEAD!
THE TIME HAS COME FOR YOU TO PAY.

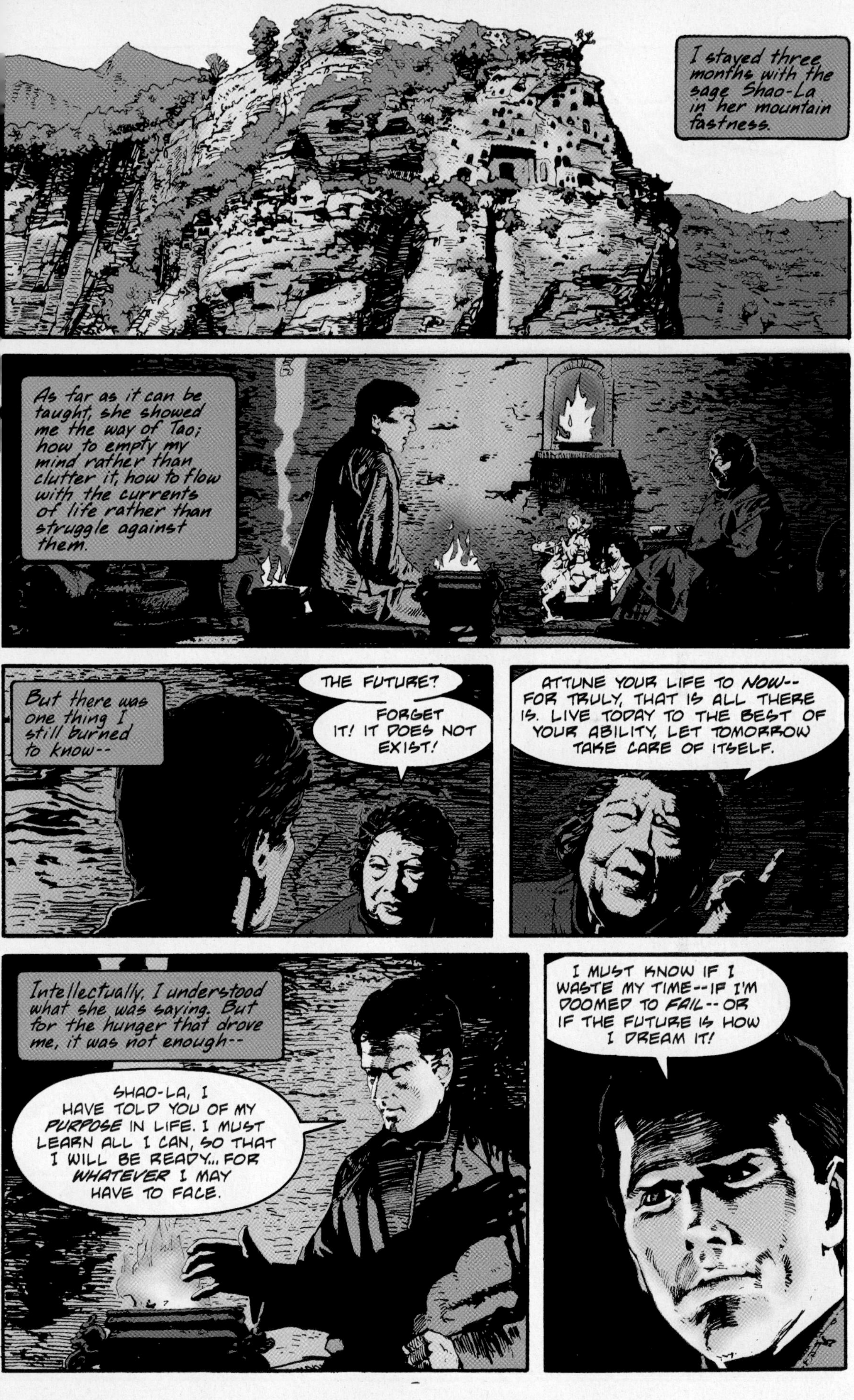
I stayed three months with the sage Shao-La in her mountain fastness.
As far as it can be taught, she showed me the way of Tao; how to empty my mind rather than clutter it, how to flow with the currents of life rather than struggle against them.
But there was one thing I still burned to know--
THE FUTURE?
FORGET IT! IT DOES NOT EXIST!
ATTUNE YOUR LIFE TO NOW-- FOR TRULY, THAT IS ALL THERE IS. LIVE TODAY TO THE BEST OF YOUR ABILITY, LET TOMORROW TAKE CARE OF ITSELF.
Intellectually, I understood what she was saying. But for the hunger that drove me, it was not enough--
SHAO-LA, I HAVE TOLD YOU OF MY PURPOSE IN LIFE. I MUST LEARN ALL I CAN, SO THAT I WILL BE READY... FOR WHATEVER I MAY HAVE TO FACE.
I MUST KNOW IF I WASTE MY TIME-- IF I'M DOOMED TO FAIL-- OR IF THE FUTURE IS HOW I DREAM IT!

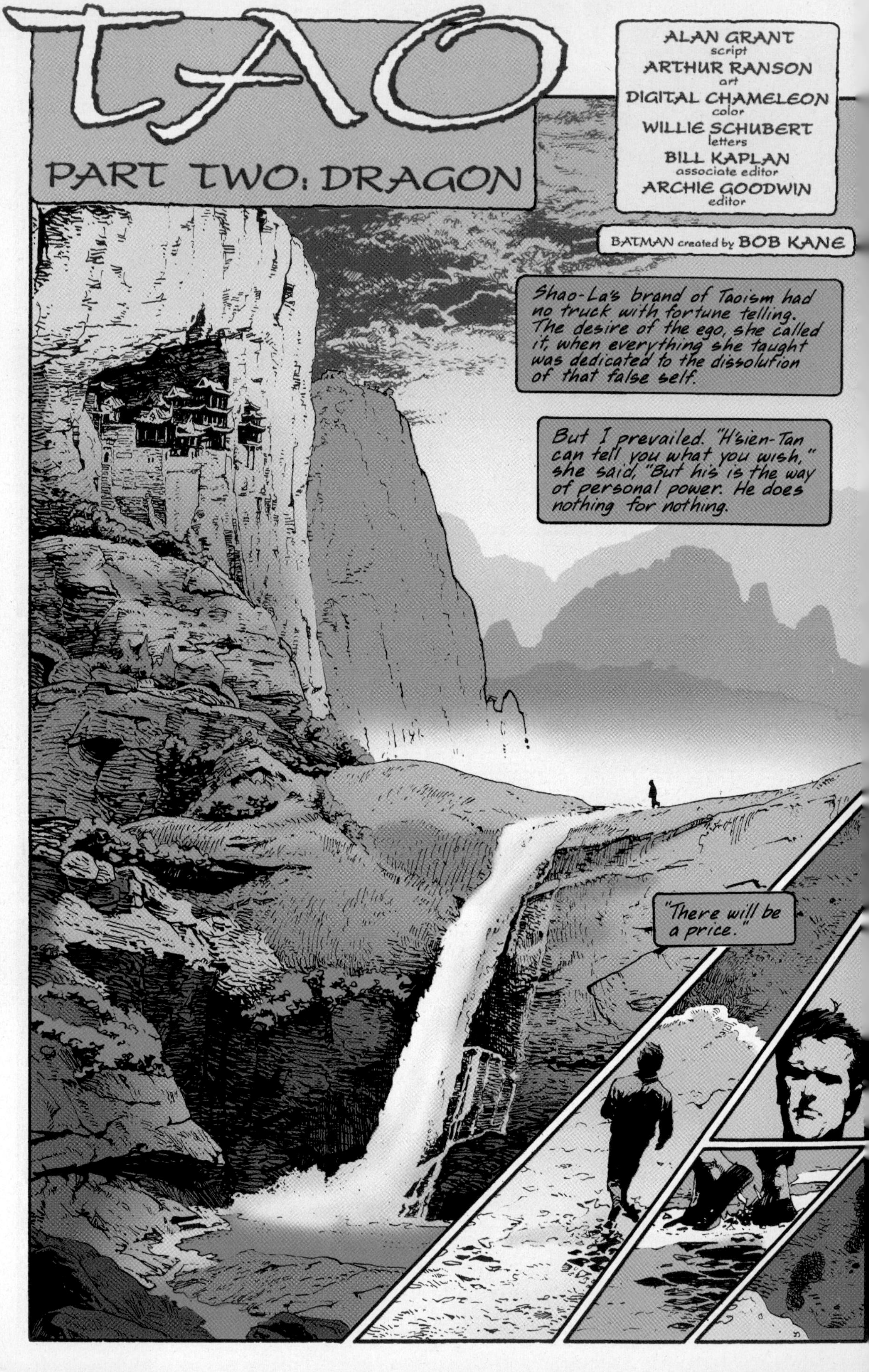
TAO
PART TWO: DRAGON
ALAN GRANT script
ARTHUR RANSON art
DIGITAL CHAMELEON color
WILLIE SCHUBERT letters
BILL KAPLAN associate editor
ARCHIE GOODWIN editor
BATMAN created by BOB KANE
Shao-La's brand of Taoism had no truck with fortune telling. The desire of the ego, she called it, when everything she taught was dedicated to the dissolution of that false self.
But I prevailed. "H'sien-Tan can tell you what you wish," she said, "But his is the way of personal power. He does nothing for nothing.
"There will be a price."

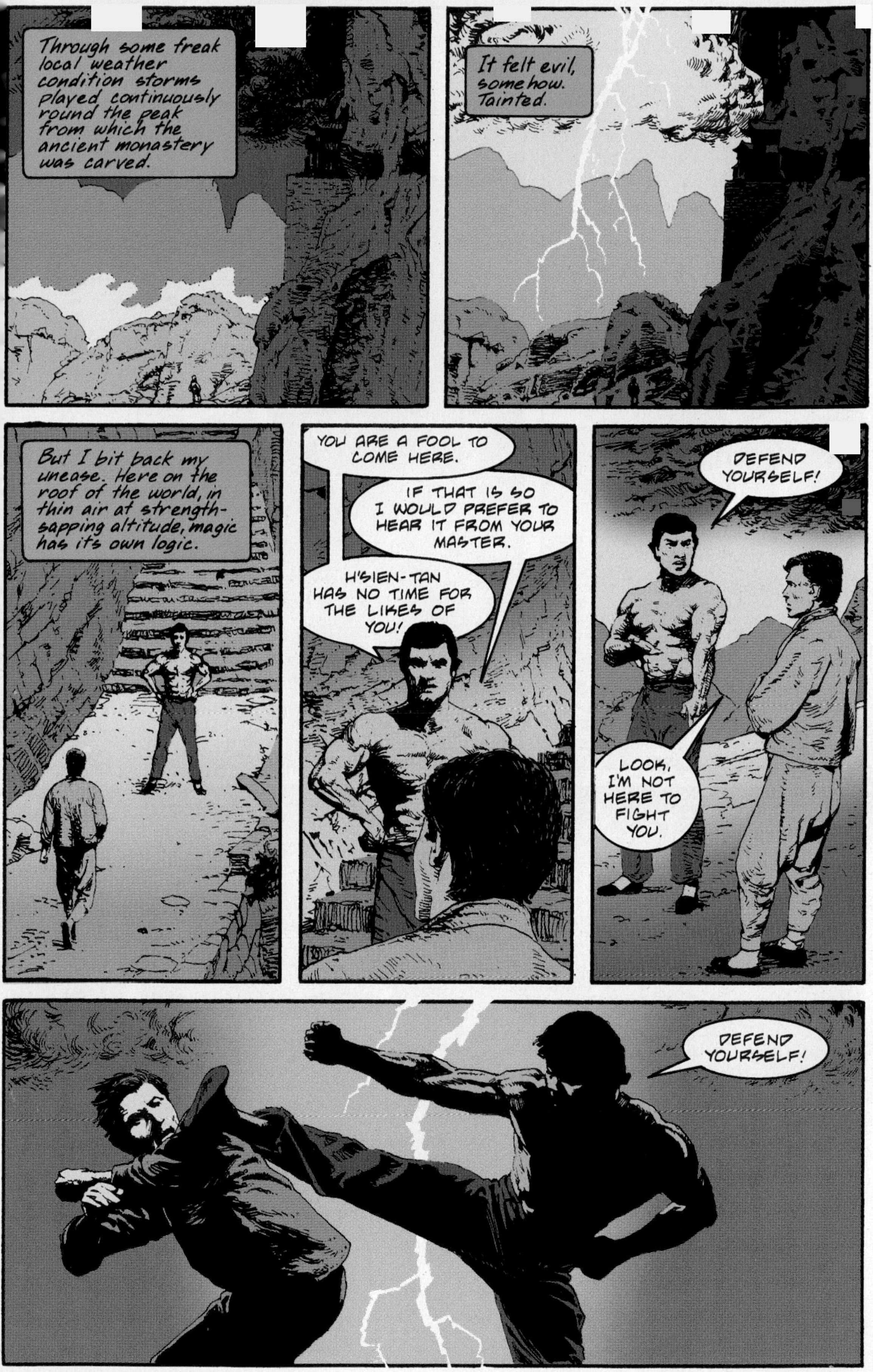
Through some freak local weather condition storms played continuously round the peak from which the ancient monastery was carved.
It felt evil, somehow. Tainted.
But I bit back my unease. Here on the roof of the world, in thin air at strength-sapping altitude, magic has its own logic.
YOU ARE A FOOL TO COME HERE.
IF THAT IS SO I WOULD PREFER TO HEAR IT FROM YOUR MASTER.
H'SIEN-TAN HAS NO TIME FOR THE LIKES OF YOU!
DEFEND YOURSELF!
LOOK, I'M NOT HERE TO FIGHT YOU.
DEFEND YOURSELF!

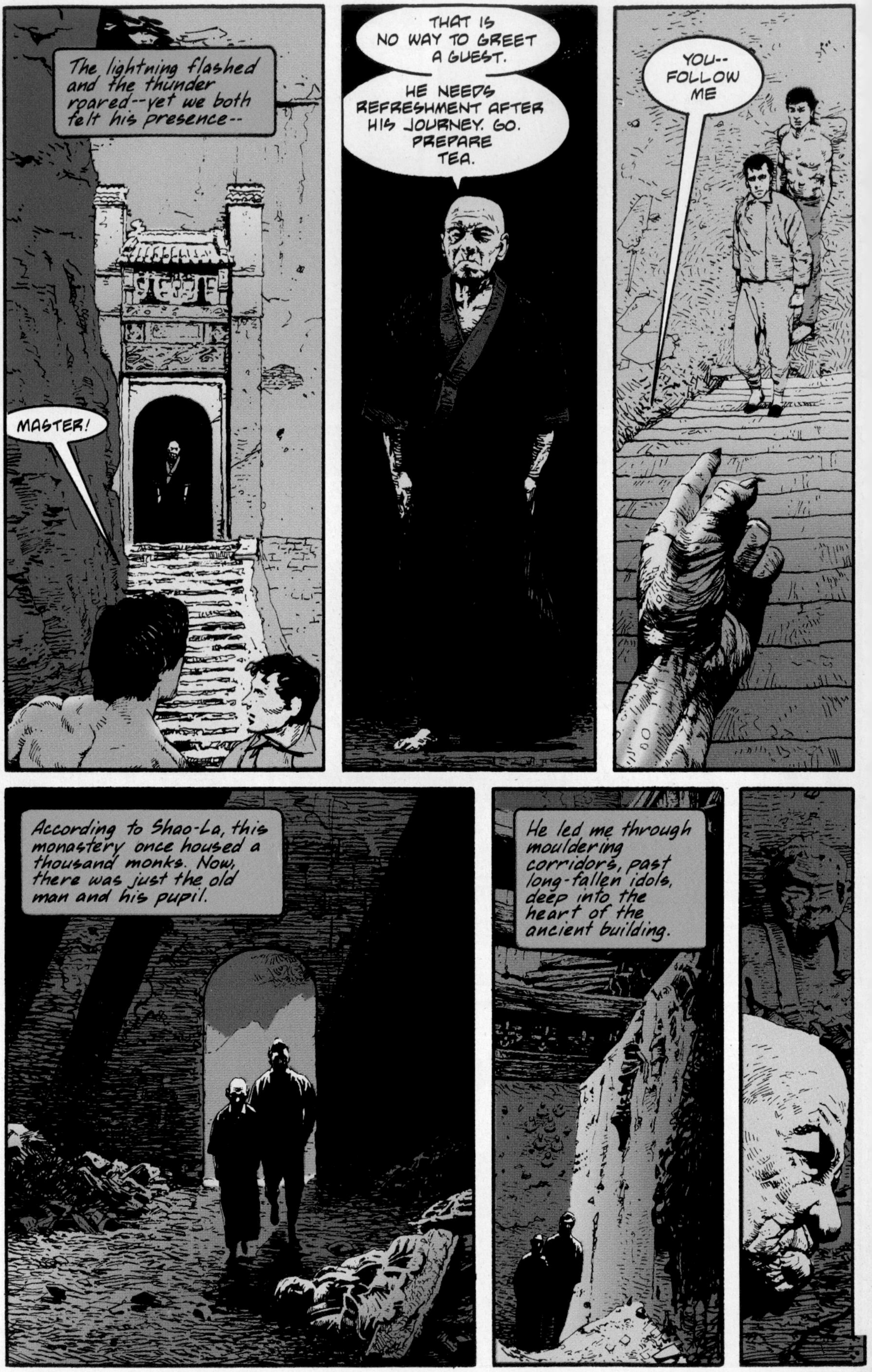

The lightning flashed and the thunder roared--yet we both felt his presence--
MASTER!
THAT IS NO WAY TO GREET A GUEST.
HE NEEDS REFRESHMENT AFTER HIS JOURNEY. GO. PREPARE TEA.
YOU-- FOLLOW ME
According to Shao-La, this monastery once housed a thousand monks. Now, there was just the old man and his pupil.
He led me through mouldering corridors, past long-fallen idols, deep into the heart of the ancient building.

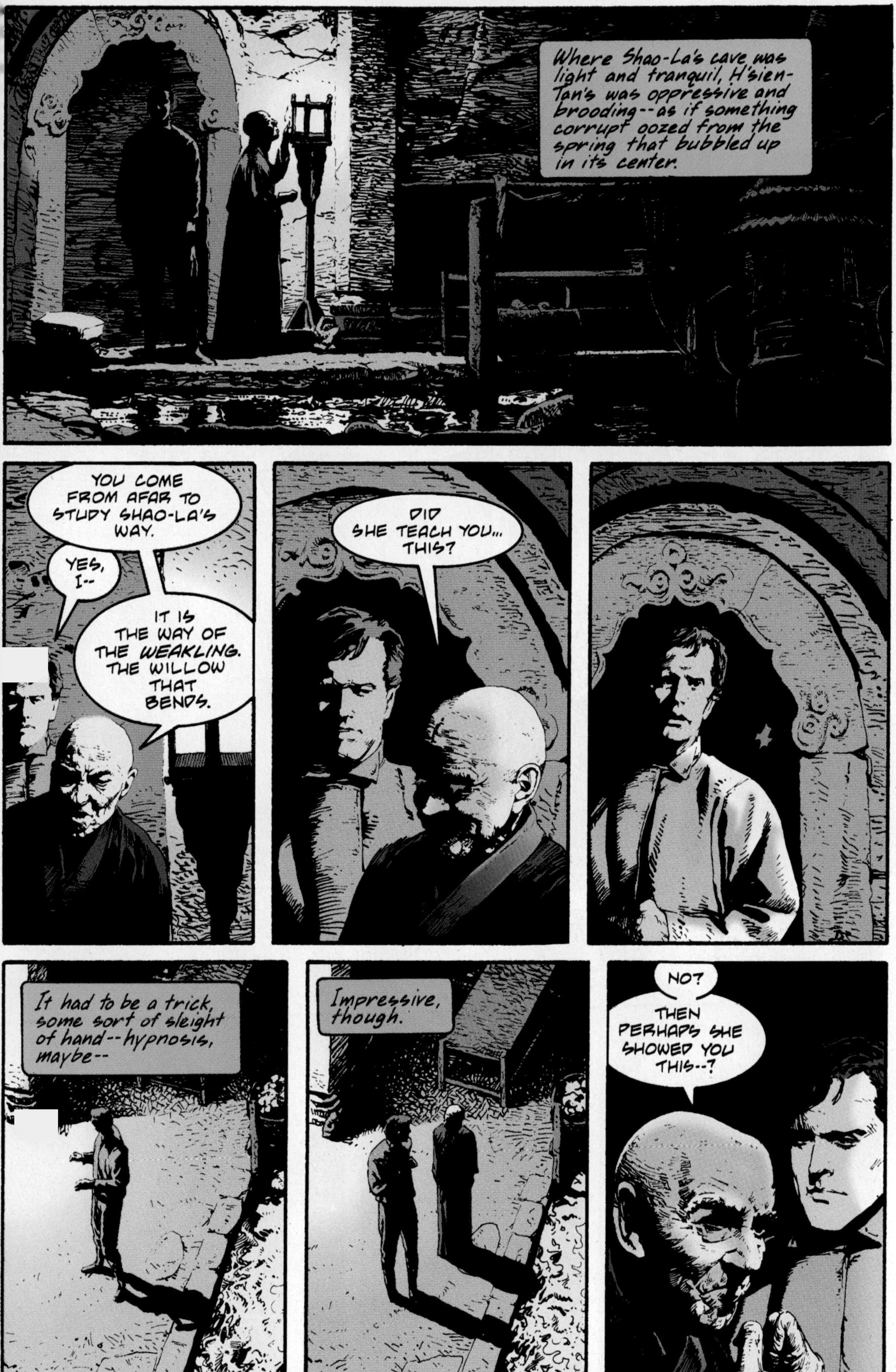
Where Shao-La's cave was light and tranquil, H'sien-Tan's was oppressive and brooding--as if something corrupt oozed from the spring that bubbled up in its center.
YOU COME FROM AFAR TO STUDY SHAO-LA'S WAY.
YES, I--
IT IS THE WAY OF THE WEAKLING. THE WILLOW THAT BENDS.
DID SHE TEACH YOU... THIS?
It had to be a trick, some sort of sleight of hand--hypnosis, maybe--
Impressive, though.
NO?
THEN PERHAPS SHE SHOWED YOU THIS--?

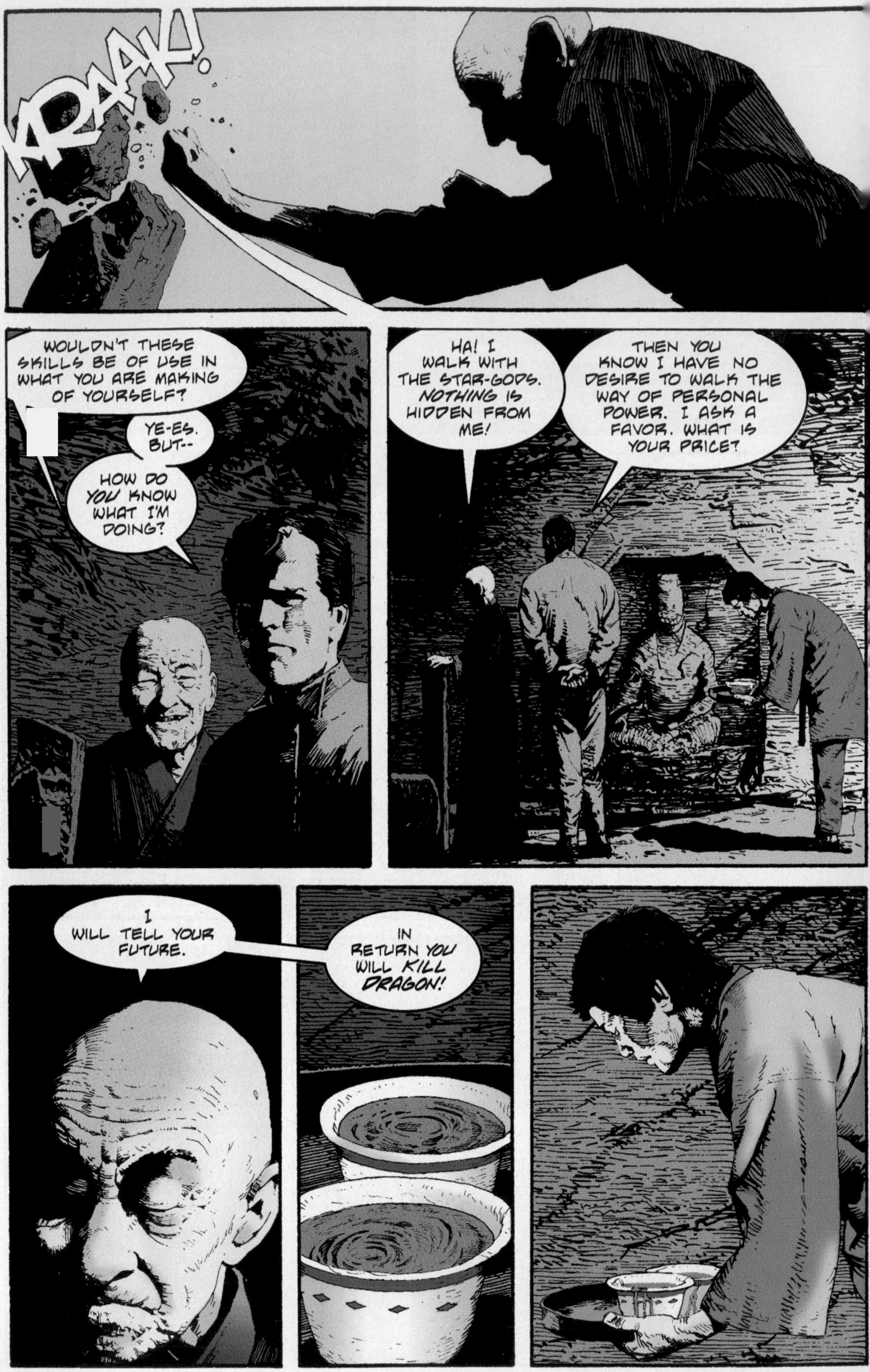
KRAAK!
WOULDN'T THESE SKILLS BE OF USE IN WHAT YOU ARE MAKING OF YOURSELF?
YE-ES. BUT--
HOW DO YOU KNOW WHAT I'M DOING?
HA! I WALK WITH THE STAR-GODS. NOTHING IS HIDDEN FROM ME!
THEN YOU KNOW I HAVE NO DESIRE TO WALK THE WAY OF PERSONAL POWER. I ASK A FAVOR. WHAT IS YOUR PRICE?
I WILL TELL YOUR FUTURE.
IN RETURN YOU WILL KILL DRAGON!

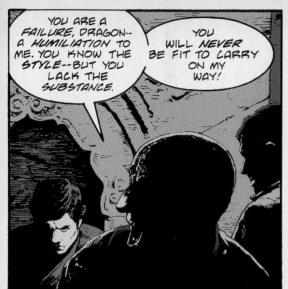

YOU ARE A *FAILURE*, DRAGON-- A *HUMILIATION* TO ME. YOU KNOW THE *STYLE*--BUT YOU *LACK* THE SUBSTANCE.

YOU WILL *NEVER* BE FIT TO CARRY ON MY WAY!

IF YOU KNOW AS MUCH AS YOU CLAIM, H'SIEN-TAN. THEN YOU KNOW MY DECISION IS ALREADY MADE.

I WILL *NOT* KILL ANYONE. NOT *EVER*.

NEVER IS A LONG TIME, BOY!

YOU WOULD MAKE A GOOD PUPIL. NO MATTER. EACH MUST FIND HIS OWN PATH.

SIT.

BUT WON'T YOU GO TO *HELL* FOR THIS? ONLY YOUR *GOD* IS PERMITTED TO KNOW THE FUTURE. WON'T *DEMONS* BREAK YOUR NECK AND TWIST IT BACKWARDS AS PUNISHMENT?

IN MEDIEVAL TIMES, MAYBE. NOT NOW.

BESIDES, HE MIGHT NOT BE *MY* GOD.

BEFORE MAN COULD READ OR WRITE, THE YELLOW EMPEROR SHOWED HIM HOW TO INTERPRET THE MARKS ON A TORTOISE SHELL--

HE TAUGHT HOW EVERY MOMENT IS A MICROCOSM OF THE WHOLE UNIVERSE, HOLDING THE SEEDS OF WHAT WAS, WHAT IS...

...WHAT WILL BE.

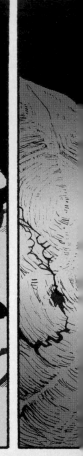

TWO PATHS ARE OPEN TO YOU...

TWO PATHS ARE OPEN TO YOU.

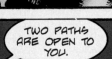

KILL ME...OR DIE!

AND JOHNNY KHAN...?

HE WAS ONLY BAIT, TO STOP YOU FLEEING.

A YEAR AGO, HE KILLED A DAUGHTER'S FATHER. SHE OFFERS PAYMENT FOR REVENGE IN BLOOD.

BECAUSE OF YOU, THIS IS WHAT I AM REDUCED TO-- KILLING MEN FOR MONEY--

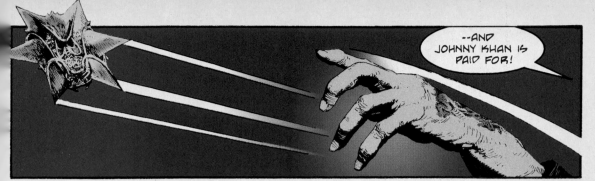

--AND JOHNNY KHAN IS PAID FOR!

KCHING!

YOUR MISTAKE!

SAVING KHAN WILL COST YOUR OWN LIFE!

WHUMP!

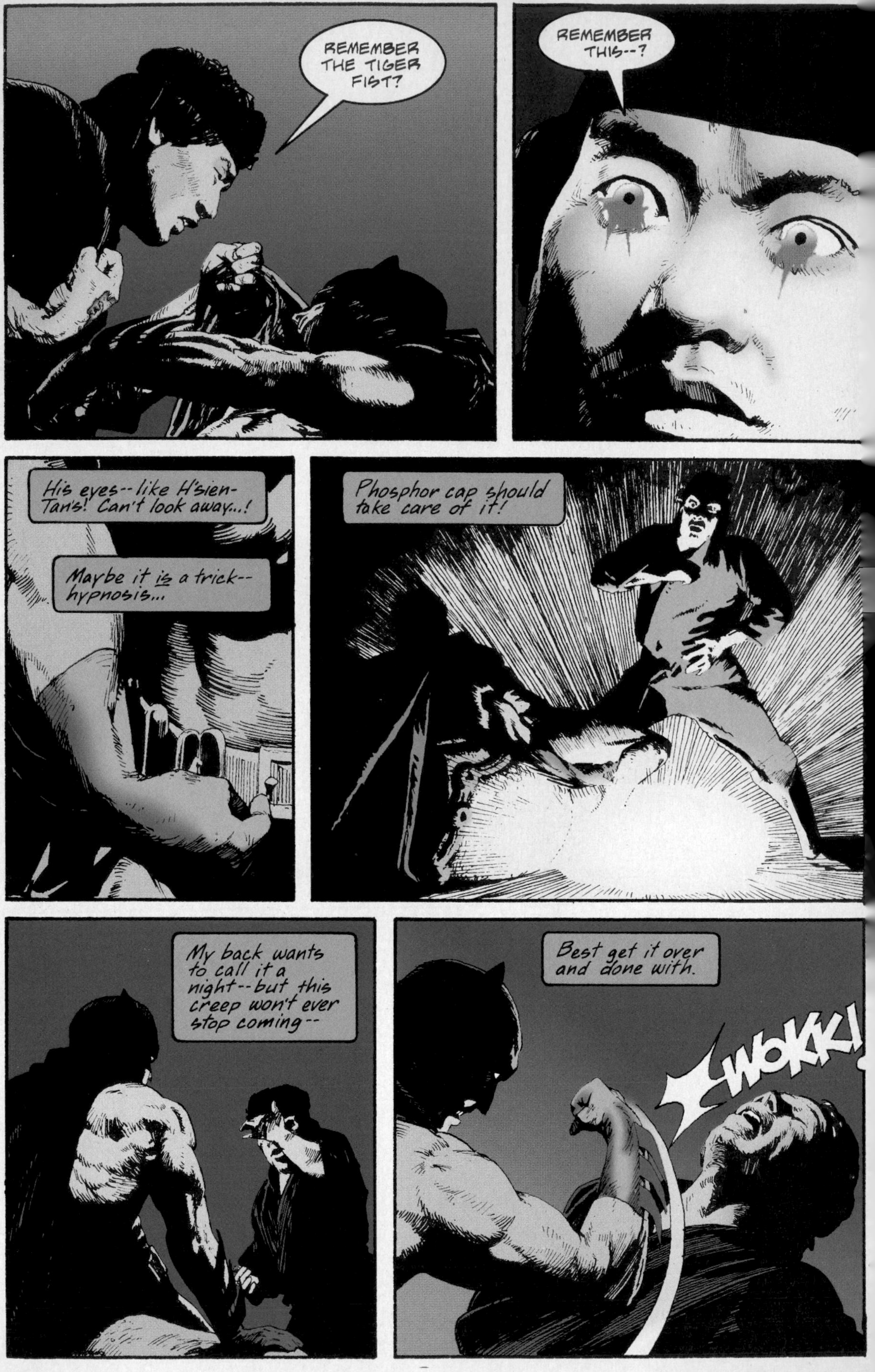
REMEMBER THE TIGER FIST?
REMEMBER THIS--?
His eyes--like H'sien-Tan's! Can't look away...!
Maybe it *is* a trick--hypnosis...
Phosphor cap should take care of it!
My back wants to call it a night--but this creep won't ever stop coming--
Best get it over and done with.
WOKK!

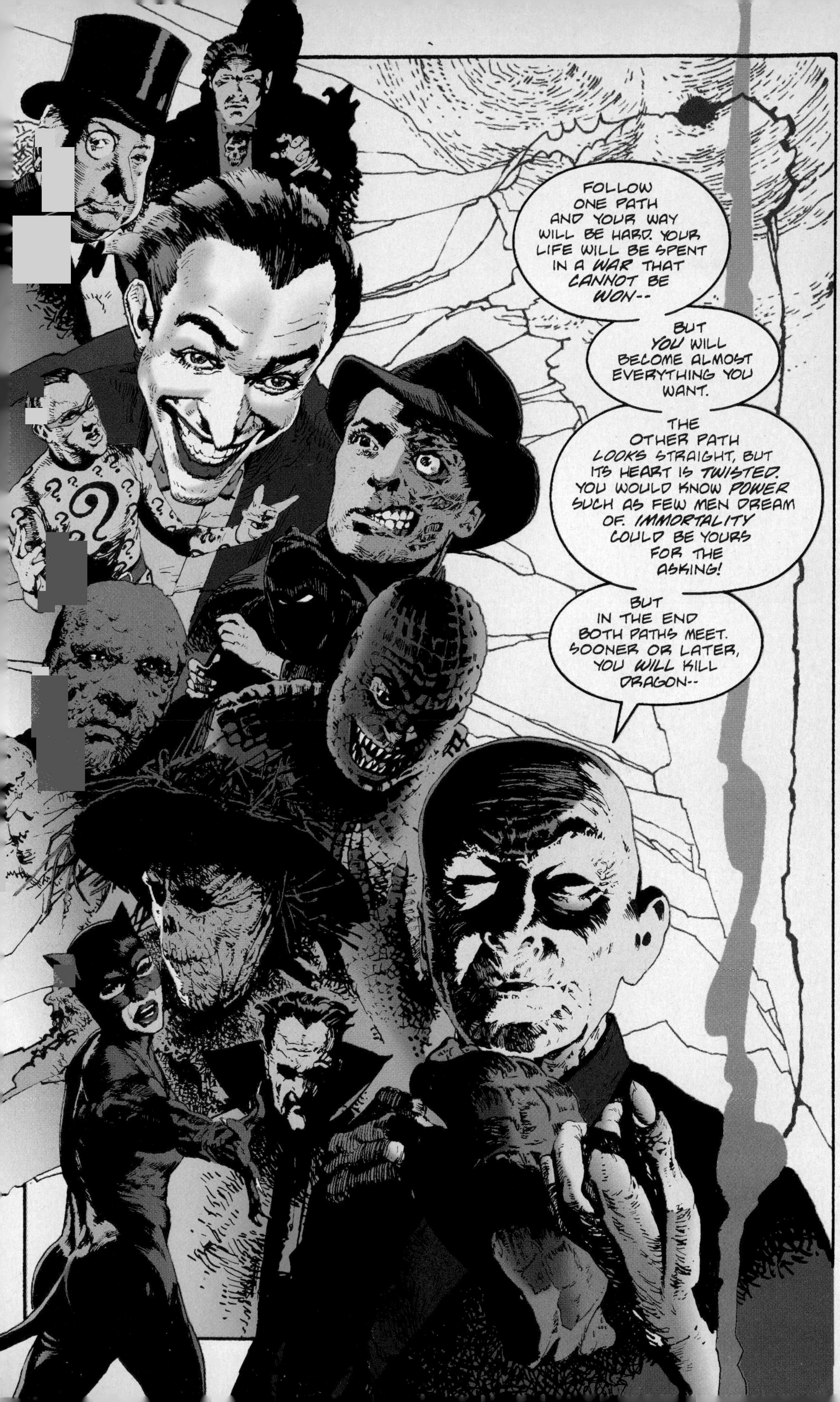
FOLLOW ONE PATH AND YOUR WAY WILL BE HARD. YOUR LIFE WILL BE SPENT IN A WAR THAT CANNOT BE WON--
BUT YOU WILL BECOME ALMOST EVERYTHING YOU WANT.
THE OTHER PATH LOOKS STRAIGHT, BUT ITS HEART IS TWISTED. YOU WOULD KNOW POWER SUCH AS FEW MEN DREAM OF. IMMORTALITY COULD BE YOURS FOR THE ASKING!
BUT IN THE END BOTH PATHS MEET. SOONER OR LATER, YOU WILL KILL DRAGON--

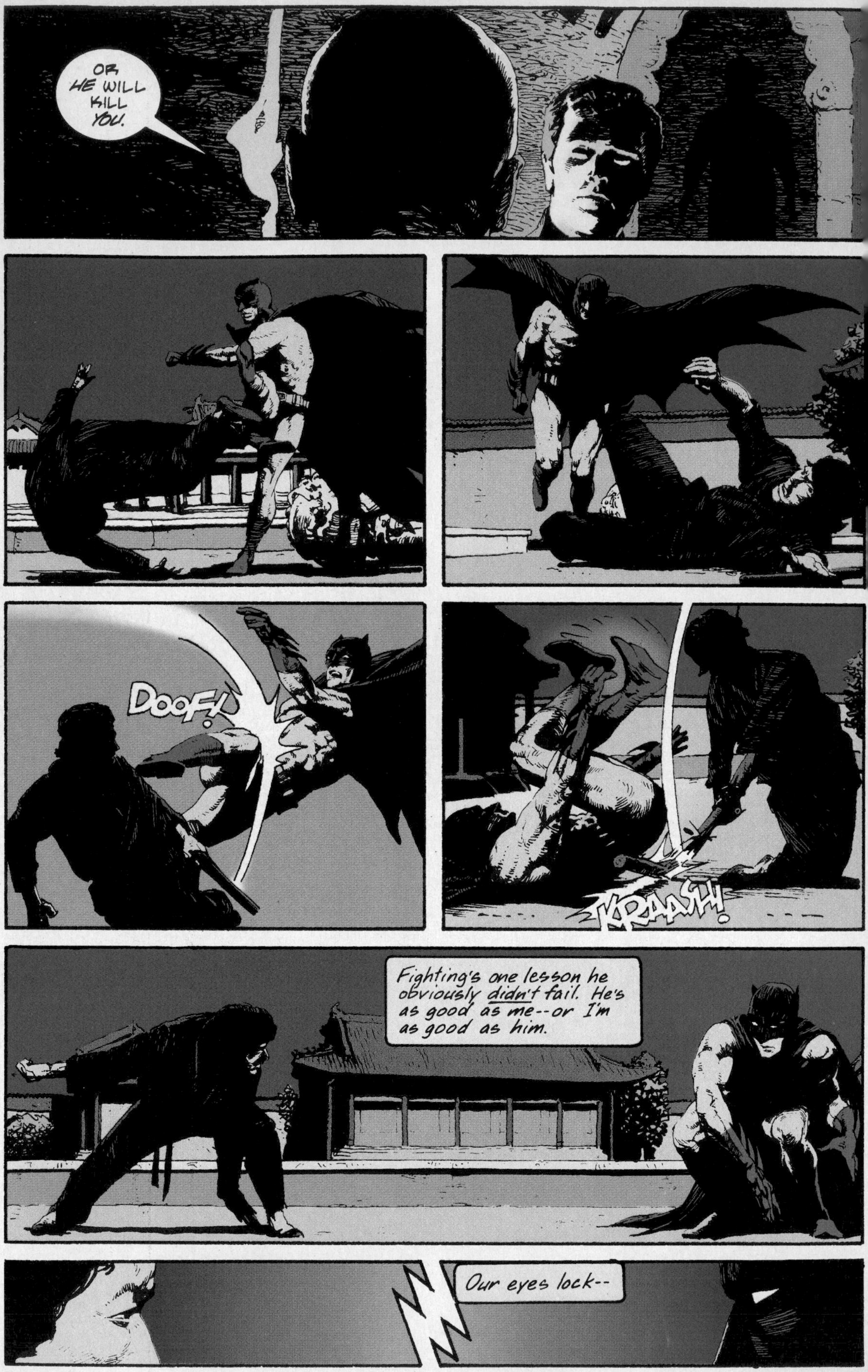
OR HE WILL KILL YOU.
DOOF!
KRAASH!
Fighting's one lesson he obviously didn't fail. He's as good as me--or I'm as good as him.
Our eyes lock--

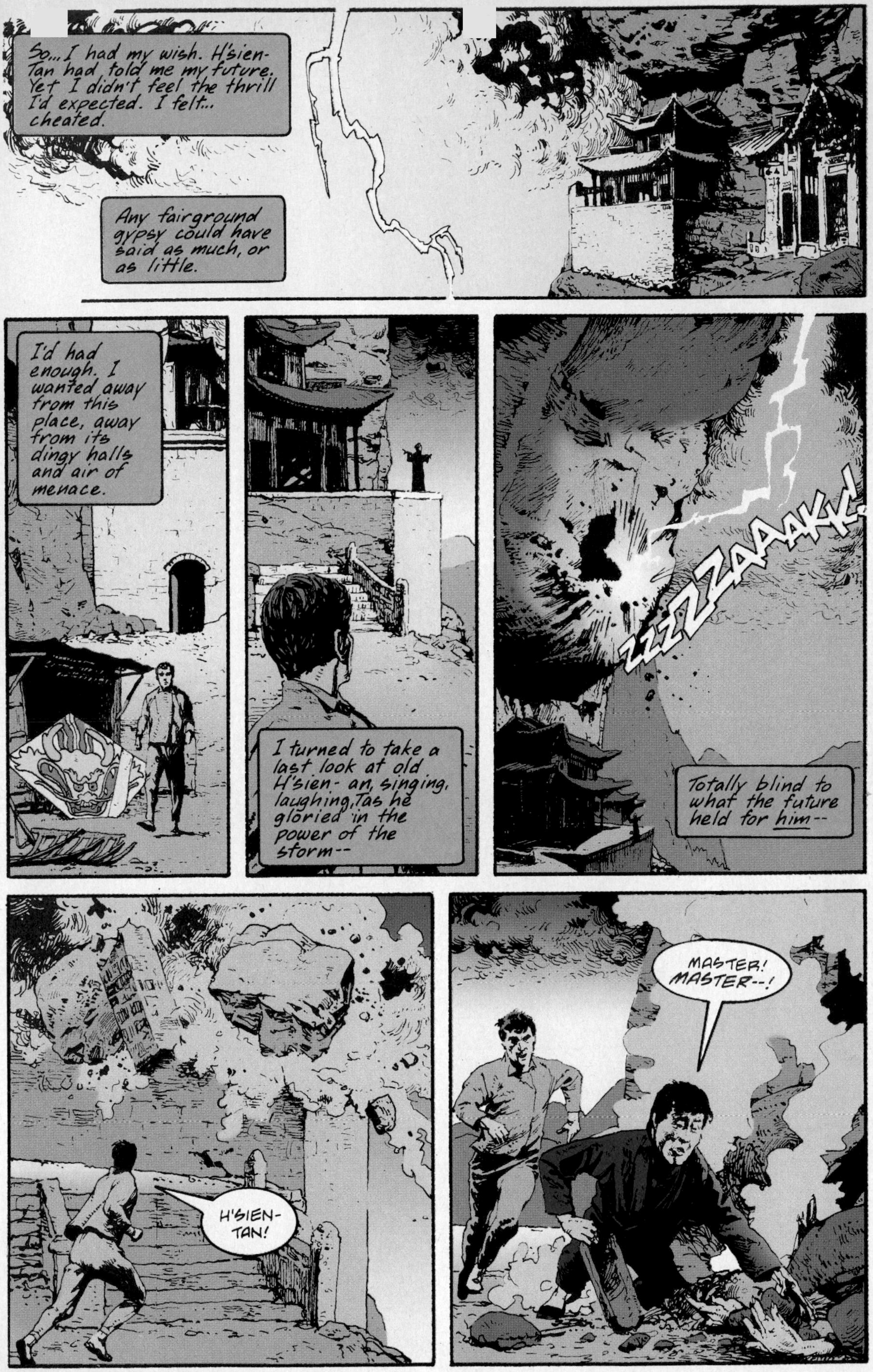
So... I had my wish. H'sien-Tan had told me my future. Yet I didn't feel the thrill I'd expected. I felt... cheated.
Any fairground gypsy could have said as much, or as little.
I'd had enough. I wanted away from this place, away from its dingy halls and air of menace.
I turned to take a last look at old H'sien- an, singing, laughing, as he gloried in the power of the storm--
ZZZZZAAAAKK!
Totally blind to what the future held for him--
H'SIEN-TAN!
MASTER! MASTER--!

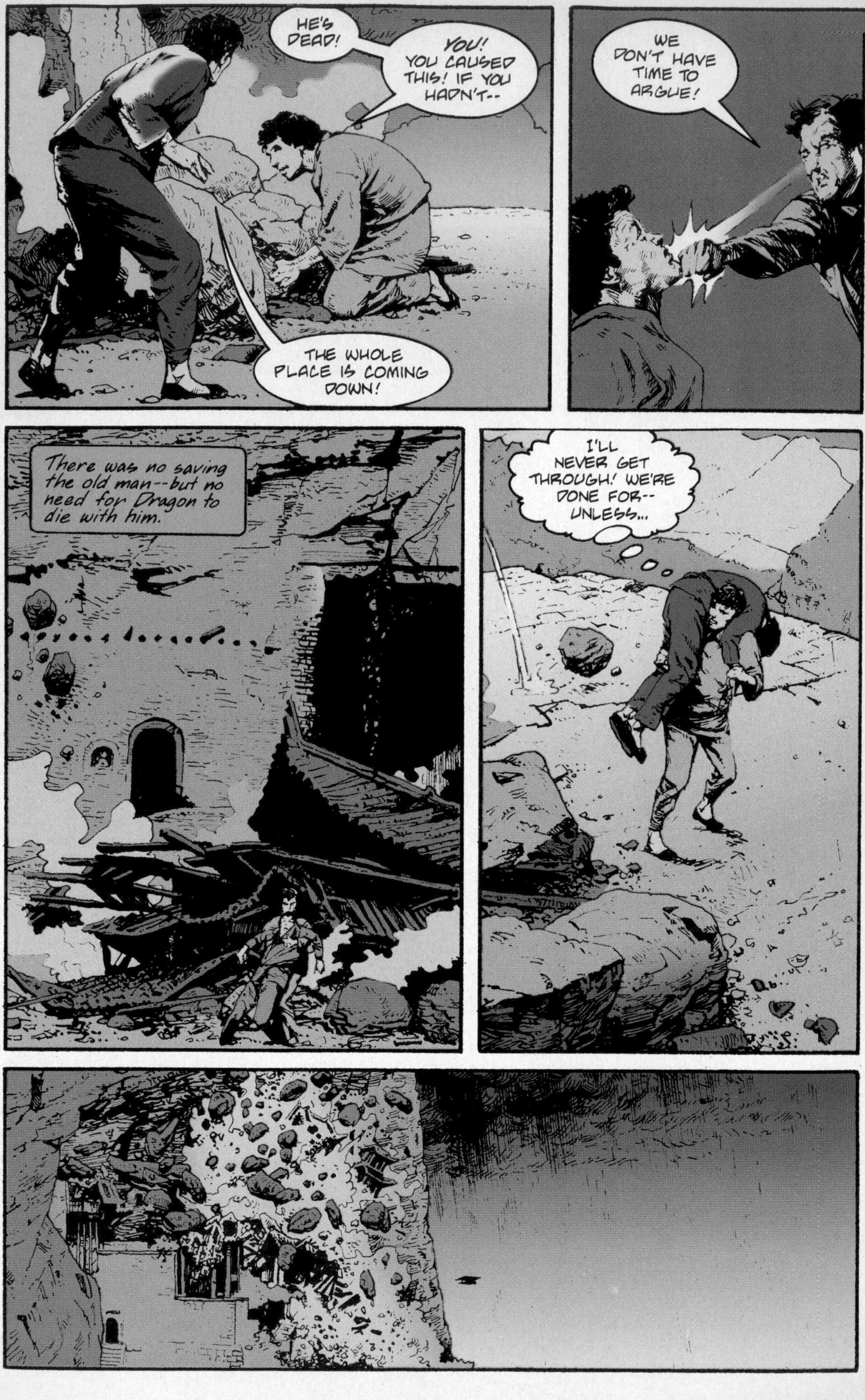
HE'S DEAD!
YOU! YOU CAUSED THIS! IF YOU HADN'T--
THE WHOLE PLACE IS COMING DOWN!
WE DON'T HAVE TIME TO ARGUE!
There was no saving the old man--but no need for Dragon to die with him.
I'LL NEVER GET THROUGH! WE'RE DONE FOR-- UNLESS...

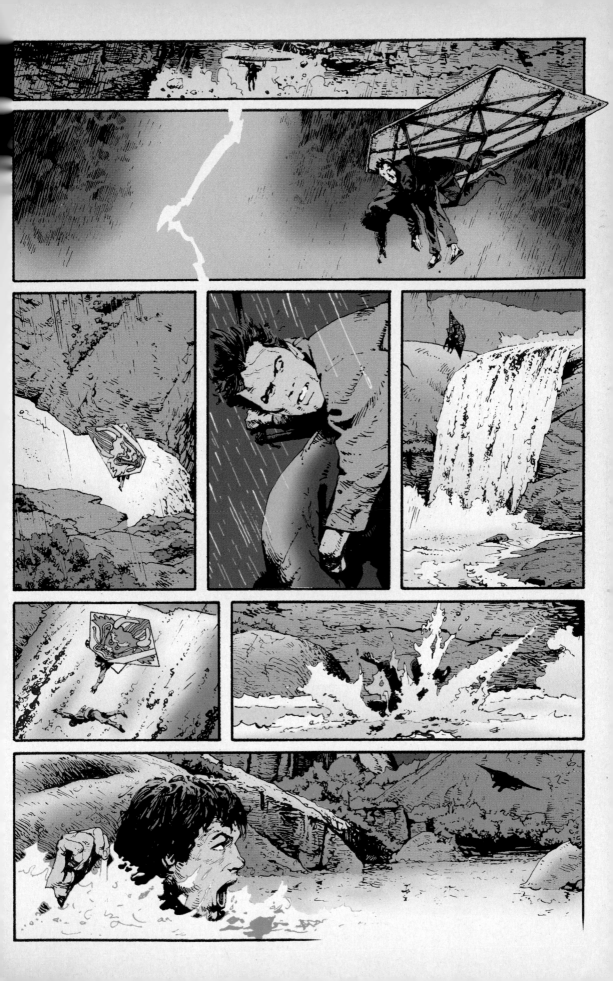

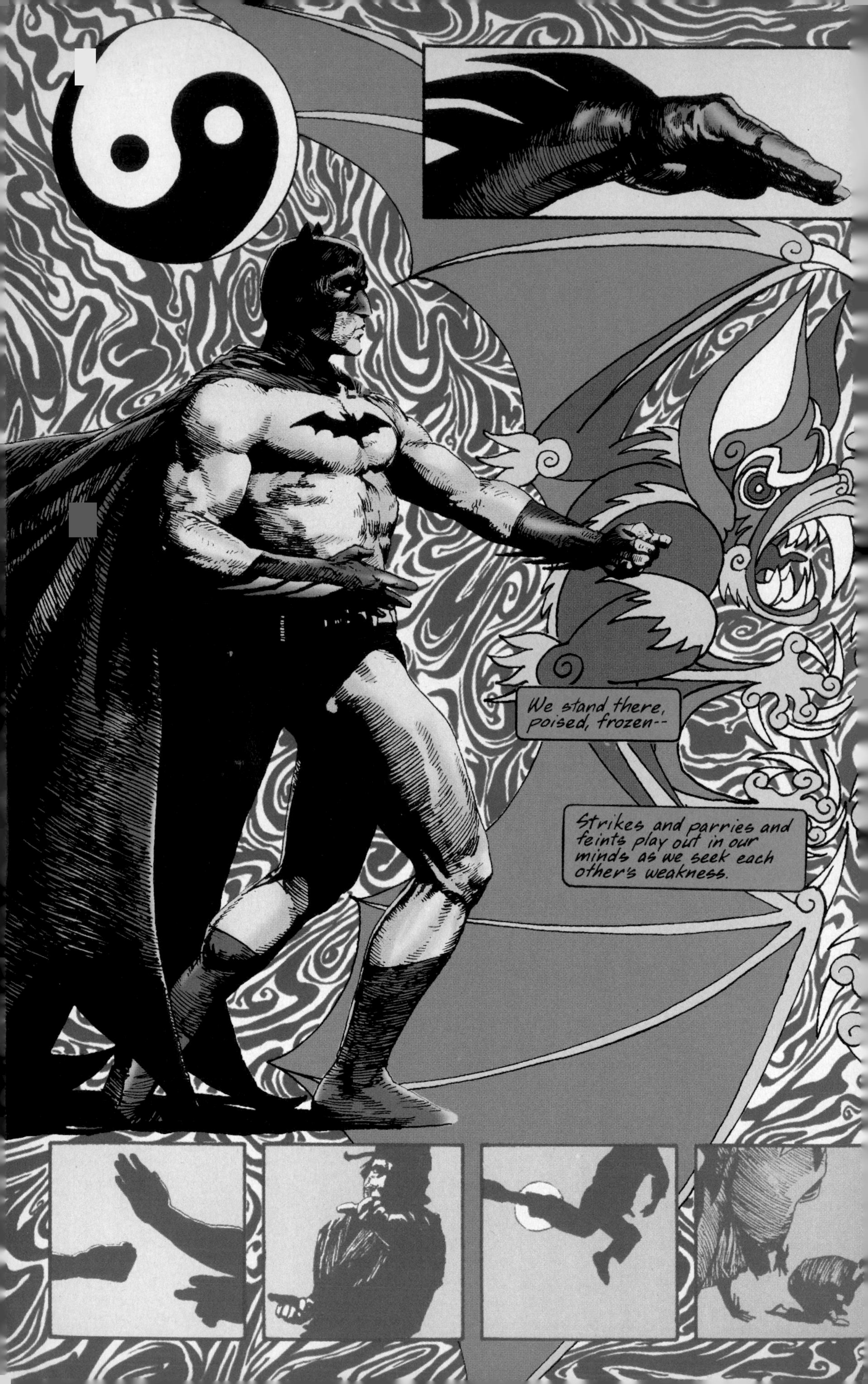
We stand there, poised, frozen--
Strikes and parries and feints play out in our minds as we seek each other's weakness.

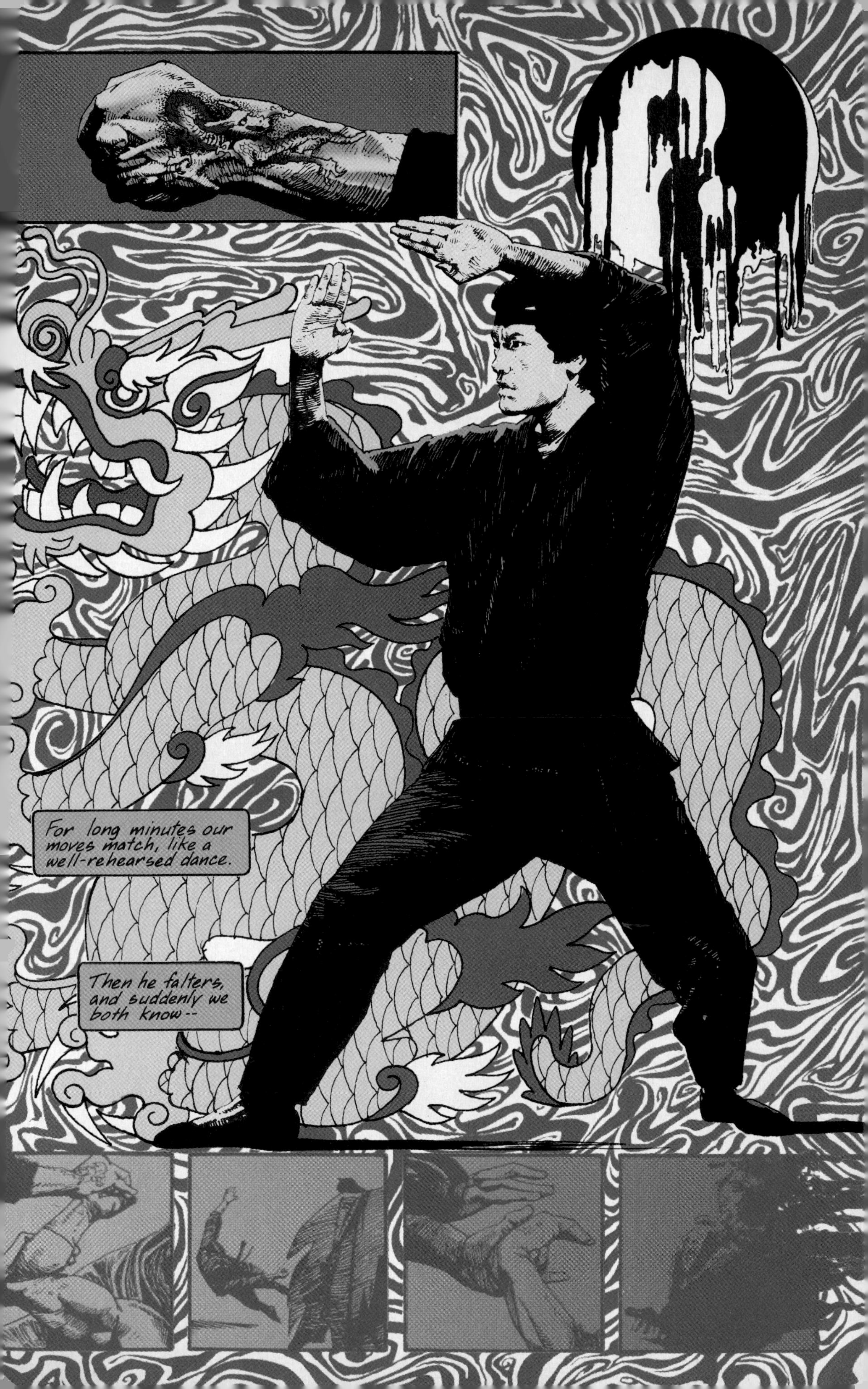
For long minutes our moves match, like a well-rehearsed dance.
Then he falters, and suddenly we both know--

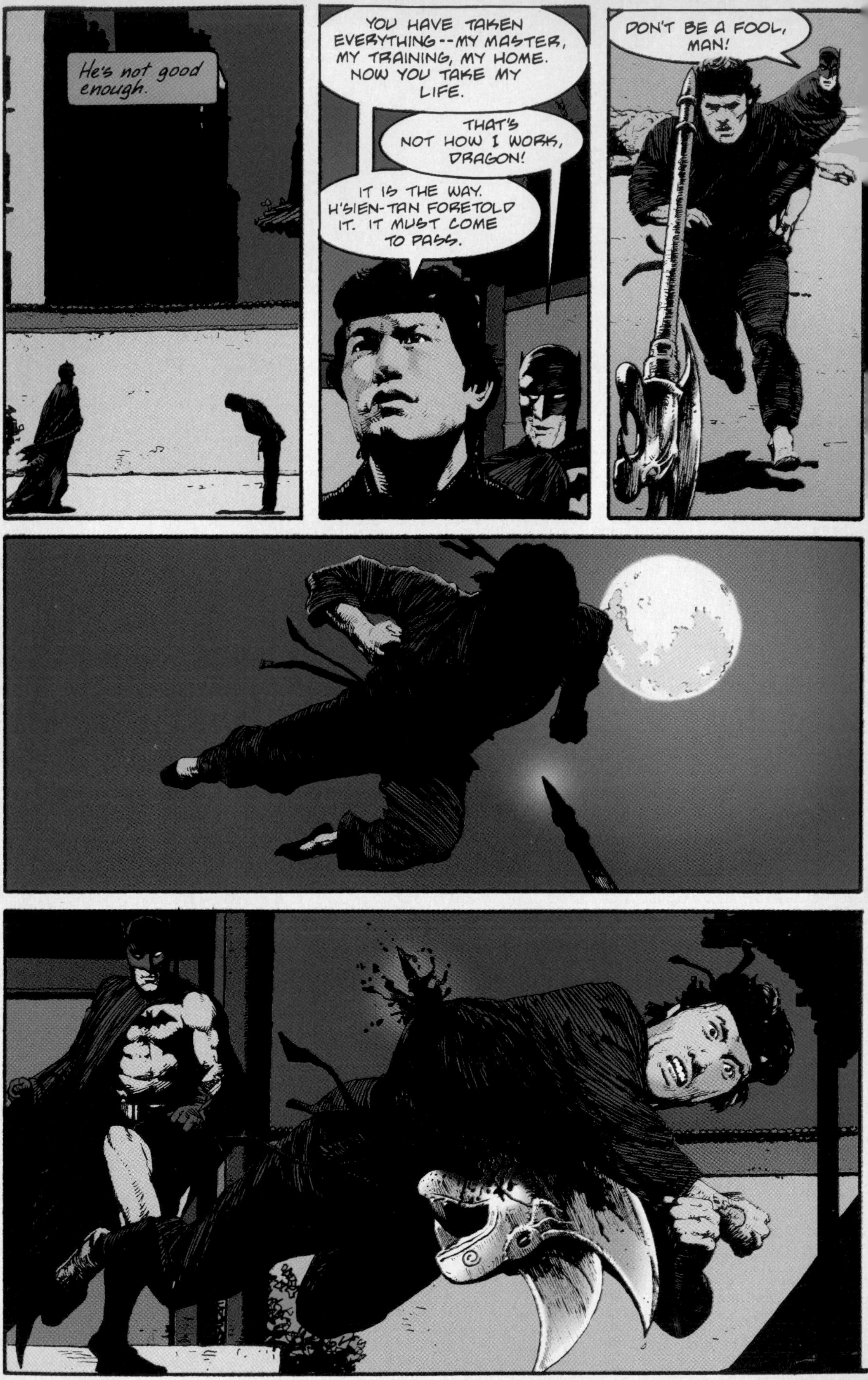
He's not good enough.
YOU HAVE TAKEN EVERYTHING--MY MASTER, MY TRAINING, MY HOME. NOW YOU TAKE MY LIFE.
THAT'S NOT HOW I WORK, DRAGON!
IT IS THE WAY. H'SIEN-TAN FORETOLD IT. IT MUST COME TO PASS.
DON'T BE A FOOL, MAN!

Y-YOU DID THAT! YOU JUST--LOOKED INTO HIS EYES...AND MADE HIM KILL HIMSELF!

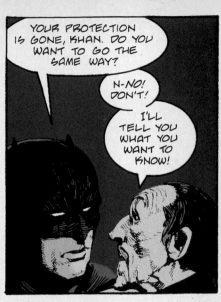

YOUR PROTECTION IS GONE, KHAN. DO YOU WANT TO GO THE SAME WAY?

N-NO! DON'T!

I'LL TELL YOU WHAT YOU WANT TO KNOW!

JUST--PLEASE DON'T KILL ME!

"The Way never acts, yet nothing remains undone." —Lao Tzu.